LIVING STREETS

Strategies for Crafting Public Space

LIVING STREETS

Strategies for Crafting Public Space

Lesley Bain, AIA, LEED AP

Barbara Gray

Dave Rodgers, PE, LEED

WILEY

John Wiley & Sons, Inc.

Published by John Wiley & Sons, Inc., Hoboken, New Jersey

Published simultaneously in Canada

For general information about our other products and services, please contact our Customer Care Department within the United States at (800) 762-2974, outside the United States at (317) 572-3993 or fax (317) 572-4002.

Wiley publishes in a variety of print and electronic formats and by print-on-demand. Some material included with standard print versions of this book may not be included in e-books or in print-on-demand. If this book refers to media such as a CD or DVD that is not included in the version you purchased, you may download this material at http://booksupport.wiley.com. For more information about Wiley products, visit www.wiley.com.

Library of Congress Cataloging-in-Publication Data:

Bain, Lesley, 1955-
  Living streets : strategies for crafting public space / Lesley Bain, Barbara Gray, Dave Rodgers.
      p. cm.
    Includes bibliographical references and index.
    ISBN 978-0-470-90381-0 (acid-free paper); 978-1-118-18008-2 (ebk); 978-1-118-18009-9 (ebk); 978-1-118-18181-2 (ebk); 978-1-118-18200-0 (ebk); 978-1-118-18201-7 (ebk)
  1. City planning. 2. Sustainable urban development. 3. Community development. I. Gray, Barbara, 1966-
II. Rodgers, Dave, 1969- III. Title.
  HT165.5.B35 2012
  711'.4—dc23

                                                                                               2011040421

Printed in the United States of America

10 9 8 7 6 5 4 3 2 1

*This book is dedicated with great love
to my father, Bill Bain.*

CONTENTS

ACKNOWLEDGMENTS   xi

OVERVIEW   xiii

Chapter 1 **PLACEMAKING IN THE PUBLIC RIGHT-OF-WAY**   **1**

The Function of Places   2

Why Invest in a Quality Public Realm?   4

Placemaking and Design   5

Encouraging the Use of Public Space   11

Reclaiming Right-of-Way for Public Places   14

Considering All the Elements in the Right-of-Way   21

Chapter 2 **MOBILITY**   **23**

Connecting People to Places   24

Why Have Walkable, Bikeable Communities?   25

The Size and Shape of Movement   26

The Pace of Movement   34

A Shift in Thinking   35

Chapter 3 **NATURAL SYSTEMS**   **39**

Reconnecting Cities to Nature   40

Urban Biodiversity   41

Natural Systems and Opportunities in the Right-of-Way   42

Why Reconnect Nature and the City?   49

Chapter 4 ELEMENTS 51

Places to Move Through   52

Materials   58

Intersections   59

Bicycle Facilities   61

Signage   68

Street Furniture   70

Street Trees and Landscaping   74

Swales and Rain Gardens   74

Curbs, Gutters, and Alternatives   77

Parking   79

Chapter 5 INFLUENCES 83

Considering Context   84

Policy Foundation—Policies That Influence Street Design   87

Codes, Guidelines, and Standards   93

Reality Factors   99

Chapter 6 TYPOLOGIES 113

Typologies Overview   113

Residential Streets   115

Green Streets   123

Alleys   139

Main Streets   154

Thoroughfares   171

Shared-Use Streets   182

Festival Streets   193

Chapter 7 **CASE STUDIES**   **207**

Mint Plaza   208

Nord Alley   217

Central Annapolis Road   225

78th Avenue SE Shared Use   235

High Point   243

Barracks Row   255

New York City   263

Terry Avenue North   271

Chapter 8 **WHAT'S NEXT**   **285**

Biophilic Cities: More Nature in the City   286

New Technologies   287

Building the Dream   290

Conclusions   296

RESOURCES   301

INDEX   311

ACKNOWLEDGMENTS

MANY THANKS TO MY HUSBAND, JOE IANO, my role model for becoming an author, and a great support in every way. This book would never have happened without him. Thanks to Allen, for his excellent editing skills; to Paul, for his willingness to climb fire escapes for a good photo angle; and to Ethan for his patience.

Thanks to the Silva boys—Alexander, Sam, and especially A.J.—for creating the time and space to make this project happen and for graphic expertise.

Many thanks to Grace Crunican for lending a quiet place to work for a few weeks, to Peg Staeheli for input and counsel, to the Gray family, especially Neil and Ellen, who read, listened, and gave great advice, to Kirk McKinley who takes great photos and was willing to give up a sunny Saturday to sort through them for us, and to Darby Watson who found the right word at the right time.

A shout out to i-sustain, and Patricia Chase in particular, as well as the SCAN Design Foundation, for helping decision makers in the Northwest see some of the world's best streetscapes first-hand, and bringing inspiration back home. Thanks to the Northwest Institute for Architecture and Urban Design (NIAUSI), for the time as a fellow to study and ponder the intimate streetscapes of Civita and Tuscany. Thanks to Todd Vogel and the International Sustainability Institute, for the vision and tenacity to change unused spaces into great gatherings and galleries. Thanks also to the Sustainable Cities Design Academy, for bringing together innovative minds to make better cities and public spaces, including the Central Annapolis Road project.

Thanks to all who spoke to us about their projects to make better streets and cities, and to those who shared their photos.

We hope that this book can be one of many contributions to a shift in thinking about the right-of-way as public space. Kudos to those who are on the forefront of using streets for new public places, for transportation choices, and for reconnecting our cities with nature. Their examples and hard lessons learned can foster wide-scale adoption of better use of the network of land for a significant improvement in the quality of life in our communities.

OVERVIEW

Photo courtesy of Gustafson Guthrie Nichol

FOR DECADES, THE CAR HAS REIGNED OVER AN ASPHALT AND CONCRETE REALM ON CITY STREETS. With the quality of urban living and sustainable development becoming increasingly important, communities are discovering new potential for urban streets.

More is being demanded from land in the right-of-way, and in some cities, demand is beginning to outpace available space. Pedestrian space has taken on increased value, not only for walking from one destination to the next, but for space in which to linger and interact. Cyclists are demanding more and safer bicycle routes. How much parking is to be provided, where it is to be located, and who is to be able to use it has sparked controversy. Transit typically uses the same lanes as private cars, but transit-only lanes help buses navigate more efficiently and safely on streets designed primarily for private vehicles. Streets are increasingly being seen as a resource for conveying and infiltrating stormwater, rather than taking away runoff in drains and below-grade storm sewer pipes.

As the structure of city form, streets are critical to urban transformation. For most of the past century, we have taken for granted that the primary purpose of a street is to move cars and other vehicles safely and efficiently, and to provide places to park near every destination. Through most of history, this has not been the case. Our approach to street use and design is not a given, but a choice, and its costs have been high in terms of the quality of urban life, social interaction, health, and the natural environment. Today, as society hopes to move toward a more sustainable way of life, it is necessary to challenge the assumptions embedded in current thinking. Those necessary challenges are beginning to be made by a growing range of people.

There has long been a disconnect between transportation engineers and the urban design community regarding the place of the automobile in the city. Generations of urbanists have valued the aesthetic qualities of towns and squares, and the age-old public places where people have met for exchange and interaction. In this way of thinking, the proliferation of the car has acted as a destructive force on irreplaceable community spaces.

> "The main issue is that the right to have access to every building in the city by private motorcar, in an age where everyone possesses such a vehicle, is actually the right to destroy the city."
>
> —*Lewis Mumford, 1957*[1]

There is no doubt that people across the globe value the historic, human-scale environments developed before the age of the automobile. Travelers regularly choose to spend time in venerable pedestrian environments, including car-free Venice, Italy, and the pedestrian-friendly streets of Paris, France. Even the top destination for world travel, New York's Times Square, with 35 million visitors, has recently chosen to pedestrianize its famed intersection.

While urban advocates such as Jane Jacobs and Lewis Mumford have long declared the automobile to be a problem in the city, professional transportation planners viewed vehicle efficiency as the problem to be solved, with progress easily measured in traffic volumes, travel time, level of service, and safety statistics. The tools developed for transportation planning in the latter half of the twentieth century only reinforce that the primary function of any transportation system is to make vehicle access safe, easy, and efficient.

---

[1] The Highway and the City, 1957.

Citizens have aligned with both of these conflicting points of view, often simultaneously and with an unintended dose of hypocrisy. For instance, people want to be able to drive everywhere, but they also don't want anyone else to park in their neighborhood. Many suburban neighborhoods forbid parking on the street, even with roads that are double the width needed for residential traffic.

To this paradox is added the new shift toward sustainable living. This factor brings more potential contradictions into the mix. Should we make greener cities and towns, or denser cities and towns? How much of the street should be for pedestrians, for bicycles, and for cars?

Designers and planners everywhere are beginning to recognize the importance of taking new approaches to streetscape design. Often, ideas for street reuse come out of local community efforts, and encounter resistance from City Hall. Many designers—civil engineers, transportation engineers, architects, landscape architects, and urban designers—are pushing to accommodate multiple uses in the street. People in local government are trying to promote change in street design, but are finding obstacles to the acceptance of alternative designs for the right-of-way.

In the course of researching the various innovative ways that people are using the right-of-way, we have found that there are three ways to utilize the space in the street well. First is *mobility.* Mobility has expanded to include multiple modes of travel—not just the car, but also pedestrians, bicycles, and transit. Second is *placemaking*. There are many opportunities for people to enjoy streets as memorable public spaces for sitting or gathering. Third is supporting *natural systems*. The space in the right-of-way is rich in opportunity for reconnecting the city to the functions and beauty of nature.

This book is intended for the full range of people looking for new ways to use the public right-of-way. Examples of streets that successfully contribute to more sustainable communities are growing in number, adding to an increasing body of knowledge that can help others identify and overcome obstacles to new approaches.

This book covers a wide range of approaches to streets that are healthier, more pleasant parts of public life: greener streets, pedestrian-friendly streets, bicycle-oriented streets, and streets that contribute to a vibrant community. Streets and communities are intertwined, and neither can successfully be considered in isolation of the other. We can do better than the singular approach of auto-dominated streets for every condition that has until recently dominated the conversation. We hope that the discussion in this book and the examples provided will create further dialogue, inspiring more successful examples and healthier communities.

WHY SHOULD WE RECONSIDER HOW TO USE THE STREET?

When streets are healthy, people are healthy.

People have become more sedentary, often driving rather than walking between everyday destinations. Reduced physical activity contributes to the current rise in obesity and chronic diseases. This change reflects not merely a lapse in our judgment, but the long-term effects of living in the unhealthy surroundings we have designed and created for ourselves. The lack of a good walking environment and the arrangement of land uses discourage people from walking as a primary way of moving from place to place. Thoughtful planning of the location, uses, and textures of the spaces in which we live encourages people to make healthier choices.

People need options to driving.

Not everyone can drive. Young people below driving age, the elderly, people with some types of physical disabilities, and people without the means to own a vehicle comprise a significant segment of society. A walkable community makes life easier and more pleasant for everyone, but especially for vulnerable populations within the larger community, whose transportation limitations reduce access to jobs, healthy food, health care, recreation, and social interaction.

Public transit and cycling are receiving increased attention as important alternatives to driving. The "Complete Streets" movement (see Chapter 5) is one example of a growing awareness that streets need to accommodate all modes of transportation in a safe and gracious manner.

Increased density requires a better public realm.

Several demographic trends support reconsideration of street use. The popularity of the "live downtown" movement, which advocates denser residential use in cities, has brought people to city centers where a full range of activities can be found within walking distance. Denser development near transit stops is another growth area. As new places to live are built in cities, the amount and quality of open spaces have not increased in proportion to the number of new residents. Successfully addressing this need will add to the health, vibrancy, and commercial success of these urban spaces, beginning an upward cycle that benefits everyone.

Streets present opportunities to contribute to the natural environment.

From added landscape to better treatment of rainwater, streets can greatly contribute to the environment. Greenery brings multiple benefits—adding to neighborhood character, providing shade, and improving air quality. By improving the environment of our cities, we can increase the health and value of communities while simultaneously protecting the environment.

LIVING STREETS

Strategies for Crafting Public Space

Chapter 1

PLACEMAKING IN THE PUBLIC RIGHT-OF-WAY

STREETS ARE MORE THAN JUST PLACES TO DRIVE. Streets are spaces in themselves, and a valuable part of the public realm. This simple concept is lost in much of the common understanding of the right-of-way. Mobility is thought of as the only function, but movement is one of several roles that the right-of-way can play. The paradigm becomes quite different if street design is approached from a multi-use, spatial standpoint rather than a single-purpose traffic function. The right-of-way becomes more than just something to move through as efficiently as possible. It can be considered as a network of spaces with a mix of uses and users, with spatial qualities and unique contexts. Streets can be conceived and designed to best support the life of communities in a variety of roles. It is a paradigm that needs exploring.

Figure 1-1

"Placemaking" means making spaces where people want to spend time. What makes a place where people choose to spend their time? A successfully conceived place often has qualities that are memorable—someone could describe it to you and you would know exactly where they meant. Often, there is something unusual about the space, a rich character that makes the space stand out from the places around it. A beautiful and distinctive view, large trees, or historic buildings can give voice to the local community and its culture. A well-designed spot, if it reflects the character and needs of the unique local culture, can provide a sense of place and setting around which that culture can center itself. Placemaking springs from understanding the local conditions and recognizing the opportunities that these conditions and cultures offer (Figure 1-1).

THE FUNCTION OF PLACES

In a healthy city, creating good public space in the right-of-way cannot be an afterthought. "People want to live in places that cultivate connectedness—to the physical city itself as well as the people in it," says urbanist Dan Bertolet. "True cities, small and large alike, have the power to bring people together."[1] It is the interchange of ideas and shared experience that brings vibrancy to urban areas, and it takes shared spaces to accomplish what cities do best.

Great urban areas have a variety of types and sizes of public spaces. Large parks and playgrounds, libraries, community centers, and schools are public spaces outside of the right-of-way. These public spaces are important hearts of civic life. The right-of-way plays a less recognized but equally critical role as both connective tissue and as a place in its own right.

In the densest cities, the right-of-way offers opportunities for much needed open space. The City of New York has the equivalent of 64 square miles of right-of-way, occupying as much space as fully 50 Central Parks.[2] In cities as dense as New York, finding enough open space to serve everyone is very challenging. The City of New York has found that underutilized portions of right-of-way can be

Figure 1-2   A plaza created from right-of-way offers open space for a Brooklyn neighborhood.
Photographer: Paul Iano

[1] Dan Bertolet in CityTank, "Ideas for the City", http://citytank.org/2011/04/13/c200-coming-home/, accessed July, 2011.

[2] NYC DOT Plaza Program, www.nyc.gov/html/dot/html/sidewalks/publicplaza.shtml.

reclaimed for plaza spaces. These transformed spaces are an important part of the City's effort to offer quality open space within a 10-minute walk for all residents (Figure 1-2).

But it is not only the densest urban areas that need quality public spaces. The sad fact that over 60 percent of Americans are overweight is an indication that we are not getting enough exercise.[3] Place-making in the streets—creating pleasant places to be outdoors and to move between destinations—improves the odds that more people will choose to walk.

Placemaking offers a wide range of benefits to a wide range of communities. Attractive sidewalks bring shoppers to Main Streets. Landscaping and street trees that beautify the right-of-way also benefit air quality and water quality. Quality places entice people to make optional trips to walk and to enjoy time out-of-doors. Bringing people together helps build social bonds in neighborhoods. Investments in the public realm, thoughtfully sited and designed, bring many tangible and intangible returns (Figures 1-3 and 1-4).

Figure 1-3 Quality public spaces offer numerous direct and indirect benefits for communities.

Figure 1-4 Active uses along the edge and places to sit make streets comfortable and interesting.

[3] "Obese," defined at Gallup-Healthways Well-Being Index, 2009, www.well-beingindex.com/.

WHY INVEST IN A QUALITY PUBLIC REALM?

"The measure of a city's greatness is to be found in the quality of its public spaces."[4]

John Ruskin

Why does a quality public realm matter? It can be easy to take for granted the profound impact our surroundings, and the quality of those surroundings, has on our daily lives. The spaces around us shape our lives, and everyone has a stake in this—from business owners who want to see their retail districts become profitable, to health experts encouraging exercise, to a commuter who uses the sidewalk to reach the bus stop on his daily trip to work—everyone has a stake in the public realm.

The public realm can:

■ Create excellent places to live, work, and play

Good outdoor spaces make the adjacent indoor spaces better. A place to sit and eat lunch in the sunshine during lunch hour, a pleasant jogging path, or a safe way for children to walk to the playground—together spatial details like these create desirable communities.

■ Strengthen community interaction

Neighbors get to know one another when they spend time in the public realm. When people work together to create shared spaces or activities—community gardens, "walking school buses" where children walk to school together, or improved retail districts—the bonds of the community increase. This is a theme that is heard again and again in successful cases of community-building efforts.

■ Encourage healthier lifestyles

People were made to walk. Our sedentary lifestyles have become problematic, in part because walking in spaces that are unpleasant and difficult to navigate has become unpleasant and difficult. Rethinking how the right-of-way is designed and used can help to reverse this trend.

■ Develop local economies

When people live within walking distance of stores and services, then they can spend less time traveling. They can spend money in their own neighborhoods, strengthening their local communities instead of bringing their business elsewhere. Attractive Main Streets provide more human-scaled alternatives to regional malls with chain stores and vast parking lots. When the quality of the public realm is outstanding, people will also come from other neighborhoods, turning local treasures into destinations. Cities that have made active and unique public spaces, such as the Riverwalk in San An-

---

[4] Commonly attributed to John Ruskin.

tonio, Texas, or Las Ramblas in Barcelona, Spain, attract tourists from all over the world, in addition to local residents.

- Promote urban patterns that are less dependent on fossil fuels

Besides being healthier for individuals, a good public realm makes for healthier cities. Walking and bicycling should be convenient, attractive choices for many daily destinations.

PLACEMAKING AND DESIGN

Streets, like all spaces, have three-dimensional characteristics. Streets are not just a flat plane on which to travel, but a volume of space, a kind of large "outdoor room," in which the surface of the street serves as a "floor," and the surrounding buildings serve as the "walls." Like any indoor space, streets have edges and enclosure (Figure 1-5).

The edges of a space define its volumetric character. When buildings line the street, serving as its walls, the activities they offer can encourage people to use the street. James Kunstler notes that "whether in the garden at home, or on Main Street, people like to feel sheltered and protected. We're attracted to arbors, pergolas, street arcades, even awnings…Buildings, therefore, are used to define and control space, and, by making it comprehensible to the human mind, make that space appear safe and welcoming."[5] We enjoy spaces that are scaled appropriately for use by people, interpreting them as cozy, intimate, or safe. We feel invited to spend time there. When streets have poorly defined edges, large empty spaces, and are sized for cars and trucks instead of people, the space instead becomes isolating, intimidating, and even dangerous, encouraging us to move through it and leave it quickly, just as the vehicles are doing. The poorly defined boundaries make the road appear larger than it actually is, with the space "bleeding" off into parking lots or empty spaces.

Some designers feel that there are ideal proportions for street sections, with building heights proportional to the street width. For instance, a 66-foot-wide street, lined with one-story buildings, 15 feet high at both sides of the street at the property lines, would have a building height to street ratio of under 1:4. If the street had wider streets or lower buildings, the definition of spatial volume begins to be lost. Two-story buildings (about a 1:3 ratio) or three-story buildings (about a 1:2 ratio) feel more comfortable to most people. Very dense cit-

Figure 1-5   The patterned stone makes a high-quality "floor" to the space.

---

[5] Kunstler, J.H., *Home from Nowhere: Remaking Our Everyday World for the Twenty-first Century,* Simon and Schuster: NY, 1998, p. 137.

Figure 1-6 Trees in the street and the median create a volume of space that deemphasizes the travel lanes. In this case, the trees compensate for the lack of buildings along the street edge.

ies may have very high ratios of building height to street width, which shade the street for much of the day and can create wind tunnels (Figure 1-6).

There are many ways to successfully suggest edge conditions, such as lining the space with mature street trees. It is not only the height of the edge in relationship to the width of the street that matters, but also the continuity of the edge conditions. Interesting streets may have a sequence along their length, perhaps with enclosures along blocks and openings at intersections. Some of the most problematic streets have insufficient definition along their length, or large intersections with multiple streets meeting at odd angles.

The desirable proportion of enclosure varies with climate and the materials used in the space. In hot, dry climates, streets have traditionally been quite narrow in order to shade pedestrians on the streets. The City of Phoenix studied street proportions in desert climates and weighed heat gain with the ability of buildings to release heat at night and found that a ratio of approximately 1:2 balanced heat gain and release. In climates with less sunlight, streets may benefit from increased width.[6]

---

[6] *Sustainable Development in a Desert Climate*, Chapter 4 of the Downtown Phoenix Plan, July 2008, pp. 4–6.

The edges of the street are typically regulated through land use laws such as zoning codes. Many land use regulations are intended to foster walkable neighborhoods by the use of requirements for street edges—calling for retail uses on the ground level, windows for display, a continuous street wall at the property line, or placing parking away from the front of the building. Regulations calling for active street fronts can help with placemaking, but the market needs to be able to support retail uses where required by code, or the street will have vacant storefronts.

Streets that have been designed with a priority on vehicles often result in disappointing "places." In the streets themselves, the ground plane is typically asphalt or concrete, with painted traffic markings. Even where there are sidewalks, the pedestrian environment offers little more in the way of amenity than the street environment. There may be little distinction between roadway and parking lots, and no sense of human-scaled enclosure.

For contrast, consider the medieval streets of Europe. Narrow and winding, they evolved over centuries, scaled for the people that built and used them. Medieval streets were built when every destination was walkable. Medieval streets and buildings were not built with plans and regulations, but were adapted in the field over time, responding to changing conditions and changing needs. In an era where moving materials was not as easy as it is today, the ground plane and the building walls that define the space were constructed with materials that came from nearby, suggesting a sense of continuity, wholeness, and rootedness.

These streets function as narrow public spaces that lead toward and connect to the plazas where the larger-scale activities of the town occur. Unlike the directional aimlessness of our wandering parking lots and malls, these narrow streets actively *guide* the pedestrian toward the plazas, adding an interactive and intimate purposefulness to the experience.

The photographs of Ortygia, the old section of the town of Syracusa, Sicily, show narrow streets with abundant Mediterranean light bouncing off the local white stone. The intimately scaled streets open up to the spacious Pizza del Duomo, creating a dramatic contrast in volumes. It is an example of constrained "people spaces" —streets with little or no vehicle traffic—opening up into the grander "people spaces" of the plaza. The quality of these spaces has drawn visitors for centuries (Figures 1-7 and 1-8).

Figure 1-7 The narrow, winding streets of Ortygia are an intimate scale.

Figure 1-8 The narrow streets connect to and contrast with the grand pedestrian plaza.

1-9a: The figure-ground of a medieval hilltown shows the narrow routes that connect to larger plazas. All of the white space is pedestrian space.

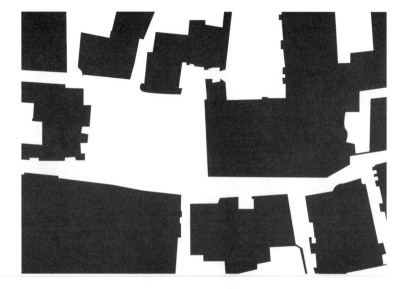

1-9b: The figure-ground of a modern city grid shows a regular pattern of land uses. Much of the white space, however, is for vehicles.

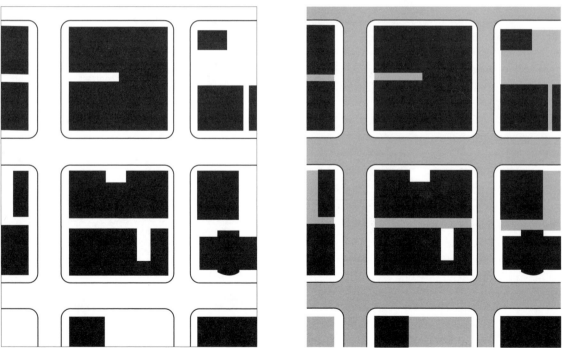

Ancient streets obviously evolved before automobiles dominated cities. But we tend to forget how much has been sacrificed in order to accommodate the car. Consider the generic urban street grid. Designers often show city "fabric" with drawings called "figure-ground" maps. The black indicates buildings, and the white is unbuilt space. In a figure-ground map of Ortygia, the white space, the void, is "people space." However, when automobiles are introduced into the "open" space, especially in high numbers and at high speeds, the space for people is confined in narrow bands up against the property lines. The people spaces—typically sidewalks—may be of higher or lower quality, but they are fundamentally different from the old streets where narrow pedestrian spaces lead to and opened up on plaza space (Figures 1-9a through 1-9c).

These narrow streets are distinct as volumes of space. This is an important concept, because many people involved in the design of streets do not fully consider the three-dimensionality of streetscape. The medieval streets—compressed volumes of space—bring people to the contrasting open space of the plaza. The variety of compressed and open space can make a very powerful and attractive network of open spaces.

1-9c: On the same city grid, vehicle areas are shown in gray, including travel lanes and parking areas. The pedestrians are on sidewalks, and the intersections are unlike the plazas where pedestrian routes historically connected.

Figure 1-10 Trees and buildings together form a volume that comfortably encloses the pedestrian space of the sidewalk.

The most successful sidewalk spaces bear a resemblance to medieval streets in that they have a volumetric character of their own. A traditional Main Street model, for instance, would have store fronts along one side with active uses, an ample space to walk and a canopy of trees with elements that buffer the traffic on the street side (Figure 1-10).

Designing for Comfort

Spaces need to be designed for year-round comfort in the particular climate in which they are located. Weather protection from harsh sun or persistent rain encourages walking in a variety of climates. Cities in colder climates cannot dismiss half the year as unsuitable for the use of public space, and many of these cities have found ways to celebrate winter with special lighting, winter carnivals, and holiday markets. Thoughtfully sited trees or other vertical elements can block pedestrians from wind. "Warmth features," such as fireplaces or glazed winter garden spaces, entice people to enjoy public spaces during winter. In Copenhagen, overhead heaters and blankets make outdoor seating comfortable even during cold months.

Thoughtful urban design also makes a difference in the attractiveness of public spaces in hot climates. There are many design solutions for providing shade, including trees and arcades. Trees have the added benefit of cooling the air with evapotranspiration. Using lighter-colored materials that retain less heat can significantly change the comfort level of a space. Water features cool spaces, and can become iconic design elements.

Public Space and Transit

Pedestrian areas adjacent to a major transit connection need space designed to accommodate the movement of people to and from the station, and waiting areas where transit is at-grade. Wide sidewalks or plaza space is very important near busy transit links. Ample space at these locations can support retail or market uses that benefit from the presence of transit patrons.

Transit stations and stops offer interesting design opportunities that can make the use of transit more appealing and can result in well-activated spaces and successful businesses. Some cities ask for amenities on the buildings adjacent to transit stops, such as weather protection, seating, or leaning rails. Transit riders then tend to congregate near the building, and property owners may resent the use of their building edge as a waiting area. Other building owners find that transit patrons create business for their retail tenants.

For the transit users, having the building up against their backs feels intuitively safer and more comfortable than waiting in an open, exposed area. When people wait alongside buildings, they must travel across the full width of the sidewalk to the curb in order to get on the bus or train. This pedestrian cross-movement interrupts the flow of people moving along the sidewalk, and can be problematic in congested areas (Figure 1-11).

Another approach to locating transit waiting areas is to place shelters near the curb, which is possible if there is sufficient circulation space between the transit shelter and the building face. Transit amenities need to be designed so that transit patrons are assets to adjacent businesses. Considerations for designing successful transit space include adequate circulation space and visibility of building entries, safety, and lighting (Figure 1-12).

Outside of dense urban areas, transit stops are opportunities for simple amenities that can be enjoyed by anyone. Tasteful landscaping, and a place to sit or perhaps to stay dry, add to the walkability of a neighborhood for everyone in the community as well as making transit use more attractive.

ENCOURAGING THE USE OF PUBLIC SPACE

Quality, safety, convenience, and interesting destinations are among the factors that determine how people choose to move around the city. As a culture and a country, our successful efforts to make driving convenient have favored the car as the most common choice for movement. This, in turn, has led to spread-out destinations that make walking and bicycling impractical. Better pedestrian environments and more compact land uses will encourage walking, and better bicycle facilities will increase the number of people who choose to cycle.

The work of Copenhagen-based Gehl Architects has distinguished between necessary activities, optional activities, and social activities. Optional activities are very dependent on the quality of the space, and in a good physical environment, a wide array of optional activities can occur. People choose to stroll, play, sit, and eat.

The attractiveness of optional trips is key to successful public space. Placemaking nurtures these optional trips, which depend heavily on the quality of the experience. Successful placemaking takes

Figure 1-11 Lean rails offer some comfort to transit patrons, but don't encourage longer stays.

Figure 1-12 Bus shelters can be located near the curb when the sidewalk is sufficiently wide.

Figure 1-13 Streets have always been places for shopping and meeting neighbors, even when cars have been added to streets designed prior to the automobile age.

advantage of the opportunities specific to a particular site and the potential of each site to contribute to the public realm. Depending on the needs of the neighborhood, this may mean creating new spaces for community activities, bringing out the identity of a neighborhood, or making enticing places that encourage people to walk from place to place. Site-specific design begins with an understanding of the natural context, and may include easy-to-overlook factors such as the light conditions and the wind and weather patterns that form the basis for comfort in the space. An understanding of the culture of the people who will use the space, through collaboration with the community, is fundamental to making places that the community wants and needs (Figure 1-13).

Streets have been meeting places throughout history. Even with the addition of vehicles into cities, many streets are still at the heart of civic life. Expanding the physical space available for public life is a critical opportunity in dense urban neighborhoods. Widened sidewalks, promenades, urban trails, small spaces for sitting, larger places for gathering—there are many types of spaces that bring people to-gether and make communities interesting places to walk and to linger. Better public spaces bring more people outside into shared activities, and build stronger communities. By creating destinations—tables and chairs near a favorite street vendor, a fountain that encourages play, or public ball courts—more people choose to spend time in the public realm. Well-designed and cared-for public spaces are a source of community pride and often generate economic benefits.

Good public spaces can make neighborhoods safer as well. An intense mixture of uses can mitigate less-than-civil behavior. The urban park that accommodates a skateboard park, water feature, seating areas, and a grassy lawn that is directly between the library and a major grocery store attracts numerous user groups—a mixture of ages, seasonal uses, and time of day uses that in combination help keep the park feeling safe.

The body of design strategies that help make public space safer is often referred to as "crime prevention through environmental design" (CPTED) or "defensible space." Good visibility, plentiful users, and a sense of local ownership of the space all help make spaces feel safer. Even so, police or security presence is a reality of managing public space, and many communities have found security "ambassadors" a worthwhile investment (Figure 1-14).

Figure 1-14 Security personnel can be part of keeping spaces safe.

RECLAIMING RIGHT-OF-WAY FOR PUBLIC PLACES

One of the most exciting recent trends in urban design is the transformation of underutilized right-of-way into successful public spaces. New York and San Francisco have been on the forefront of this movement. It is no coincidence that the country's densest urban areas have discovered the value of even relatively small parcels of land. The old adage of "location, location, location" is as important for urban planners as it is for real estate investors. Even small spaces in these desirable locations can make huge contributions to the public realm.

The use and design of repurposed spaces must be right for their context. Is the space located in a dense urban location, where people need gathering places, or is it in an industrial area? What can the space add to the context that is appropriate and needed? What problems can it help solve? If right-of-way is not contributing to mobility, then it is ripe with opportunity for placemaking or improving ecological function.

Figure 1-15   A green street, where newly planted landscape replaced a driving lane.

Right-of-way space can be used to add landscape and to improve drainage. Where there is less density, not every space needs to be "inhabited" space. Greening—adding trees, landscaping, and natural drainage—has the effect of "beautification," but goes beyond mere aesthetics by serving environmental functions, and increasing a community's sense of pride of place (Figure 1-15).

Portions of the right-of-way may be suitable for park space, for passive or active recreation. Some parks include basketball or bocce courts or chess tables. Park facilities for dogs and dog owners have proved popular with a group that needs to be outside multiple times each day. Where people are invited to stay in the space, the design needs to support comfort and safety, with clear lighting and lines of sight.

A successful mixed-use park needs plenty of people to keep it activated. Underutilized right-of-way in denser neighborhoods, where people need more open space, is a perfect opportunity for a pedestrian plaza. Places with transit connections are especially good candidates for creating successful open space because of people walking to and from transit. A mix of uses—residences, businesses, places to eat, transit—means that people come and go over most of the day and evening. That mix is critical to the health of businesses that may not be able to survive on a population that is only present during the 8-to-5 work day.

One of the challenges with creating mixed-use spaces is the amount of time needed to initiate and complete the many incremental steps required from conception to construction. The public realm is always evolving, and the best public spaces are created over time. It is often more successful to create a place with character by infilling missing pieces within a district than by launching large-scale new developments. Infill development means that there is a variety of uses and design styles, with buildings and elements from different eras, and often quirky conditions that make for interesting and attractive spaces.

The public realm is complex, and successful transformations involve policy frameworks, a supportive local jurisdiction, options for mobility, and a committed community of residents and business owners. The public-sector investments in streetscape and public places can encourage desired private development. Indeed, the goal of good urban planning is exactly that—to foster public actions that spur the private sector to take actions toward a better community.

Well-conceived, well-designed public actions can be catalysts in the creation of quality places to live and work. For instance, public transit systems can jump-start new development and new activity that, in turn, make the transit system better utilized. But new public spaces by themselves do not necessarily turn troubled places around. Cities evolve with complex interactions of private and public owners, community endeavors, and the different perspectives provided by regulatory, economic, and cultural frameworks. Public spaces need to serve a mix of users and uses. They need to support activities that are desired by a mix of users. The right-of-way is an enormous opportunity for placemaking, but like any good public space, must be in the right place, with the right design, in order to be a true community asset.

Reclaiming Right-of-Way: PARK(ing) Day

Why do it? Because it's your city!

(PARK)ing Day website, frequently asked questions

Civic actions, by individuals or small groups, can add up to the spread of significant ideas. In 2005, a San Francisco art and design studio called Rebar put quarters in a downtown metered parking space and converted it into a temporary public park for the 2-hour duration of the time allotted on the meter. The idea of the project was to challenge assumptions about the way that public space is used in the City, and to empower people to define how space is used. "Renting" a metered parking space is a cost-effective way to briefly control a piece of the City.

Figure 1-16 Park(ing) Day brings out creative ideas on how to use the street. *Eli Brownell/King County Parks*

This small-scale guerrilla action inspired people all over the world to create temporary open spaces of their own. Rebar put their idea out as an "open source" project, with a manual on how to make temporary parks out of parking spaces. The outcome, PARK(ing) Day, has become an annual, worldwide event. Just four years after the original installation, PARK(ing) Day 2009 simultaneously generated 700 parks in 140 cities on 6 continents[7] (Figure 1-16).

In some cities, there appear to be no restrictions on what can be done in a parking space, so long as the space is paid for. Other cities specifically limit what is legal within a parking space. Within a few years of the original PARK(ing) Day precedent, several cities, including Los Angeles, California, and Seattle, Washington, have created permits especially for PARK(ing) Day.

PARK(ing) Day installations have been harder to accomplish in other cities. After Louisville, Kentucky's Urban Design Studio set up their park on South Third Street, the action was shut down and the "park" moved indoors. Metro Louisville Public Works required approval from four different departments, a traffic plan, and a three-foot buffer with reflective cones for safety. "This example," wrote Brandon Klayko in the Broken Sidewalks blog, "really gets at the heart of the discussion that needs to be taking place: who are our public spaces really for?"[8]

Reclaiming Right-of-Way: New York City's Green Light for Midtown

New York City announced its Green Light for Midtown program in February 2009. NYCDOT described the program as an initiative to improve mobility and safety that would also make the area a better place to live, work, and visit. The redesign of several intersections in Midtown was based on a study showing improved traffic flow where Broadway's diagonal cuts across Manhattan's grid.

Temporary measures—paint and orange barrels—were put in place to test channelizing traffic. The channelization resulted in five pedestrian plazas along the route, creating an aggregate 2.5 acres of "found" open space. The Times Square Alliance brought in 376 folding lawn chairs to accommodate summer crowds before the more substantial furniture arrived.

The experiment in Midtown was declared a success on many levels. It may seem counterintuitive that reducing the amount of drivable space would improve traffic flow. But Broadway's angle cuts off the grid and results in a wide intersection where it cuts across the avenues that run north and south. According to the Green Light for Midtown Evaluation Report, reconfiguring these awkward intersections has improved traffic flow and reduced injuries to motorists, passengers, and pedestrians.

The new pedestrian spaces have proved to be very popular. The evaluation team found 84 percent more people are staying in the public spaces of Times and Herald Squares. They found that people were reading, eating, talking, and taking photographs in the spaces. Over a quarter of Times

[7] http://parkingday.org/, website content by Rebar, 2011, accessed July, 2011.
[8] http://brokensidewalk.com/?s=park%28ing%29+day.

Figure 1-17 The reconfiguration of Times Square increased and improved pedestrian space. *Photographer: Paul Iano*

Square employees are now leaving their offices for lunch more often. Residents report that they are shopping more in the neighborhood. Nearly three-quarters of New Yorkers felt that Times Square had improved dramatically[9] (Figure 1-17).

"New York is the world's greatest stage for urban design and streetscapes," says New York Department of Transportation Commissioner Janette Sadik-Khan.[10] These experiments have inspired new projects in all of New York City's boroughs, and become models for other cities. Chapter 7 further discusses the program and its policy foundation.

---

[9] New York City Department of Transportation, About the Green Light for Midtown Project, City of New York, 2011, accessed July 2011.

[10] "NYCDOT Launches Design Competition for Temporary Plazas in Times Square, Initiates Capital Design Process for Permanent Improvements," Press Release, March 3, 2010.

Reclaiming Right-of-Way: Pavement to Parks

San Francisco's Pavement to Parks program is an excellent model of repurposing urban right-of-way as plazas. Based on New York's conversion of excess right-of-way into pedestrian plazas, San Francisco is experimenting with new ways of using streets. Each project is "intended to be a public laboratory"[11] with the City and community working together to see if temporary changes should be made permanent. Selection criteria for the Pavement to Parks programs include space available in underutilized roadway, a lack of public space in the vicinity, community support, potential to improve bike and pedestrian safety, uses that can attract people to the space, and a steward for the space.

The first of the Mayor's Pavement to Parks initiatives—the 7,800-square-foot pedestrian plaza at 17th and Market—opened in May of 2009. DPW Director Ed Reiskin worked with the Castro Street Community Betterment District, the MTA, the City's Planning Department, the Mayor's Director of Greening, and City Supervisor Bevan Dufty. The temporary nature of the changes allowed a much easier process, and alleviated concerns expressed by some neighbors that the new space could result in crime and trash. If it didn't work, the project could easily be removed. The design work, done by Public Architecture, uses salvaged or recycled materials and is seen as an experiment—hopefully the first of many new repurposed public spaces. The local businesses have played a strong role, including setting up and putting away tables and chairs.

The success of the project shows. A year later, more permanent features were being put in place by volunteers, including Planning Department staff. The park was dedicated as Jane Warner Plaza to honor the memory of a well-loved neighborhood policewoman.

One particularly interesting initiative in San Francisco's program is the creation of "Parklets" by reclaiming two to three parking spaces. The sidewalk grade is extended, and instead of the parking space, there are benches, planters, landscaping, and bike racks. Some have tables and chairs (Figure 1-18).

Columbus Parklet is San Francisco's third Parklet. Most of the funding came from donations. The design, done by Rebar Group (the originators of PARK(ing) Day), was donated, and the adjacent cafe provides daily maintenance. The Parklet is free and open to the public.[12]

Figure 1-18 This parklet is a temporary sidewalk extension with a modular design that fits in the width of a parking lane. *Photo: Rebar Copyright © 2010 by Rebar Group, Inc. Walklet is a registered trademark of Rebar Group, Inc. Used with permission.*

---

[11] http://sfpavementtoparks.sfplanning.org/, website sponsored by Mayor's Office of Greening and San Francisco Planning Department.

[12] More information is available at http://sfpavementtoparks.sfplanning.org/.

Pedestrian Streets: Didn't We Try This Before?

As the expanding use of automobiles drew the life out of city centers in the 1960s and 1970s, some downtowns tried to compete with suburban shopping centers by offering easy parking and creating pedestrian malls. Most of these experiments failed, and cars were eventually reintroduced on the streets. It has become conventional wisdom that all American streets should have cars, regardless of the context.

While it may seem obvious, successful pedestrian streets require lots of pedestrians. American cities lost the culture of pedestrianism as they began to be shaped by the travel patterns of the car. Cities were carefully zoned into separate uses, with fewer and fewer downtown residents. Job opportunities became less concentrated in the city centers. Given the powerful magnitude of these shifts, removing cars from a shopping street was nowhere near sufficient for creating an urban renaissance.

Figure 1-19 Quality pedestrian spaces attract residents and visitors. *Photographer: Dave Knight*

In contrast, pedestrianized zones began to appear in the 1960s in Europe, with greater success than in North America. The old city centers of Europe were built before cars, and never fully adapted to large numbers of vehicles. Many of the pedestrian zones in Europe are destinations for tourists, who are attracted by the quality of the environment and character of the places. Many are located in cities with excellent transit systems. It is no wonder that places that functioned well before the introduction of the automobile would be better suited as pedestrian zones than the cities built during the height of the automobile era (Figure 1-19).

Even in Europe, these zones with little to no traffic evolved over time. Copenhagen's Strøget is a largely car-free zone that is crossed in places by through-traffic. One of the reasons that this zone works so well is that 37 percent of trips in Copenhagen are made by bicycle.[13] Many people live and work within an easy cycle, and people report that the main reason they cycle is because it is easy and fast. The reduction of

13 City of Copenhagen, Cycle Statistics, www.kk.dk/sitecore/content/Subsites/CityOfCopenhagen/SubsiteFrontpage/LivingInCopenhagen/CityAndTraffic/CityOfCyclists/CycleStatistics.aspx.

cars in Strøget happened incrementally, beginning with temporary holiday closures, and expanding as people adjusted to each round of changes.

There are some notable successes in American pedestrian streets. Most are in college towns—Boulder, Colorado; Burlington, Vermont; Charlottesville, Virginia. College campuses are some of the best pedestrian environments in North American cities, and their successful examples of pedestrian streets are also often coupled with historic downtowns.

The management and programming of pedestrian streets is an important predictor of success. Many successful pedestrian places enjoy considerable use as locations to hold performances and events. Some places have developed a tradition of grassroots activities. In Boulder, for instance, the Pearl Street Mall is filled with performers of all kinds and audiences glad to be entertained. Seattle's Pike Place Market is known for its street performers, but those activities are managed by the Preservation & Development Authority. Locations for performance are designated, and performers must pay for an annual permit badge.

The lessons to be learned from earlier attempts at pedestrian streets are important, but the failures of that effort should not be overly extrapolated. A renewed interest in urban living has blossomed since the pedestrian malls in American downtowns fell into disfavor in the 1980s and onward. Today, walkable, mixed-use neighborhoods, if not pedestrian malls, are in fashion. Streets, as well as buildings, can be mixed-use—with a diversity of activities, ways of getting around, and different kinds of places. There will be new opportunities for pedestrian-friendly streets that respond to shifts in demographics and culture. Successful streets will evolve and support the needs of the people that use them.

CONSIDERING ALL THE ELEMENTS IN THE RIGHT-OF-WAY

The right-of-way moves more than people and goods. Water, sewer, telecommunication, and power move above, on, and below the street surface. Utilities and services may not seem glamorous, but they are important components of the public realm and need careful consideration in the design and maintenance of public space.

The pipes and conduits that carry water, sewers, and natural gas run underground, usually below travel lanes in the street, but sometimes under the planting strip or sidewalk. The location of the utilities can limit the location of street trees, so the desired locations for trees should be considered when laying out new utility locations.

Electricity and cables may be underground, or on overhead poles. Electric transit also functions through overhead power transmission. In addition to the physical space this utility infrastructure occupies, it also requires safety clearances from other objects—both vertically and horizontally.

The presence of above-ground utilities impacts the type and location of street trees. Smaller trees may be the best solution below overhead wires, rather than larger species that require substantial pruning.

Power line corridors that carry high-voltage lines have restrictions on what can be placed on the surface within the corridor. Some cities have used this restriction on buildings in the corridor as an opportunity to build long stretches of bicycle or pedestrian trails, such as Seattle's Interurban Trail and Chief Sealth Trail. High-voltage lines along city streets may require setbacks from the adjacent buildings, offering additional space for pedestrians at the building frontage.

Telecommunication lines have had a large visual impact on city streets. Telephone and power poles carry a variety of lines belonging to public agencies and private companies. Some telecommunication networks are installed in underground corridors below travel lanes or parking zones. By keeping the underground utilities away from planting zones, trees stay healthier, but the pavement needs to be ripped up and replaced when changes or repairs to the utilities below are required. The new generation of wireless connections manifests itself in cabinets on the surface, competing for the often-scare resource of sidewalk space.

Utility boxes are too often an afterthought, and if they are located without thought to the pedestrian space, they can become obstacles to mobility and major detractions from the quality of a space. In many cases, traffic signal controller boxes must be placed near the street corner, proximate to the signal loop detectors and hardware. In these cases, every attempt should be made to minimize the impact of the boxes on sight lines and aesthetics. They need to be far enough away from the curb ramps so that access to the crosswalk is not impeded. The best solution is usually for the street designer to work with the traffic engineers so that the solution works both functionally and aesthetically. (Figure 1-20).

Figure 1-20 Utility boxes should be placed with pedestrian access and public spaces in mind to avoid unfortunate consequences for streetscape designs.

All utilities need to be accessed from time to time for maintenance and repair. Part of the art of good street design is arranging all the necessary elements of the street in ways that function well for the utilities but create a thoughtfully arranged streetscape that prioritizes public activities.

Waste removal is another consideration in designing the street. Garbage trucks are often oversized vehicles with large required clearances. Garbage trucks may also need access via alleys or other service drives. Some urban areas are reconsidering how waste is handled. The details of how waste is sorted, stored, and collected can encourage recycling and waste reduction. Methods of waste collection can also free up use of streets and alleys for uses other than storing garbage. See the Case Study on Nord Alley in Chapter 7 for the changes brought about in Seattle's Clear Alley Program.

Chapter 2

MOBILITY

THE CONCEPT OF MOBILITY HAS BROADENED. Instead of just thinking about transportation from the standpoint of efficiency for cars, the equation now must define how to best move people and goods. The way that people and goods are moved has major spatial implications. The amount of space needed to convey the same amount of people in private vehicles versus transit is striking. Consider moving 200 people through the city. This may take some 175 cars, or it may take 3 buses.

We love our cars. But they come at a high price in terms of efficiencies measured in health, quality of urban space, resources spent, and air and water quality. A broader view of mobility and how different modes of transportation can be balanced begins with understanding each mode and its opportunities to support healthier communities (Figure 2-1).

Figure 2-1 *Photographer: Rick Browning*

CONNECTING PEOPLE TO PLACES

People generally use streets to move from one destination to another for a specific purpose. Travel may mean getting from home to your child care, your workplace, school, or shopping district. Daily trips connect people to the land uses that make up the social, economic, and cultural fabric of their community. The right-of-way is the space that accommodates the movement from one place to another for pedestrians, cars, trucks, buses, and bicycles. Even movement that is purely recreational—walking, cycling, or driving for pleasure—has an origin and a destination.

In considering the design of streets, it is important to remember that streets need to serve land uses, rather than dominate them. This simple consideration flips the conventional approach to design in the right-of-way. Movement is generally not the goal in itself, but allows people to get to places and activities.

Standard street design assumes that the car is the most important vehicle to be accommodated. Truck and emergency vehicle access is next in the hierarchy, followed by transit, then pedestrians and bicycles. Complex modeling and data analysis is conducted to establish a baseline for efficient car movement and, given assumptions about growth in population and changes in land use, the number of cars that will need to be accommodated in the future. Traffic volumes, speeds, travel time, and turning movements are collected, access requirements imposed, and sometimes changes in land use are made or discouraged based on the ability of the proposed street to handle the envisioned number of cars.

Once the core business of accommodating the car is accomplished, other modes of transportation, such as walking and bicycling, are squeezed into the remaining space, or not considered at all. It should come as no surprise that when the street and adjacent buildings are designed first and foremost to accommodate cars, other functions are not well supported. The best way to get around becomes, by default, the car.

Another approach is to start with the types of land uses that need to be served, and then define the best way to serve them. This approach involves a more holistic look at the natural, social, cultural, and economic systems that the transportation system serves. The new approach assumes that rights-of-way should be designed to support a full range of functions—not just vehicular access. For cities and towns that value denser, more compact centers, the new approach places much greater importance on the needs of people coming by foot, bike, or on transit. If land use policy plainly favors compact mixed-use centers, the desired outcome will not be achieved by continuing to provide for cars as the first priority.

WHY HAVE WALKABLE, BIKEABLE COMMUNITIES?

If you plan cities for cars and traffic, you get cars and traffic. If you plan for people and places, you get people and places.

Fred Kent, People for Public Spaces

Living in neighborhoods that do not require driving for most daily activities has direct and indirect benefits. Portland, Oregon, has made walkable communities a priority in their Portland Plan, with the concept of a 20-minute neighborhood. The idea is that people can get to the places that they need to go to on a daily basis in a convenient pedestrian environment: school, shopping, transit, parks, and social activities. This is actually an old idea. Before cars were prevalent, many people could walk to the places that they needed to get to (Figure 2-2). Many of these indirect benefits are similar to the list in

Figure 2-2 Walkable, bikeable communities are comfortable places to spend time with neighbors. *Courtesy of SvR Design*

Chapter 1, and include: better places to live, stronger communities, and better individual health. There are also direct benefits to families and individuals. Creating walkable, bikeable communities can:

- Reduce transportation costs

  American households spend a large portion of their resources on transportation. Transportation costs are second only to housing for the majority of families, and low-income families spend a disproportionate share of their income on transportation costs. Walkable communities can save families the cost of gasoline, car repair, and the cost of a second or third family vehicle.[1]

- Reduce time spent in the car

  Sprawling communities translate into a lifestyle that requires long hours behind the wheel. Long commutes to work, time spent in traffic jams, driving between errands, and hours shuttling youngsters to activities are typical of suburban living. Walkable, bikeable communities are appealing to many people tired of spending too much time in the car.

- Offer mobility options for everyone

  Not everyone can drive. Children, seniors, and people with disabilities need to find ways to get around without using a car. Walkable, bikeable communities allow independence for people who cannot or choose not to drive, and reduces the burden on family members who do drive.

- Increase property values

  Walkable neighborhoods are more attractive to home buyers. Walk Score® is a computer-based algorithm that rates places and has been used to look at the value of homes within easy walking distance of multiple destinations. A report done for CEO's for Cities found that walkability increased home values from a few thousand dollars up to $34,000.[2] Even accounting for the various factors in comparing home prices, it showed that people value neighborhoods with options for mobility.

THE SIZE AND SHAPE OF MOVEMENT

Streets and space within the right-of-way include functions other than just movement. Streets are both conduits for movement and places in themselves. Different types of streets accomplish the balance of functions to different degrees. Highways and roads are given over almost entirely to movement

---

[1] Surface Transportation Policy Project (STPP). "Transportation Costs and the American Dream: Why a Lack of Transportation Choices Strains the Family Budget and Hinders Home Ownership." STPP, July 2003, www.transact.org/library/decoder/american_dream.pdf.

[2] "Walking the Walk: How Walkability Raises Home Values in U.S. Cities." Joe Cortright, Impresa, Inc., for CEOs for Cities, August 2009, accessed via http://blog.walkscore.com/wp-content/uploads/2009/08/WalkingTheWalk_CEOsforCities.pdf.

and connecting one destination to another. Plazas, squares, parks, and some streets are destinations in and of themselves, even though people do move through them on their way to another destination. As a designer of streets, understanding the interplay of the full range of functions is critical (Figure 2-3).

The level of movement that can be expected on a street is the basis for categorizing streets into a system of street classifications. Most jurisdictions classify streets as principal arterials, minor arterials, collectors, and local streets. These categories are based on measurements of travel speed and time, traffic volume, distance traveled, and the typical land uses served (e.g., residential versus industrial versus commercial).

Engineers also measure the "level of service" for vehicles. The highest level of service describes the condition where traffic flows at or above the posted speed limit and drivers have full mobility between lanes. Level of service is also measured at intersections, ranking from a high of Level A to a low of Level F, based on the number of seconds of wait time for motorists at signalized and unsignalized intersections.

Figure 2-3 Light rail, density, and a mix of uses on the street are hallmarks of new transit-oriented communities.

Traffic modeling uses empirical data from existing conditions to set a baseline condition and then predict future or revised traffic volumes. These models provide a way to analyze and measure proposed changes to a street system. Travel demand forecasting is intended to help make informed transportation policy decisions using demand modeling and network modeling.

Street classifications and level of service indicated by traffic modeling are significant measures because they affect decisions regarding street design as well as the allocation of resources. For example, a principal arterial with a level of service of "D" today that is anticipated to have a level of service of "F" in the future is likely to attract more resources for new improvements and repair, than a local street with low volumes and relatively free-flowing traffic.

The improvements might come in the form of wider travel lanes, additional turn lanes, more complex intersections with multiple traffic signal phases, and more "green time" for traffic signals

Figure 2-4 Pedestrian measures are quite different than measures for cars. People may choose active streets, but no one chooses to be stuck in traffic.

on the main road. Although these improvements satisfy the need to move the volume of vehicles generated by unrestricted demand as efficiently as possible, they do so at the expense of movement for other modes—especially pedestrians and bicyclists, as well as natural system elements such as street trees, landscaping, and stormwater.

Movement of vehicular traffic has been the core mode of developing a transportation system. Significantly less time and effort has been placed on assessing the qualities and needs of pedestrian and bicycle movement. Recently, methods that parallel the measurements used to assess and analyze car movement are being applied to measure pedestrian and bicycle movement.

The level of service framework has been applied to both pedestrian and bicycle movement, but because the characteristics of movement for these modes is drastically different than those of the car, the resulting measures have not been as successful. For example, pedestrian level of service rates the volume of pedestrians on a sidewalk using the same structure as vehicle level of service. The sidewalk that received the highest ranking—level of service A—had free-flowing pedestrian movement with minimal delay and maximum space between people. In contrast, pedestrian level of service F describes a crowded sidewalk where movement is not free-flowing. This would indicate that a sidewalk devoid of interaction is preferred (Figure 2-4).

In reality, the opposite is true: Sidewalks with free-flowing movement and few pedestrians are not the markers of a healthy, vibrant pedestrian environment. Pedestrian level of service F is much more descriptive of the type of bustling sidewalk characteristic of a desirable place for pedestrians. Clearly, pedestrian movement needs a different set of analytic tools.

Potential tools are being developed to fill the void—although none have yet been formally approved or recommended to take the place of the traditional tool set. These new techniques measure both the quantitative and qualitative aspects of the pedestrian realm. Part of the impetus for developing these techniques is to help elevate interest in, and funding for, improvements to the pedestrian environment. Several are designed to be used by community groups interested in better understanding and improving the walkability of their neighborhoods and include walkability audits and public space surveys.

Each element in the right-of-way has a spatial dimension. These dimensions are manifested as travel lane widths, bridge heights, curb radii, tree canopy, and sewer trunk line dimensions. The size and movement characteristics also set dimensions where the network plugs into private buildings—loading docks, side sewers, car and bicycle parking, and entryways.

Spatial needs of modes frequently conflict with one another. Considering the basic needs of each mode separately helps to understand the affinities and challenges that occur when they are integrated within the right-of-way.

The Personal Vehicle

Ranging in size from the diminutive compact to the large-scale sport utility vehicle, the dimensions of personal vehicles vary widely. A mid-size car is about 15 feet long, 5 feet high, and approximately 6 feet wide. A light truck, sport utility vehicle, or minivan is two to three feet longer, requiring more space to navigate, drive, and park. As the shortest vehicles on the road, the personal vehicle does not typically dictate minimum height clearances.

The driver of the typical personal vehicle values a quick, easy trip that is safe and reliable. Minimal obstructions, inconveniences, or stopping points enhance the experience. The single-purpose roadway with limited access maximizes these goals. On streets that allow turning movements, vehicles can move most quickly with wide curb radii and slip lanes. Synchronized traffic signals are preferred—nothing is finer to a driver than seeing a string of green lights into the distance. When stopping at a light is required, the right turn on red is expected.

At the end point of a trip, the driver seeks secure, free or low-cost comfortably sized parking spaces, as convenient as possible to the front door of their destination. On-street parking spaces are also desirable and if you ask neighborhood business owners, they will tell you that on-street parking in very close proximity to their front door is a necessity for their business to succeed. A clear path from the car to the walking area of the sidewalk is also desirable.

Parking requirements for personal vehicles have been reduced in many jurisdictions. Even so, the parking requirements have often taken a "worst case scenario" attitude, providing ample parking for the most intense usages, and are often sparsely utilized.

In large parking lots, there are typically few, if any, accommodations for pedestrians. The slow volumes and limited number of cars actually allow a reasonably safe co-existence of vehicles and pedestrians in the same way that a shared-use street functions. Because we are accustomed to the mix of pedestrians and cars in large parking lots, we consider it safe, even though other shared use conditions seem foreign and potentially dangerous.

Trucks

Trucks and service vehicles range from small delivery trucks with basically the same needs as the larger end of the personal vehicle scale, to oversize freight vehicles that require special permits to operate on city streets. Trucks, like cars, prefer limited access highways with roadway dimensions that are wide, multilane, and have at least 20 feet of height clearance from the roadway to the underside of a bridge or other overhead element. Cities often create freight routes that allow for movement of vehicles with extra width, height, or weight, with wide clearances and larger turning radii. Moving freight and goods in an urban environment with a tight street grid and narrow lanes is very challenging, especially for the larger end of the truck spectrum.

For those moving goods from one place to another, fast travel times and minimal delay are ideal. Hazardous materials are often relegated to certain roadways and restricted on others. Wide turning radii make it possible to turn large vehicles without going into the adjacent lane. Large curb cuts make for more direct access. At the end of a trip, trucks are best supported by loading zones close to the main delivery entrance, or loading docks in large buildings that are easily accessible from the street.

Trucks are found to some extent on most streets. Even residential neighborhoods have occasional moving trucks or larger deliveries. Other streets are frequently used by trucks, and some jurisdictions classify streets as various types of truck or freight routes. These may include regional truckways, freight or industrial districts, routes for oversize vehicles, priority truck streets, or local truck routes.

There can be a distinction made between streets designed for trucks and streets that accommodate use by trucks. The City of Portland uses this distinction in their publication *Designing for Truck Movements and Other Large Vehicles in Portland*. When streets are designed for trucks, the curb radius allows the truck to make a turn without needing to use space in adjacent or opposing lanes. When trucks use streets infrequently, streets may accommodate trucks with a tighter turning radius, allowing trucks to move outside of their lanes while turning. Mountable curbs that large vehicles can navigate are another possible solution for accommodating low volumes of trucks.[3]

[3] City of Portland Office of Transportation. "Designing for Truck Movements and Other Large Vehicles in Portland." http://www.portlandonline.com/transportation/index.cfm?a=357099&c=54899, adopted October 8, 2008.

Emergency Vehicles

**America's public spaces are sized by the biggest fire engine
the community can afford to buy.**

Andres Duany

Police vehicles and fire trucks need to be able to access properties without delay. Fire trucks are a particular challenge because of the size of the vehicles and the need to stabilize them with outriggers. Fire department requirements often dictate minimum street widths. Twenty feet of clear pavement is typically considered a minimum dimension for private fire lane access in urban areas. Codes often require fire lanes, color-coded red, at the main access points to commercial, industrial, and institutional buildings.

Fire trucks vary in size, but most are just over eight feet wide with an outrigger spread of approximately sixteen feet. Some jurisdictions have increased the size of their fire trucks to accommodate the ever-expanding duties of firefighters, including hazardous material cleanup and medical response. Although these duties could be managed independently by smaller, more nimble vehicles, placing all of the equipment on one truck necessitates a larger, heavier vehicle that is ill-suited to narrow streets, tight corners, and changes in the pavement plane.

When designers and fire departments work together, there are solutions to accommodating emergency vehicles in narrower streets. For example, fire fighting operations that require a 20 foot width can be created every 200 to 300 feet, rather than continuously. "Skinny streets" and alleys may have limited or no parking so that emergency access is unimpeded, but the streets are comfortable widths for bike and pedestrian orientation. Traditional neighborhood streets are often narrower than the widths required by more recent regulations, and have functioned adequately for years. There are resources available with specific research on accommodating emergency vehicles in narrower streets, including the Local Government Commission's "Emergency Response, Traffic Calming and Traditional Neighborhood Streets," written by Dan Burden with Paul Zykofsky.[4]

Transit

Buses, streetcars, and light rail vehicles range from 30 to 60 feet in length and require a level access point, typically adjacent to the curb, so that passengers can enter and exit the vehicles. Buses prefer 12- to 14-foot travel lanes, wide curb radii, and an over-street height clearance of approximately 14 feet.

---

[4] Burden, Dan, and Zykofsky, Paul. "Emergency Response, Traffic Calming and Traditional Neighborhood Streets," Local Government Commission and Center for Livable Communities. Available online through the Local Government Commission, www.lgc.org.

Electric transit vehicles are usually energized through overhead catenary systems that are costly to move and to expand. These overhead systems typically require 16 feet of overhead clearance and can limit the ability to add trees with canopy coverage over the roadway. Because these systems have little to no fumes, they have advantages in dense urban settings.

Unless they travel in a dedicated right-of-way, transit vehicles typically share the right-of-way with other modes of transportation. With the desire of many urban areas to shift drivers toward transit, there are situations where transit may have priority over single-occupancy vehicles with transit-only lanes during part or all of the day. Vehicles that run on rails may share a lane with cars, or have dedicated space within the right-of-way. Traffic signals can be optimized for transit, through the use of signal queue jumps, to increase transit speed and reliability.

Figure 2-5 Well-integrated transit is essential to urban streets. *Photographer: Rick Browning*

Transit riders are pedestrians as they move to and from transit stops, and while they wait at the transit stop. For this reason, the linkages to transit and the area surrounding the transit stops merit particular design attention (Figure 2-5).

Bicycles

Bicycles have been using streets since before the automobile was invented. Cycling interest groups began advocating for improved roadway conditions in the late nineteenth century. The car has eclipsed the bicycle as a primary means of travel, but bicycle advocates are a dedicated group and continue to lobby hard to ensure that their needs and demands are seriously considered as transportation funds are allocated and new policies developed.

A flat, direct route is preferable for most cyclists. Those riders who are fit and experienced are typically comfortable riding in a bicycle lane adjacent to traffic, or sharing the lane with cars and other vehicles. More casual riders prefer a separated facility such as a trail, cycle track, a low-speed residential street, or other physically separated bicycle facility.

Bicycle facilities include a network of roadways, bike lanes, and paths for travel; access for bicycles on transit;

and end-of-trip facilities—most notably places to park bicycles both on street and in buildings. American use of bicycles for commuter trips has been growing, but the low mode share has been seen as a reason to favor using resources for vehicles—a self-fulfilling scenario since the lack of resources spent on bicycle facilities has not encouraged a significant shift in America's traveling public to make more of their trips by bicycle.

The presence or absence of high-quality bicycle facilities makes a tremendous difference in the likelihood of people to choose a bike trip over a car trip. The number of people commuting by bicycle varies from place to place, with almost 6 percent of Portland, Oregon, commuters using bicycles.[5] Not surprisingly, cities with a foundation of pro-bicycling policies are seeing the largest growth in bicycle ridership.[6]

New York City has recently altered their transportation policies to favor walking, bicycling, and transit use, and has made a substantial investment of public dollars in the infrastructure needed to support these policies. They have increased the lane miles of bike lanes in their network, improved end-of-trip facilities, and added cycletracks (physically separated bicycle lanes) to grow users of the system. The New York City Department of Transportation released a NYCDOT Commuter Cycling Indicator in 2009, tracking commuter cycling use by counting the number of cyclists crossing a set of "screenlines" throughout the City between 1984 and 2009. The report documents a 35 percent increase in commuter cycling between 2007 and 2008 alone[7] (Figure 2-6).

Figure 2-6 Cycling and density can work well together. *Photographer: Paul Iano*

[5] http://public.sheet.zoho.com/public/bikeleague/70largest-cities-1.

[6] www.bikeleague.org/resources/reports/pdfs/acs_08_summary.pdf.

[7] NYCDOT, NYC Commuter Cycling Indicator, 2009.

Pedestrians

Like cyclists, pedestrians are extremely sensitive to the conditions in the street right-of-way. Weather, light, and hills make a tremendous difference to someone who is about to embark on a walking trip. Wide, level sidewalks are highly desirable for pedestrians. Safety and security are other significant concerns. The presence or absence of light, perception of safety, noise, and fumes from traffic all have a much more significant impact on a pedestrian than they do on the driver of a car traveling within a protective steel environment at a much higher rate of speed. Streetscape elements that shorten crossing distances such as curb bulbs or fewer, narrower travel lanes improve the pedestrian trip, as do elements that require vehicles to travel more slowly, such as tight corner turn radii and traffic calming devices.

Like cycling, walking can be a transportation option or a recreational activity. The quality of the environment is especially important in optional trips—those that are made by choice, rather than be necessity. Based on the type of trip, people may favor a direct route versus a less direct route that has more points of visual interest. For the pedestrian who is walking for a transportation purpose—to work, to school, or to run an errand—a direct route is usually preferable. Walking trips made for recreational purposes may place direct connections somewhat lower on the priority scale after comfort and visual interest.

Pedestrians are harder to predict than drivers. For example, one person may feel unsafe on a route with heavy tree coverage that blocks out the light and creates dark, shadowy spaces. That same street may feel inviting to other people who find the dense, green canopy as shady, quiet, and beautiful. Given the less predictable nature of the pedestrian trip, it is much harder to measure. The old adage, "what gets measured is what gets done" may apply directly in this case. It is harder to accurately predict pedestrian travel patterns, and hard to measure the qualitative issues that nurture walking. As a result, it is harder to make the case that transportation resources should be spent on improving pedestrian infrastructure.

THE PACE OF MOVEMENT

Human locomotion—its pace and scale—is central to the development of cities. Prior to the advent and widespread use of the car, walking distance and bicycling distance was one of the determining factors in the layout of new cities and towns. People generally travel at three to four feet per second. At that pace, proximity has huge value. This is still true today. The number of important and relevant destinations accessible within a short walk makes the difference between a quick and efficient trip on foot, or the decision to give up on walking and drive. Town centers enable efficient "trip chaining"—reaching multiple destinations in proximity on foot. By bicycle, the travel-shed and pace of travel increases substantially. Public transit further expands the zone of travel, but places restrictions on routes and schedules.

The personal vehicle typically provides the most freedom of choice. But as our mode choices have increased and our freedom and flexibility have grown, the humble walk and bicycle trips have suffered. Cars require lots of space for movement and storage, and they typically move at a rate of speed that so far surpasses the pedestrian that it is uncomfortable to walk in proximity to a roadway that carries even moderate volumes of cars. Noise and exhaust fumes are side effects of this speed of movement, as is the maintenance required to keep roads in good conditions when they are heavily traveled by vehicles. Gravel, dust, and dead grass don't mean much to a car driver traveling along at 25 to 30 mph, but an unpleasant walking environment may mean the difference between the choice to walk or drive for a pedestrian.

Moving at three to four feet per second, every detail matters. The materials used to articulate the path in the pavement—the plantings, the sound and experience of water—these details encourage movement by foot. When asked what it would take to get people to make more trips on foot, bicycle, or transit, the topic of quality frequently comes up: quality of materials, quality of experience, noise and sound, interesting diversions, and quality of destinations.

A SHIFT IN THINKING

Communities around the country are changing the way they think about streets. Quality communities—those that provide many of the same walking trip efficiencies that the historic town center did—are becoming the new model. More and more people want the freedom to choose how to move from place to place without needing to rely on a car. Walking, bicycling, and connections to transit are becoming increasingly desirable. People are getting more adamant that walkable communities are worthy of public dollars.

Often, transportation professionals downplay the importance of quality, broadly referring to place-making elements as "amenities." In contrast, safety is typically at the heart of a group of issues often referred to as "core transportation business." Other items in the core category include infrastructure preservation, navigational features such as signs, markings, and signals, and, of course, pavement. None of these elements should be downplayed as they are critical to core transportation business.

However, placemaking features and quality design should also be seen as necessary components of core transportation business, if your business is about giving the traveling public more choices, about creating a greener and cleaner environment, and about being the catalyst for change. Successful transportation projects that are well loved and continually discussed all across the nation have made walking, cycling, and transit more attractive. The best, most exciting transportation projects have clearly put the emphasis on quality of place.

In tight budget times (which are most times when transportation infrastructure is the topic) communities are often faced with the news that the quality elements that make public spaces appealing are just "nice to haves" rather essential elements. But in order to create vibrant streets where people choose to walk and bicycle for most of their trips, placemaking features are necessities, not amenities. Quality materials, landscaping, public art, benches to sit on, and lighting to improve visibility at night are crucial infrastructure for walking. Dedicated space, ample and secure parking, and signal priority need to be included as crucial infrastructure for bicycling. Accessible and comfortable stops, frequent and reliable service, and an excellent walking environment are equally crucial for transit riders who all start their trip as pedestrians or bicyclists (Figure 2-7).

Figure 2-7 Cities around the world, including this street in Japan, have found ways to integrate bicycles. *Photographer: Rick Browning*

PEDESTRIAN MEASURES

How many people are walking, and where do they choose to walk?

Pedestrian counts are very useful, indicating pedestrian preferences of routes. Pedestrian counts can be done by using cameras, or by observers on the ground. The number of children walking indicates a level of comfort perceived by both children and their parents.

How much space is given over to pedestrians?

The amount of sidewalk or pedestrian space is measurable, and can also be analyzed in terms of a network of connections. Fixing gaps in the network of pedestrian routes can be an effective way to increase walkability.

How many destinations are nearby?

The number of nearby amenities has been shown to be the best predictor of whether people choose to walk.[8] Walk Score® is a proprietary methodology that uses an algorithm to determine a level of walkability based on proximity of amenities. It doesn't measure the qualitative aspect of the pedestrian environment.

How safe is the walking environment?

Statistics can usually be obtained from municipalities in terms of pedestrian/vehicle collisions and incidents of crime. Lighting levels can also be measured. However, quantitative measures may not be sufficient; people's perception of the walking environment may feel different than the statistics alone would show.

How comfortable is the street for pedestrians?

There are some quantitative measures of comfort, such as the speed of traffic adjacent to the pedestrian realm. Amenities, such as seating and weather protection, are beginning to be considered necessities rather than optional elements in the streetscape and the presence of street furnishings can be documented. There are various methods that practitioners and communities have employed in order to find usable measures for determining the quality and comfort of the walking environment. These methods include surveys or audits used by community members to rate the quality and comfort of the pedestrian network. DIY Community Street Audits, developed by Living Streets in the UK, is one method. Consulting firms, such as London-based Intelligent Space, have developed special expertise in analyzing pedestrian movements and designing with pedestrian movements in mind.

[8] "Perceived and Objective Environmental Measures and Physical Activity Among Urban Adults"; Christine M. Hoehner, PhD, MSPH; Laura K. Brennan Ramirez, PhD, MPH; Michael B. Elliott, PhD; Susan L. Handy, PhD; Ross C. Brownson, PhD.

Chapter 3
NATURAL SYSTEMS

UNTIL RECENTLY, NATURAL SYSTEMS WERE NOT CONSIDERED TO BE FUNCTIONS REQUIRING SPACE IN THE STREET. Stormwater was directed to curbs, drains, and pipes. Most of the infrastructure of drainage was below ground and out of sight. Landscaping was sometimes valued as an aesthetic plus, but rarely considered from an ecological standpoint.

The land in the right-of-way is now seen as a resource for handling rainwater, keeping it out of the sewer system by capturing, infiltrating, or transpiring water. Streetscapes are beginning to be seen as opportunities to restore habitat and clean the air. Where new development is replacing natural areas, well-designed landscape and natural drainage systems can minimize the impacts of that development. In areas that are already urbanized, thoughtfully designed natural systems can even begin to restore the natural ecology or hydrology of a site. However, the successful use of natural systems requires much more space on the surface than underground hard-piped utility systems. It is another function that must compete for space in the right-of-way (Figure 3-1).

Figure 3-1 *Photographer: Rumi Takahashi*

RECONNECTING CITIES TO NATURE

It is particularly ironic that the battle to save the world's remaining healthy ecosystems will be won or lost not in tropical forests or coral reefs that are threatened but on the streets of the most unnatural landscapes on the planet.[1]

Worldwatch Institute

The relationship of cities and nature is critical on a global scale. Urbanization is fast occurring across the world, especially in developing countries. Consider that in 1800, at the dawn of the industrial revolution, only 3 percent of the world's population lived in cities. One hundred years later, by 1900, that figure had grown to 14 percent. In 1950, some 30 percent of people in the world lived in cities. By 2008, fully half the world's population lived in urban areas,[2] and that number continues to grow. Home to so many, the cities of the world need to be humane places to live, not sterile places that threaten and encroach on nature while isolating their residents from its psychological and physical nourishment. But with good planning and design, cities can interact in a healthy way with the natural world. If managed well, concentrated population centers can actually limit the negative effects of development by preserving areas with habitat better than sprawling development.

"The battle for a sustainable environmental future is being waged primarily in the world's cities," according to the World Watch Institute. "Right now, cities draw together many of Earth's major environmental problems: population growth, pollution, resource degradation, and waste generation. Paradoxically, cities also hold our best chance for a sustainable future."[3]

We often perceive a dichotomy between cities and the natural realm of the countryside, viewing these realms as fundamentally opposed. Part of the challenge of reenvisioning cities is to invite natural systems back into urban areas. As publicly owned land, usually covered in impervious surface material, streets are an obvious place to look for opportunities to reintroduce landscape and natural drainage. Streets also inherently form an interconnected network of places, and are thus well-suited to improvements relying on connectivity throughout a district or region.

---

[1] Worldwatch Institute. 2007. "Preface," p. xxiv. *State of the World 2007: Our Urban Future.* New York and London: W. W. Norton and Company.

[2] Population Reference Bureau. "Human Population: Urbanization," www.prb.org/Educators/TeachersGuides/HumanPopulation/Urbanization.aspx.

[3] Worldwatch Institute. 2007. "Preface," p. xxiv. *State of the World 2007: Our Urban Future.* New York and London: W. W. Norton and Company.

URBAN BIODIVERSITY

What does the quantity and biodiversity of vegetation mean for urban areas? The living plants and organisms provide ecological services—cleaning the area's air and water, pollinating its plants, and regulating its climate. In less quantifiable realms, urban biodiversity makes for better places to live, connects people to the environment, and resonates with the human spirit. Even small fragments of green space can have significant effects.

Emerging work promoting the health of urban ecosystems crosses many professional and political boundaries. Scientists, landscape architects, engineers, planners, and policymakers need to bring together their expertise, supported by an engaged public that values nature in the city. The U.S. Long Term Ecological Research Network (LTER) has ongoing projects in place tracking ecological changes. More than 1,800 scientists and students are involved in this collaborative network investigating diverse ecosystems.[4] The LTER Network focuses on two urban environments in the United States—Baltimore and Phoenix. Phoenix is an arid inland ecosystem, and Baltimore is an urbanized area within the Eastern deciduous forest.

The Baltimore Ecosystem Study (BES), part of the LTER Network, integrates the sciences and community-based activities, including urban design efforts. Cities are, to some extent, designed systems. The relationship of the active design decisions and an understanding of natural and urban ecosystems could go a long way toward better places to live and environmental health. The Baltimore Ecosystem Study (BES) Urban Design Working Group is exploring critical topics through collaborative research and design studios. For example, metropolitan Baltimore is used as a case study for applying patch dynamics theories of landscape ecology to a systems approach to urban design. BES has brought together designers, scientists, professional planners, students, and faculty to share information on the ways that ecosystem science can be applied through planning and design.[5]

Another connection between communities and the urban environment is through organizations that engage and educate people about their environment. Citizen-scientists are a powerful resource for projects that monitor and support habitat and ecosystems. Volunteers are working on projects such as the Audubon Society's Christmas Bird count, and the Chicago Wilderness Habitat Project, which monitors populations of frogs, birds, and butterflies in the Chicago area. These citizen-scientists monitor the urban ecosystem, while the program trains them to be habitat stewards and activists.

The design and use of land in the public right-of-way has a role to play in the quality of urban biodiversity. The new streets and communities which replace habitat have a localized and cumulative impact

---

[4] The U.S. Long Term Ecological Research Network (LTER Network). www.lternet.edu, accessed on July 17, 2011.
[5] The Baltimore Ecosystem Study, www.beslter.org/, accessed on July 17, 2011.

on natural systems. However, they can be designed in ways that reduce impacts by preserving intact areas of the most productive habitat. Simply introducing additional plantings into already urbanized land holds promise for both people and nature at once: It creates living space for human well-being while simultaneously improving ecosystems. The science underlying the way in which vegetation is restored into the city can be used to make the efforts most productive. The art of bringing back nature into the city is an exciting work in progress.

NATURAL SYSTEMS AND OPPORTUNITIES IN THE RIGHT-OF-WAY

There are many ways in which streets and other right-of-way land can contribute to healthier cities. Often, benefits to one natural system directly or indirectly improve other natural functions. For example, by replacing paving with a rain garden, plant materials can be used to cleanse water while simultaneously reducing the area's heat island effect. Creative thinking can expand the potential positive effects. For instance, the same plants used to filter the water may be selected to benefit particular wildlife habitats. Just as transportation planners view the network of streets as a system, looking at the network of streets in terms of natural systems will help encourage good decisions about specific places and the priorities of uses for particular portions of the right-of-way.

Trees and Vegetation

Streets have long been lined with trees, primarily for aesthetic reasons. But trees bring huge benefits to streets, meeting diverse and overlapping goals. Tree canopy coverage manages the heat island effect in urban areas where paving has replaced much of the green spaces that existed long ago. Trees also sequester carbon and reduce green house gases. A single tree may sequester an average of 13 pounds of carbon a year.[6] Airborne pollutants such as sulfur dioxide, ozone, carbon monoxide, and nitrogen oxides are also partially controlled by trees through absorption and uptake by inner leaf surfaces (Figure 3-2).

Trees provide the urban environment with such value that both Los Angeles and New York City have set out a goal to plant one million new trees within their boundaries. In Seattle, a 30-year goal to increase urban forest cover from 18 percent to 30 percent is projected to increase annual economic benefits—stormwater management, cleaner air, and carbon storage—by $15 million to $44 million.[7]

---

[6] Coder, Dr. Rim D. "Identified Benefits of Community Trees and Forests." University of Georgia: 1996.

[7] "Building the Biocarbon Economy: How the Northwest Can Lead; Re-Greening Cities: The Carbon Landscape, Greenspaces and Green Infrastructure to Build Biocarbon and Climate Resiliency While Saving Energy and Tax Dollars," Patrick Mazza, Research Director, Climate Solutions. July 1, 2010.

Figure 3-2 Street trees make the median a place that can be used and enjoyed. *Photographer: Dave Knight*

Street trees have a positive effect on mobility as well. Linear tree canopy adjacent to the street calms traffic as the shadows cast on the pavement by the tree branches often encourage vehicles to slow down as they navigate the patches of light and dark on the street.

Too often, vegetation alongside streets and roads is selected primarily for ease of maintenance. Grassy medians are ecological monocultures regularly treated by an array of fertilizers, pesticides, and herbicides. Designers are just beginning to see the "extra" spaces in the right-of-way as natural resources. Landscaped swales, rain gardens, and bioretention planters can provide efficient solutions for treating stormwater, controlling localized flooding, and improving water quality.

In the 1990s, the city of Berlin, Germany, created a program called the Biotope Area Factor as a creative way to improve urban ecosystems. The Biotope Area Factor (BAF) is a point-based regulation that requires incorporating greenery in developments. Developers are required to reserve a portion of the land for plants or other ecosystem functions, with flexibility in how the point-based BAF is achieved. Surfaces are classified from sealed surfaces (no credit), to vegetated surfaces unconnected to soil below (partial credit), and vegetated surfaces connected to the soil (full credit). Credit is also given for providing for the infiltration of rainwater from the roof, and the inclusion of vertical greenery (green walls) and green roofs.

Malmo, Sweden, and Seattle, Washington, have also adopted similar requirements. The adoption of Seattle's Green Factor program created a significant shift in thinking regarding development requirements. Prior to the 2007 enactment of the Green Factor program, developers were actually discouraged from making most improvements in the right-of-way. The Green Factor now allows landscaping on both private property and in the right-of-way, with points awarded for trees, landscaping, and permeable paving. Trees are weighted in the point system by size, and credit is added for landscaping that is visible from the public realm.

Air

Trees and vegetation provide multiple environmental functions, including removing pollutants from the air. Trees offer shade in warm months and help block winds in winter. As a side benefit, shading also reduces energy use in buildings. Like all benefits, designing with the unique attributes of a site in mind maximizes effectiveness. These may be attributes of the climate, of the particular uses in the area, or a need to respond to a point pollution source. The value of trees for pollution removal depends on the length of time the tree is in leaf, climate, amount of tree cover, and pollution concentration.[8] Trees that shade adjacent buildings are particularly beneficial in warm climates, as they considerably reduce the need for air conditioning.[9]

---

[8] "Air pollution removal by urban trees and shrubs in the United States", by David Nowak, Daniel E. Crane, Jack C. Stevens. USDA Forest Service, Northeastern Research Station, 5 Moon Library, SUNY-ESF, Syracuse, NY 13210; Available online at www.sciencedirect.com, Urban Forestry & Urban Greening 4 (2006), 115–123.

[9] Science for Environmental Policy, European Commission News Alert Issue 96, February 2008.

Water

Cities are beginning to reconnect their natural systems at both localized levels and on the larger scale of their watersheds. The rainwater that falls on the urban environment is beginning to be considered an amenity and a resource rather than a problem. Models that use landscaped areas in the right-of-way are being developed and tested by forward-thinking jurisdictions, and serve as models for subsequent efforts worldwide.

As interconnected grids or networks, streets can form a system for moving water. Streets are already used as utility networks—the standard piped infrastructure of stormwater management typically lies below the street. At grade, streets often channel excess water naturally, whether intentionally or not, because of the slope of the street or variations in the surface of the street. It can thus be wiser to incorporate runoff into the design intentionally.

Natural drainage systems actually have many advantages over piped systems. When designed correctly, natural systems can be used to filter pollutants from water, reduce flooding, improve the water quality of receiving lakes and streams, and cool the air.

Cities are finding that natural drainage solutions are not necessarily more expensive, and may actually be more affordable than standard stormwater management systems. Utilizing natural processes can extend the life of the existing below-grade systems and prevent the large expenditures required to repair or expand "gray" infrastructure below the street. Traditional systems are very expensive, and green stormwater infrastructure is looking increasingly attractive to municipalities that are short on funding.

Some cities are putting the costs on private developers, creating regulations that require property owners to reduce impervious surface, or to retain an increment of the stormwater which falls onsite. For example, the Philadelphia Water Department enacted regulations that make property owners responsible for retaining the first inch of rainfall onsite. The Department estimates that it has reduced billions of gallons of water from entering its sewer system through the use of this technique.[10]

Streets can offer a place for swales, rain gardens, and other elements that slow and treat water. Cisterns in the right-of-way can be connected to drains from adjacent roofs. These projects can be much more than simply a drainage improvement—they can be artistic expressions of water flow and neighborhood values. The Growing Vine Street project in Seattle, Washington's Belltown neighborhood was initiated by residents who spent years advocating, working to change regulations, and raising

---

[10] "Green Infrastructure Case Studies: Municipal Policies for Managing Stormwater with Green Infrastructure," www.epa.gov/owow/NPS/lid/gi_case_studies_2010.pdf.

Figure 3-3 Artist Buster Simpson's Beckoning Cistern takes water from the rooftops into the set of cisterns along Vine Street. *Courtesy of SvR Design*

Figure 3-4 Viewlands Cascade slows and filters runoff with a series of 16 vegetated cells.

funds. The result is a local icon, with artist Buster Simpson's "Beckoning Hand" bringing water to the cisterns from the adjacent rooftop. The cisterns spill down the steep street, and connect to the community P-patch (Figure 3-3).

Habitat

Cities that are healthy for people are also healthy for birds, insects, and other animals. While cities are not always suitable habitat for animals that require large undisturbed territory, there are many species that survive, and even thrive, in urban settings. Some well-adapted species are problems, and municipal efforts regarding wildlife are often targeted at eliminating problem species. But animals of all kinds inhabit developed areas, and many of them are beneficial to humans. Using right-of-way, where appropriate, to support healthy habitat merits attention from scientists, designers, and communities.

While the narrowness of the right-of-way limits its usefulness to many species, street trees and other plantings should be selected with habitat in mind. Some trees are food sources for birds—the flowering dogwood's red berries attract songbirds such as cardinals, robins, and cedar waxwings. The Washington Hawthorn's dense thorns provide nesting sites and fruit. Other trees, such as the Honeylocust, offer little wildlife value.[11]

Tree-lined streets can be useful as connections between larger habitat areas, primarily for birds. A study done in Madrid looked at the way that birds used tree-lined streets, and found that over half of the species found in a local park were also seen in the streets. The tree-lined streets had a significantly higher number of species than streets without trees. The birds were using the streets to move between the fragmented areas of urban habitat[12] (Figure 3-4).

Bats are an interesting example of animals in urban settings. Bats play an important role in the food chain as predators of nocturnal insects, including many pests. As urbanization has diminished their natural habitats, bat colonies have found refuge under bridges and highway structures. At least 24 of the 45 species of bats in the United States have been documented using highway structures as roosts, and the design characteristics that attract bats have been studied and well documented by Bat Conservation International, the Federal Highways Administration, and the Texas Department of Transportation.[13]

Austin, Texas, has embraced its bat colonies. When the Congress Avenue Bridge was renovated in 1980, the bats found the narrow, deep openings below the bridge to be well-suited to colonization. From March through April every year, thousands of Mexican free-tail bats migrate from Mexico

---

[11] Marylanders Plant Trees, State of Maryland website: www.trees.maryland.gov/pickatree.asp.

[12] Fernandez-Juricic, "Avifaunal use of wooded streets in an urban landscape." Conservation Biology 14: 513–521. 2000.

[13] Bats in American Bridges, Bat Conservation International, Inc. Resource Publication No. 4, Brian W. Keeley and Merlin D. Tuttle, 1999. www.batcon.org/pdfs/bridges/BatsBridges2.pdf.

to Texas to give birth, and stay until early fall. Up to a million and a half bats have been recorded during the height of the season. In Austin, these months have become bat-watching season, and a well-known tourist attraction. Around sunset, clouds of bats come out to feed. An observation center is available for picnics, the lake-side restaurants offer decks for viewing, or people can watch from cruise boats.[14]

Light

Although it is difficult to get an accurate count of street light numbers, it is safe to say that there are literally millions of street lights in the United States alone. In addition to their safety functions in keeping streets safe and functional, these lights consume energy, cost money, and send light not only downward to create safe streets, but—uselessly for people and harmfully for the environment—into the night sky.

Light pollution contributes to various environmental problems, disrupting ecosystems and animal behavior. Artificial light attracts some birds, insects, and invertebrates. Many of the flying insects attracted to street lights die, including species that are important sources of food in the food chain.[15]

Dark skies are particularly valued in the arid southwest where the star-filled skies are considered one of its finest characteristics. Flagstaff, Arizona, became the world's first "International Dark Sky City" in 2001. Flagstaff is the home of the Lowell Observatory, which was founded in 1894. It has attracted over a million people to its Steele Visitor Center since it opened in 1994, and has been a model for educating school children and community members about astronomy.[16] Flagstaff's commitment to aggressively replace their existing streetlights with full-shielded low-pressure sodium fixtures was one of the reasons cited for the designation.

Agreeing on lighting levels that create safe conditions but minimize light spill can be complicated. But reducing energy costs, using more energy-efficient fixtures, and using fixtures that minimize upward light spill are commonly accepted goals. A number of states, including Arkansas, California, Colorado, Connecticut, Georgia, Maine, New Jersey, New Mexico, and Texas, have enacted laws that cover lighting of highways and state projects.[17]

The National Park Service now sees reduced light pollution as part of its mission. City dwellers who can barely make out the Milky Way at home are astounded to see the beauty of a star-filled sky.

---

[14] Common information from City tourism and other sites.

[15] *Ecological Consequences of Artificial Night Lighting,* edited by Catherine Rich and Travis Longcore, Island Press, 2006.

[16] Lowell Observatory Press Release, August 28, 2008, www.lowell.edu/media/releases.php?release=20080828.

[17] International Dark-Sky Association, Directory of Lighting Ordinances, www.flagstaffdarkskies.org/idsc.htm.

WHY RECONNECT NATURE AND THE CITY?   49

WHY RECONNECT NATURE AND THE CITY?

If one way be better than another, that you may be sure is Nature's way.

Aristotle, Nichomachean Ethics

Reconnecting nature and the city can:

- Improve water quality

  Green stormwater infrastructure slows and filters rainwater, reduces erosion, and removes pollutants in the water that enters lakes, rivers, and streams (Figure 3-5).

- Improve air quality

  Trees and plants sequester carbon, filter pollutants, and provide shade along streets and neighboring buildings. In addition to providing shade, trees provide cooling for the area around them by pumping water from the ground into their leaves, where it evaporates from the surface, cooling the tree and the air around it.

- Reduce urban heat island effect

  Heat builds up in urban areas, where natural vegetation is replaced by buildings, roads, and other paved areas that absorb heat during the day, such as parking lots. Reintroducing green materials helps make a more comfortable urban environment for people and lowers energy consumption.

- Improve habitat

  Greening the city provides shelter and food for wildlife. Selecting the species of trees and plantings to be used in the right-of-way for their habitat value helps to support healthier urban ecosystems.

Figure 3-5 Maynard Avenue, in Seattle's old Japanese neighborhood (Nihonmachi), is a green street with cisterns, art, and landscape that draw on the area's culture and history. *Photographer: Rumi Takahashi*

■ Improve well-being of people who live in the city

The shade, cooling, and aesthetics of a green city contribute to comfort. Beyond comfort, people connect with nature in the city, whether through gardening, bird-watching, or enjoying the local park bench.

■ Create economic benefits

People value living in green neighborhoods with tree-lined streets. Studies show that people are willing to pay more for homes with trees.[18] Commercial properties also increase in value when trees are present.

■ Engage children, citizens, and decision makers

There are many ways that people engage with nature as individuals and groups. The more connected people are to the natural environment, the more they commit to keeping it healthy. As children are increasingly spending time with digital toys instead of outdoor play, environmental education has taken on great importance. And because the majority of decision makers live in urban environments, the awareness of environmental benefits in cities is critical to preserving urban and nonurban areas (Figure 3-6).

[18] Orland, Vining & Ebreo 1992, The Effect of Street Trees on Perceived Values on Residential Property. *Environment and Behavior,* 24(3), 298–325.

Figure 3-6 Even the youngest community members can be involved in turning the medians into usable habitat. © *The Pollinator Pathway, Photographer: Jenny McIntosh*

Chapter 4
ELEMENTS

THE ELEMENTS THAT MAKE UP THE PUBLIC RIGHT-OF-WAY are critical to creating streets that support placemaking, mobility, and natural systems. Not only are the elements themselves important—the way they are designed, the relationship between them, and the messages that they send to their users require equally serious attention. The choice of which materials to use—an asphalt walkway versus a concrete walkway, a textured cobblestone sidewalk versus a continuous expanse of pavement—makes a difference in the look and feel of a space, as well as its longevity and durability (Figure 4-1).

Figure 4-1

The materials used to create a space and the ways in which they are used indicate which of the space's possible functions take priority. Asphalt and white paint are the "language" of vehicles, and visible turning radii show that the space is designed for the needs of cars and trucks. Higher-quality materials signal that the space is considered important enough to be a worthwhile investment, that it has importance as a place. Materials such as cobblestones and pavers are smaller-scale elements suggestive of a place that might be pleasant to spend time in or to move through slowly on foot. Elements such as hanging flowers or retail displays indicate that someone cares enough about the place to tend to it.

This chapter focuses on the various elements of the right-of-way, and the issues that designers should weigh and consider when designing a project. This information is by no means exhaustive—there are numerous resources, including standards manuals and material guidelines available to guide specific choices about the material tolerances and qualities that need to be considered.

PLACES TO MOVE THROUGH

Sidewalks and Pathways

Sidewalks, pathways, and trails are the connective tissue of the public realm. They connect you from your front door to shops, friends' houses, the park, or the bus stop. They provide spaces for vending, for signage, for plantings, and for seating. Sometimes they become a place of refuge for the homeless. Sidewalks are where public and private uses interface. In fact, it is often unclear who actually owns the sidewalk and who is responsible to maintain it—the local jurisdiction or the adjacent property owner. At the edges of the streets, and the edges of private property, the sidewalk is a microcosm of the interactions and decision-making challenges in the public realm.

For people on foot, the elements of an urban area through which they move include the city's many sidewalks and its less formal paths and trails. Ideally, these elements form a complete network linking a full range of destinations with safe and pleasant routes. Where these elements do not exist, people will create their own "goat paths" by walking in parking lots, yards, or along travel lanes or roadway shoulders. The completeness and the quality of the pedestrian network are fundamental to walkable communities.

Width

The *total width* of the sidewalk includes the curb, planting area, walking area, and frontage zone directly adjacent to buildings. The width of the walking area itself is called the effective sidewalk width, or *walk zone*.

A wider sidewalk can accommodate more pedestrians, street furniture, large street trees, utilities, and bicycle racks. In walkable areas visited by many pedestrians—such as neighborhood business districts or urban hubs—sidewalks become mixing zones for a wide range of activities, all of which need space to exist. Retail activities, signage, seating, landscaping, art, utilities, and other uses compete for space.

In lower-density areas, five-foot-wide walk zones are adequate for two people to walk together comfortably, or for people traveling in opposite directions to pass one another. Five feet allows room for two wheelchair users to pass one another, or for one wheelchair user to turn around. Some jurisdictions prefer a more comfortable six-foot sidewalk as the standard. It is important to keep utility poles, tree branches, and other obstructions out of the walk zone, especially for people with limited vision.

The perceived comfort of the walkway for pedestrians is dependent on context, not just width alone. In situations where a narrow sidewalk is constrained on one side—perhaps by a wall or change in grade—and is near heavy traffic on the other side, a minimum sidewalk width can be very uncomfortable. If there are many of these constrained and uncomfortable walking routes in an area, people are less likely to walk (Figure 4-2).

Figure 4-2 This street is well buffered from traffic, and includes overhead weather protection for comfort.

Zones

Urban designers subdivide total sidewalk width into zones. Along the building face, people interact with buildings and the activities that occur at street level. Glassy storefronts offer interest for "window shopping" in retail areas. The areas adjacent to the building can form eddies of space connected to sidewalks at entries, or they can provide space for sidewalk displays. Building facades can provide structure for overhead weather protection, seating, and lighting.

The walk zone is usually the space in the center of the sidewalk—a clear area that follows a straight path, where people can move without obstruction.

Between the walk zone and the vehicle travel lanes, there is often a "buffer zone," which may include landscaping, signage, utility poles, parking meters, fire hydrants, benches, newspaper racks, or other street furnishings. Items in the buffer zone are subject to various regulations by local jurisdictions, such as setback requirements from moving traffic and utilities. On-street parking also helps buffer sidewalk areas from traffic, but the buffer zones need to be designed to allow people to move from the sidewalk to their cars easily (Figure 4-3).

The curb and gutter typically distinguish the pedestrian zone from the vehicle zone. They create a clear separation, meet requirements for people with limited vision, and offer a hard edge to deflect vehicles from sidewalks. Gutters take stormwater from the travel lanes and convey it to drains and underground pipes. The sidewalk, approximately 6 inches above the gutter, stays dry. This type of section is discussed in the Barracks Row Case Study presented in Chapter 7.

Treating pedestrian zones as more than just narrow, linear corridors opens up new options for designers. Rather than a section that remains the same along the length of the street, as "extruded" sections, zones can be clustered rather than simply extended. For example, a plaza space may be located near a transit stop. Landscape may take on less of a linear quality and feel more like a "grove" than a continuous line of trees. This clustering can create a variety of spaces that interact with adjacent buildings and streets. Larger groupings of landscaping can mean healthier trees and plantings. A clustered approach to streetscape is discussed in the Terry Avenue North Case Study in Chapter 7.

Figure 4-3 Street elements need not be perfectly aligned in order to have a usable walk zone. Informal elements that are connected to the place itself are often the most interesting.

CLUSTERS AND LINEAR ZONES

Streets tend to be linear connections, with linear buffers that separate pedestrians from fast-moving traffic. The curbs, buffers, on-street parking, street trees, walk zones, and building interface zones are typically linear as well. Shared-use streets can move toward clusters of uses and space. For instance, plaza space could be created near building entries. Groups of angled parking are located where most needed. Large landscape zones with substantial trees can be created rather than the standard line of street trees. The diagrams shown here illustrate how linear and clustered streetscape can work both in plan and in section (Figures 4-4, 4-5, 4-6, and 4-7).

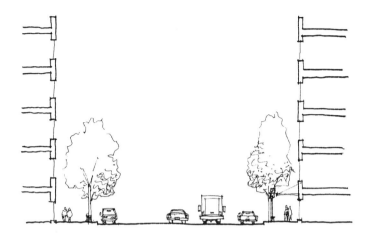

Figure 4-4 Standard street design: section.

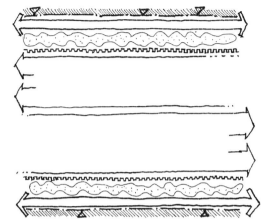

Figure 4-5 Standard street design: plan diagram.

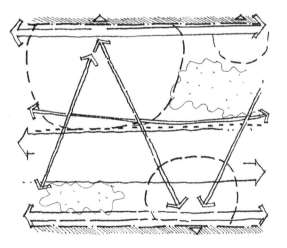

Figure 4-6 Inhabited street design: plan diagram.

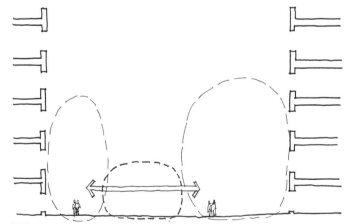

Figure 4-7 Inhabited street design: section.

Trails

Trails are usually in a separate right-of-way from cars. They are widely used within and outside of urban areas, and have become important elements in pedestrian and cycling networks. Spaces below utility corridors or along former rail corridors may be appropriate for trails because they are linear spaces designed for movement, usually with plenty of unused empty space and few obstructions.

Solana Beach, an oceanfront community north of San Diego, created the Coastal Rail Trail by transforming an unused strip of land squeezed between Highway 101 and a deep trench where Amtrak and freight trains pass. Joggers, strollers, roller-bladers, and cyclists have enjoyed the mile and a half of landscaped trail since its completion in 2005. Generous amounts of public art bring interest to the trail. The designers, San Diego's Schmidt Design Group, selected plantings that were drought-tolerant and native to southern California. Solana Beach property owners voted to create a special assessment district to pay for ongoing maintenance of the Coastal Rail Trail, and someday the Solana Beach segment of the trail could connect to a 40-mile route stretching from Oceanside to downtown San Diego (Figure 4-8).

Another place to capture underutilized space for cyclists and pedestrians is below power lines. Seattle turned over three and a half miles of unused space below power lines into the Chief Sealth Trail in

Figure 4-8 Shared-use trail in Solana Beach, California.

2007, using recycled concrete and excavated soils from the light rail project on nearby Martin Luther King Jr. Way. Residents of the south Seattle neighborhoods had expressed the desire for such a trail for many years, and the light rail contractor, RCI/Herzog, offered the idea of reusing the construction materials. The bike trail connects neighborhoods in south Seattle to the Rainier Beach light rail station.

Privately Owned Through-Routes

Although large-lot developments are not part of the public right-of-way, public decision makers often look for ways to break down the scale of large blocks. Urban places are defined by systems of streets and connections, and many areas that have been developed in the automobile era have lost those connections. Jurisdictions are suggesting or requiring finer-grained connections within new developments, turning car-oriented places into walkable neighborhoods. Where platting has created large blocks, pedestrian through-routes can greatly improve the scale and connectivity of the area. For well-designed and managed developments, through routes allow more retail space and other active uses (Figure 4-9).

Travel Lanes

Cars, trucks, buses, and emergency vehicles share vehicular travel lanes. Increasingly, lane space is being dedicated to bicycles, both on arterial and residential streets. In the United States, travel lanes are typically 12 feet wide when possible. For highways, widths of 12 to 14 feet allow for large trucks and high speeds. Ten- to eleven-foot lanes suffice for most urban conditions. In residential areas or on low-volume, low-speed roads, lanes can be as narrow as eight feet. Narrow streets can be found in towns and cities built before the automobile era, and cars have adapted to all but the very narrowest streets. America's historic districts have narrow streets that are well-loved by residents and tourists, such as Boston's Acorn Street in Beacon Hill or Philadelphia's Elfreth Alley.

Figure 4-9 Pedestrian through-routes in private developments break down scale and can help support retail uses.

Where streets have multiple lanes, the lane adjacent to the curb is typically wider to accommodate buses, or to provide more space for cyclists. A wider curb lane also provides a few extra feet of separation between moving traffic and pedestrians traveling on the sidewalk.

There are several strategies for reconsidering the arrangement and function of travel lanes in order to balance the space in the right-of-way. When accommodating bicycles, a shared lane marking or sharrow may be added on an existing lane, or general purpose lanes may be reduced in width to create a bike lane. Rechannelizations, or "road diets" reduce the number of lanes, and offer space in the right-of-way for bicycles or pedestrians. These strategies are discussed in more detail in Chapter 6.

MATERIALS

Materials in public spaces must stand up to heavy use and continue to look good and function well over time. Materials that are durable can stand up and be a source of pride for generations, exemplified by older cities across the world.

Sidewalk materials include concrete, asphalt, brick, and stone. Life-cycle costs, construction costs, durability, maintenance issues, color, and permeability are all factors to be considered when paving a sidewalk or pathway. To meet accessibility requirements, pedestrian routes in the United States must have firm, stable, and slip-resistant surfaces. This is an important consideration when choosing brick or stone that is prone to becoming slippery when it gets wet.

Concrete is commonly used for sidewalks, especially in American cities, because it is durable, available, and relatively affordable. Concrete's light color contrasts with the asphalt of a roadway and reflects light. The manufacturing of concrete has a high carbon footprint because of the heat required for the process, but it can last for decades if well maintained. New concrete mixes include additives such as fly ash that reduce the green house gases that are released in the production of typical Portland cement. The trade-off for using these mixes is their longer curing time, which can impact a project's schedule.

Concrete has a tendency to crack with movement of the ground or the growth of tree roots. It is impervious, and keeps water from moving into the soil beneath, unless it is specifically designed to be porous.

Color can be added to concrete, and it is possible to create a variety of textures by using an exposed aggregate or a different surface finishing. Some cities have a standard color and scoring pattern for sidewalks in order to maintain consistency. Standardized details allow predictable sidewalk replacement and repair over its lifetime. This is especially important in urban areas where utility cuts tend to occur more frequently.

Interlocking pavers made of precast concrete are another material option that can be attractive and durable, but one with a higher cost than standard concrete. Pavers can accommodate some settlement without cracking, and can also offer some permeability. In order to repair a section of pavers, the crew can pull out the pavers, repair the utility, and then, if the pavers are in good condition, they can be put back in place.

Cost certainly plays a role in choices about material selection. Asphalt prices fluctuate with the price of oil. Standard asphalt is dark in color and absorbs heat rather than reflecting it like a light-colored concrete will do. There are methods of stamping and coloring asphalt to make it look lighter in color, or more like brick. In general, asphalt does not typically last as long as concrete, although since the loads placed on sidewalks are relatively light, some asphalt walkways have been in place for 25 years or more and are still functioning well. Asphalt advocates note that it is a recyclable material, and that it can be designed as a porous pavement. Some asphalt contains recycled materials including asphalt shingles, rubber tires, and glass.

In historic districts and older cities, or in places where a higher level of quality and craftsmanship is desired, sidewalks are made with brick, cobblestones, or granite. Without solid underlayment, bricks and stones can become loose or uneven and in some cases create a tripping hazard for pedestrians. This situation commonly occurs in areas that have a frequent freeze-thaw cycle which causes certain stones to settle, or in locations where there are tree roots that have heaved the sidewalk.

In addition to the standard materials that have long been used, new materials are being developed. A new product made of recycled tires has recently been used for sidewalk pavers and tiles. These pavers can be installed directly on prepared ground rather than on a hard base, and have more flexibility to accommodate tree root growth, but are not currently in widespread use.

When selecting materials for locations where pedestrians share space with vehicles, paving materials are a key design feature. They can be used consistently across the ground plane to create a more plaza-like feel to the right-of-way, or they can be used to distinguish the driving area from the walking area and in doing so may help address ADA requirements for color contrast between walking and driving areas (Figure 4-10).

Figure 4-10 The varied materials in the street may reveal history and indicate pedestrian and vehicle zones.

INTERSECTIONS

Intersections must balance the needs of vehicle and pedestrian movements. For intersections along critical portions of the pedestrian network, it may make sense to favor the needs of pedestrians and allow longer wait periods for vehicles. For all intersections, pedestrians should be able to cross safely and without long waits as they are exposed to the elements. Crossing time is especially important for people

Figure 4-11 This crosswalk is slightly elevated, emphasizing pedestrian movement. *Courtesy of SvR Design*

who walk slowly. There are many ways to design intersections which shorten crossing times or allow points of refuge for pedestrians. Visibility for all modes of travel is key at intersections (Figure 4-11).

Accessibility

Walking environments must provide enough information to the visually and physically impaired to ensure their safe mobility. Consistency in design allows people to move safely in unfamiliar places. Critical information, including the detection of obstacles and hazards, can be universally understood if it is visual, auditory, and tactile. Some jurisdictions require a 30-inch-wide strip of truncated domes, in highly contrasting colors, along areas where pedestrians move from walking zones into zones where vehicles are allowed.

Where high-contrast truncated domes are required, they present a design challenge. Because they need to be visible to sight-challenged people, these strips of domes can visually overwhelm places where there is a desire to eliminate curbs. Other elements may be used to distinguish car-free zones and vehicle zones, such as landscaped planters, textures, and bollards. Meeting the requirements of the Americans with Disabilities Act is a central concern when designing the interface of car-free and vehicle zones.

Crosswalks

Crosswalks are the critical location where pedestrians cross through the realm of vehicles. Safety is paramount. Crossings may be either marked or unmarked. Marked crossings use paint or other contrasting materials to indicate pedestrian zones to motorists and to people walking. Most transportation departments use the Manual of Uniform Traffic Control Devices (MUTCD) guidelines for marking crosswalks with high visual contrast. The commonly used "ladder" design has been found to be highly visible.

Thermoplastic paint is commonly used for crosswalks and other traffic indications. The fairly rapid deterioration of paint is often an indicator of deferred maintenance on city streets. Varied materials with integral contrasting colors, such as brick, stone, or concrete, last longer and may also provide tactile guidance. These materials are frequently used along with more standard crosswalk markings that are reflective and therefore much easier to see in low light or at night.

BICYCLE FACILITIES

Bicycle Lanes

Bicycle lanes are a striped segment of the right-of-way, usually adjacent to the curb, dedicated for use by cyclists. They are usually five feet wide. Bicycle lanes can also be accomplished adjacent to parallel parking by extending the lane to accommodate bikes between parked cars and the vehicle lanes. Part of the challenge with this approach lies in creating enough space to keep cyclists well outside the "door zone," where cyclists will not be impacted by drivers who neglect to look for bikes when getting out of their cars after parking. This is easy to accomplish when right-of-way is plentiful, but is challenging on narrow urban arterials where space is at a premium.

Painted bicycle lanes are showing up in many U.S. cities—modeled after pavement markings that have been used in Europe for decades. The colored bicycle lane can be used along the length of a bicycle lane, or in spot locations to highlight areas where bicycles and cars cross paths, and where drivers should be alert that they need to expect cyclists and yield the right-of-way.

Cycletracks, Separated or Buffered Bike Lanes

As the number of bicycles using the roadway increases in many cities, new engineering tools are emerging. Cycletracks, based on successful European models, are dedicated bicycle lanes separated from traffic. Cycletracks may be separated by parked cars or by a short curb—typically three inches. Copenhagen, Denmark, has a robust network of cycletracks that supports a city where approximately 37 percent of trips are made by bicycle.[1]

New York City has over 400 bicycle lane miles in the city, part of a major effort that built 200 bike lane miles in all five boroughs in just three years. Just under five miles of this system are bike paths physically separated from car traffic lanes. A number of these protected bicycle paths are separated from vehicular traffic by parked cars. The bicycle is ridden between the curb and the passenger side of a parked car. Turn movements need to be managed at the intersections so that drivers have a clear view of cyclists when they are preparing to make a right turn.[2]

Another type of buffered bicycle lane can be accomplished by painting a striped, cross-hatched area between bicyclists and motor vehicles. This approach is a good choice for routes without enough space to accommodate a separated lane between the parking and the curb, or where on-street parking is not available (Figure 4-12).

Shared Lane Markers or Sharrows

San Francisco, California; Portland, Oregon; and Seattle, Washington, are among the jurisdictions that have formalized shared lanes for bicyclists. The "sharrow" or shared lane marker on the pavement indicates to bicyclists and drivers that bikes can be expected to share the lane. Sharrows are placed within the lane so that they guide cyclists toward the best position to ride—outside the door zone. Signage reminding drivers to share the road with cyclists is another appropriate addition to shared bike lanes which helps raise driver awareness that cyclists should be expected on this route.

Signed Routes

Another type of bicycle facility is the signed route. Signed routes have consistent informational signage that formally marks the corridor as a bicycle route, and often includes the direction and distance to key

---

[1] Cycle Statistics, City of Copenhagen, www.kk.dk/sitecore/content/Subsites/CityOfCopenhagen/SubsiteFrontpage/LivingInCopenhagen/CityAndTraffic/CityOfCyclists/CycleStatistics.aspx, accessed July, 2011. See also www.copenhagenize.com/,the "Copenhagenize: Building Better Bicycle Culture" website produced by Copenhagenize Consulting, Copenhagen, accessed July, 2011.

[2] www.nyc.gov/html/dot/html/bicyclists/bikenetwork.shtml, New York City Department of Transportation, Bicycle Network Development, City of New York, 2011, accessed July 2011.

Figure 4-12 The cross-hatched painted area serves as a buffer. *Photographer: Paul Iano*

destinations. Many signed routes have no other indication on the street that they are part of a bicycle facility, but the designation may figure into a jurisdiction's decision regarding design treatments, such as signals at arterial crossings. Cities or nonprofit organizations may direct cyclists to these routes through the use of bicycle maps or other educational materials.

Bike Boxes

Bike boxes are pavement markings used at an intersection to give cyclists more visibility and help prevent bicycle/car collisions. In Seattle, the bike box is a painted green space on the road with a white bicycle symbol inside. In some locations it includes a green bicycle lane approaching the box. The box creates space between motor vehicles and the crosswalk, allowing bicyclists to position themselves ahead of motor vehicle traffic at an intersection.

Figure 4-13 Midtown Greenway in Minneapolis. *Courtesy of SvR Design*

The main goal of the bike box is to improve cyclist safety by increasing awareness and visibility of cyclists, and help them make safer intersection crossings. This is especially necessary when drivers are turning right and bicyclists are traveling straight. Bike boxes encourage cyclists to approach and cross intersections more predictably. The box also provides space at the front of an intersection where cyclists can avoid breathing vehicle fumes.

Greenways

Greenways usually refer to linear open spaces with paths or trails which connect communities and parks for cyclists and pedestrians. Greenways often take advantage of unused railroad right-of-way or utility corridors, and have proved to be very popular for both recreation and commuting (Figure 4-13).

Some notable greenways include the Midtown Greenway in Minneapolis, Minnesota, which connects the Mississippi River to the Chain of Lakes in the City's Uptown District. It includes a six-foot-wide pedestrian path and a fourteen-foot-wide bike path.[3] Another successful large-scale urban greenway is the Ohlone Greenway, a bicycle and pedestrian route running between Berkeley and El Cerrito, California, in the East Bay area. The Ohlone Greenway uses both railroad right-of-way and the area under the elevated BART tracks.[4] An ambitious effort called the East Coast Greenway is underway, aiming to connect some 3,000 miles from eastern Canada to Key West, Florida, with a trail system.[5]

Neighborhood Greenways

Greenways need not be continent-spanning efforts which connect multiple cities. A growing number of smaller, less ambitious projects have

[3] Midtown Greenway Coalition website, Frequently Asked Questions, www.midtown greenway.org/faq.html, accessed July 2011.

[4] TrailLink.com, powered by Rails-to-Trails Conservancy, Ohlone Greenway www.traillink .com/trail/ohlone-greenway.aspx, accessed July 2011.

[5] Website by East Coast Greenway, Durham, North Carolina, 2011 www.greenway.org, accessed July 2011.

been easier to launch and just as successful in their own scale and context. Neighborhood Greenways use low-speed, low-volume residential streets to make safe and pleasant corridors that prioritize cyclists and pedestrians. The City of Portland began this concept as "bicycle boulevards" but expanded the idea to include a broader range of nonmotorized movement, as well as the idea of more pleasant residential streets. Using engineering measures and additional landscaping, neighborhood greenways are intended to benefit the people who live and move along the route.

Part of the task of a successful neighborhood greenway is to slow vehicles and reduce their number. Streets that parallel busier arterials are good candidates for neighborhood greenways, because fast-traveling cars can use the higher-speed arterials, leaving the parallel street for local traffic and greenway use. Traffic-calming elements can create larger areas within the right-of-way for trees, vegetation, and natural drainage. The habitat, community, and transportation functions of these corridors improve the quality of life for the residents and users of the space, and tend to improve desirability of the neighborhood and the street.

Establishing bicycle and pedestrian priority is important if neighborhood greenways are to function as intended. Residential side street crossings of the greenway should be controlled, allowing the bicycle movement to continue uninterrupted. Existing stop signs along the greenway route should be removed. Where the greenways cross arterials, a balance must be struck between keeping the arterial traffic moving, and ensuring that bicycle and pedestrians on the greenway have a predictable crossing. Maintaining arterial operations helps to keep vehicles on the arterials rather than using neighborhood streets as cut-through routes.

There are various ways to address the arterial crossing of a greenway. A simple crosswalk with warning signs can be used for roadways less than three lanes across. Stop lines for the crosswalk need to be set far enough back so that if a vehicle tries to pass a stopped automobile, pedestrians and cyclists in the crosswalk will be visible. Short medians are also used to restrict turn movements onto the greenway by cars, and provide a refuge for cyclists and pedestrians when crossing the busier street. Signalized crossings at intersections are less likely on neighborhood greenways, because low-volume residential streets are unlikely to meet the federal criteria, or warrants, necessary to install signals using federal funds. Since neighborhood greenways are a new facility type, they do not currently have an adopted signal warrant. Signal strategies along the greenways vary, with cities taking advantage of the experience of their peers and the recent development of a variety of experimental warrants.

Neighborhood greenways can be built in phases. Starting with signage, paint, and simple traffic diversion, a neighborhood greenway can be put in place with little funding. Active neighborhood support is a critical element in creating a successful greenway—both to advocate for the route's recognition as a greenway, and to help spread the word and generate use. Over time, as funding allows, more resource-intensive improvements can be added, such as rain gardens associated with curb bulbs, planted traffic diverters, and traffic signals.

End-of-Trip-Facilities—Parking and Showers

Successful bicycle facilities provide for the functions that cyclists need at the end of their trip. Convenient and plentiful bike parking is necessary for trips to work, recreational areas, and shopping destinations. Places to shower and change clothes are vital ingredients for people who wish to bicycle to work but are employed in offices where bicycle attire would not be appropriate.

One of the reasons that people love to ride bicycles is convenience. This means that if at the end of their trip, the bike parking is not convenient, people may not choose to cycle. Successful bike parking is addressed by considering a few factors: Is the bicycle parking located very near the entrance to frequently used destinations? Would a cyclist feel secure accessing their bike throughout the day, implying that the location is well-lit and convenient to access from the street? Is there enough parking to meet the demand of the nearby destinations? Do most of the cyclists parking their bikes need long-term or short-term storage? Is the parking protected from the weather? Would there be a market for secure bicycle parking? Answering these questions early in the design of the bicycle parking facility will more likely result in a well-used facility.

Bicycle parking comes in many forms. On-street racks typically house one to four bicycles, and are located on sidewalks where there is enough room to keep them out of the area where pedestrians walk. Many designs exist—from utilitarian, off-the-shelf products that can be modified to fit the space available, to custom designed racks. Musician, author, and bicycle enthusiast David Byrne designed bicycle racks as part of New York City Department of Transportation's Urban Art Program. Initially designed as temporary installations, these racks are durable and iconic and are now approved by the City's design commission as permanent installations.[6]

Bike corrals are on-street facilities where multiple bikes can park in one location. Bike corrals have several benefits over on-sidewalk racks. A corral can fit within the same space as a single on-street parking space, converting a previously car-oriented space to a space for bikes. If located on the street, adjacent to the intersection, a bike corral can improve visibility at intersections by eliminating the option for cars to park in close proximity of the crosswalk.

Bike corrals work very well in locations where bicycle parking demand is high and sidewalks are constrained—for example, outside of restaurants with sidewalk cafes, or in neighborhoods with narrow sidewalks flanked by tree pits and assorted street furniture. By concentrating bicycles in one spot, bike corrals can reduce clutter along busy sidewalks. Bike corrals can also be covered to provide weather protection for parked bicycles (Figure 4-14).

[6] www.nyc.gov/html/dot/html/bicyclists/bicycleparking.shtml. New York City Department of Transportation, City of New York, 2011, Bicycle Parking, accessed July 2011.

Figure 4-14 Bike parking near the train station in Washington, D.C.

Secured bike parking is another type of facility that has emerged—and is often membership based. Membership usually guarantees secure 24-hour bicycle parking. Benefits often include access to amenities such as showers, changing rooms, maps, and information, or even vending machines with patch kits, tubes, and other bicycle necessities. Secured bike parking can be staffed—such as the premier facilities of Washington D.C.'s Union Station, or those in Chicago's Millennium Park—or unstaffed, such as the bike cages found in a number of BART rail stations in and around San Francisco. Bike cages and lockers are frequently used at transit stations. They provide secure bicycle parking for commuters who may shift transportation modes from bike to bus as they finish their trip, necessitating longer-term parking that is well located and secure enough that they can count on their bike being there when they make their return trip.

Bicycle parking requirements that are part of local land use or building codes ensure that new construction includes the appropriate amount of bicycle parking to support the uses in the building. This issue is discussed in more detail in Chapter 5.

SIGNAGE

At the beginning of the automobile age, there was no directional signage and no common system for warning or informing drivers. Bicycle groups in the UK put up some of the first modern road signs in the early 1880s. providing directions to destinations and warning of potential hazards, such as steep hills. As the importance of signage became clear with the growing number of drivers, automobile clubs and other organizations took on the task of creating signposts. The first stop sign was installed in 1915 in Detroit, Michigan.[7] Detroit put the first three-color traffic light in place in 1920.[8]

During the 1920s, standardization of traffic signs began, with colors and shapes of signs delivering messages to drivers. Round signs indicated danger, such as railroad crossings. The familiar octagon of the stop sign represented the need to stop at intersections. Diamonds call for caution, and rectangular signs provide regulatory information. In 1935, the first MUTCD (Manual on Uniform Traffic Control Devices) volume consolidated guidance into a nationally accepted set of standards. Subsequent editions of MUTCD have evolved regulations that control higher volumes of traffic, higher speeds, and new technologies (Figure 4-15).

Figure 4-15 Signage for a bike lane in Vancouver, B.C.

New Signage Philosophies

Signage is part of the mindset that separates uses and clarifies zones and speeds. When driver behavior is problematic, the road-planner's urge is often to add more and more signage. At some point, the amount of signage overwhelms the environment and becomes counterproductive. The idea of separation and clarity in signage is so ingrained in the planning community that challenging it philosophically can be almost heretical. But where cars are few, and traveling slowly, this assumption is being challenged.

In shared-use zones, where all modes of movement occur at similar speeds, the "naked streets" movement has come to mean the removal of signage. Environmental clues are used instead to provide information and to increase driver awareness of the context that they are passing through.

---

[7] Cyclists' Touring Club. The UK's National Cyclists' Organisation website, "History of the CTC," http://www.ctc.org.uk/desktop-default.aspx?tabid=3666.

[8] Manual on Uniform Traffic Control Devices (MUTCD), U.S. Department of Transportation Federal Highway Administration website, "Knowledge: The Evolution of MUTCD," http://mutcd.fhwa.dot.gov/kno-history.htm

Hans Monderman advocated for less signage in Holland. Signs, he felt, were an admission that the environment carried insufficient information for drivers. Better to change the environment than to keep adding signage.

In Drachten, a growing town with some 45,000 residents, Monderman removed the traffic signals from an important intersection known as the Laweiplein. The intersection handled about 20,000 cars a day. One of the priorities for the plan was improving the character of the space itself. The Noordelijke Hogeschool Leeuwarden (NHL) University of Applied Sciences undertook a complete evaluation of the conditions of the intersection both before and after the construction. The study examined traffic volumes and movements, efficiency, methods of communication between users, accident reports, and opinions of residents and bus drivers.

The report found that, after implementation of Monderman's plan, traffic—including vehicles and bicycles—circulated more freely, and moved at a fairly consistent low speed. Capacity had improved, despite an increase in the traffic volumes. The average time taken by pedestrians to cross the intersection decreased from 50 seconds to about 30 seconds, and there are fewer bus delays. With slower speeds, pedestrians and cyclists cross the intersection without waiting. The character of the space has improved, and early data appears to show a safer condition.[9]

The project has succeeded in making Laweiplein both a functional traffic element and a quality public space for Drachten. According to the study's surveys, people are pleased with the improved character of the space, and feel that congestion has been reduced. Respondents reported an increased perception of personal safety, but a reduced opinion of traffic safety despite an actual reduction in the number of accidents. Local bus drivers were generally positive about the redesigned intersection, but had some worries about unpredictable movements from cyclists.[10]

Although not addressed in the study, the user group that has been most challenged by shared space concepts is people with limited vision. The cues for drivers and pedestrians negotiating the intersection with reduced signage are primarily visual. The curbs that distinguish pedestrian and vehicular zones are gone, and European regulations do not require the truncated domes and color contrasts of American regulations.

Martin Cassini, the report's author, concluded:

> Removing lights removes barriers to traffic flow and improves behavior. If you observe a junction where the lights are out of action, there is rarely congestion. People approach slowly, wave each other on, and filter in turn. Lights and other controls hamper instead of harness human nature, causing untold delay and harm.[11]

---

[9] "Full Report: The Laweiplein: Evaluation of the reconstruction into a square with roundabout." January 2007 Noordelijke Hogeschool Leeuwarden; retrieved from www.fietsberaad.nl/library/repository/bestanden/Evaluation%20Laweiplein.pdf
[10] Ibid.
[11] Ibid.

STREET FURNITURE

Street furnishings include benches, kiosks, magazine racks, planters, pedestrian-scale lighting, wayfinding signs, and other elements that make people comfortable in a place. High-quality spaces require the integration of these elements so that they are both attractive and functional. Art and cultural elements that are rooted in their communities create character and make for more interesting, human-scale places.

Some street furnishings are fundamental for simple comfort. But the aspiration for furnishings is to give places character, to encourage people to walk and to enjoy the outdoors. Seating is important even in places where people are primarily moving, since there will be people who simply need a spot to rest. Elements such as trash receptacles help keep streets clean, and lighting is needed for safety at a minimum. Street furnishings also address particular needs, such as a place to sit and be protected from the weather while waiting for transit.

Figure 4-16   A few simple plantings make a big difference in making a human scale. It shows that someone cares about the place.

Figure 4-17   This public space, designed by Gustafson Guthrie Nichol, incorporates a water feature that is welcome in the summer months, but is invisible when not in use during other seasons.

Street furnishings can shape spaces and the way that people interact. For example, benches can be perpendicular to foster conversations. There are many examples where benches go unused because they are oriented to traffic, or located in places that are undesirable to sit. Landscape planters can shape space by creating nooks where people can sit and talk out of the flow of people walking.

A question often arises about which street furnishings should be consistent, and which should be unique to a particular location. There is no one answer to this question, but some elements benefit by consistency. For instance, streetlights are usually best as consistent elements, for lighting quality, aesthetics, and for keeping the variety of bulbs to a minimum for maintenance. Signage also benefits from consistency. Trees are often consistent, but planting monocultures can mean that the street trees are vulnerable to disease or pests. Some of the most interesting streetscapes allow for personalization of elements, so that property owners can add interest and the "quirky" elements that make one place different than another.

The following photos illustrate a variety of street furnishings that are appropriate responses to their particular circumstances (Figures 4-16 through 4-23).

Figure 4-18 Street furnishings need not be fancy or expensive to be effective.

Figure 4-19 Games and other activities can be fun for participants and for people-watchers.

Figure 4-20 Street furnishings can draw on the culture of a place, such as these planters that line a shared-use area at an Asian grocery.

Figure 4-21 Art in the streetscape offers character and interest.

Figure 4-23 The humble trash receptacle is an important urban element. This design encourages recycling. *Courtesy of SvR Design*

Figure 4-22 Elevators and escalators can help people negotiate steep topography.

STREET TREES AND LANDSCAPING

Street trees and landscaping in the right-of-way provide a wealth of benefits. Adding greenery to urban environments helps to clean the air, filter the water, and creates humane and pleasant places within the city. The message that well-landscaped streets send is that the place itself is cared for; that people, birds, and animals are invited, and that the city is linked with its natural setting.

In his *22 Benefits of Urban Street Trees,* Dan Burden reports, "We are well on the way to recognizing the need for urban street trees to be the default design, rather than a luxury item to be tolerated by traffic engineering and budget-conscious city administrators."[12]

But advocating for retaining existing street trees and adding new ones still requires effort. Street trees get some negative press from local business owners when they block signage, heave the sidewalk, and present a tripping hazard. Maintenance staff complain that the leaves, berries, and fruit which drop at various times during the year create too much work (Figure 4-24).

The adage "right tree, right place" is a good rule. Selecting species that will be successful, allowing them sufficient space to grow, and ensuring that they are planted correctly are critical. Without sufficient care, urban trees contend with harsh conditions and have short lifespans.

Because the value of urban trees is becoming more widely understood, new products that improve urban growing conditions are coming on the market. One interesting technology is modular underground framework that holds soil and allows roots to spread within the framework. These systems take the loads from the surface and prevent soil from being compacted, so that root systems can expand below the pavement without causing heaving or cracking.

SWALES AND RAIN GARDENS

Bioswale

Stormwater runoff carries particulates from the roadway or parking area. Bioswales are used primarily for removing those particulates. A typical swale has a level bottom width at least two feet wide, and a length designed to accommodate the expected stormwater flows. Traditionally, bioswales have had grass plantings, but lists of acceptable plant types have expanded in many jurisdictions. The plant selection should be chosen with site-specific soil, moisture, and shade conditions in mind.

---

[12] *22 Benefits of Urban Street Trees,* Dan Burden, Senior Urban Designer, Glatting Jackson and Walkable Communities, Inc; May 2006.

Figure 4-24 This street tree helps create a sense of privacy for residents on the lower floor.

The swale should have a longitudinal slope (usually less than 5 percent) that fully drains after each storm event. Flatter swales and highly infiltrative soils may require a liner to keep the flows in the swale. The swale's sides tend to be sloped at a maximum of 3:1, allowing maintenance access and mowing as needed.

Bioretention Swale

A bioretention swale is used both to slow the flow of stormwater and to treat it. Bioretention swales usually have a level bottom with 3:1 side slopes. The side slopes may be combined with short rockeries or walls. Bioretention swales are designed in concert with the actual infiltration rate of the native or imported soils. The soil mix has an expected infiltration rate that is modeled in conjunction with the native soil. In cases where slower infiltration rates predominate, the swale may need an underdrain connected to the storm system. Vegetation may include a palate of plant material, chosen for aesthetics and performance, or simply grass.

Figure 4-25 A portion of this alley was redone as a rain garden.

Rain Gardens

Rain gardens are planted depressions that receive and absorb rainwater from impervious surfaces such as sidewalks, roofs, and streets. Rain gardens tend to be less linear than swales, and are well suited for adding stormwater treatment, traffic calming, and improved habitat to existing streets.

Rain gardens typically include a thick layer of engineered soil over a layer of gravel. The surface of the rain garden is below the surrounding grade by about four to eight inches, which is enough to allow the water to be retained while it infiltrates, but not so deep that it becomes a pond or a tripping hazard. Overflow structures can handle the extra water during the largest storms. Plants with deep, fibrous roots are ideal for cleaning and filtration, and native species are preferred. Smaller, distributed rain gardens are better than larger, concentrated facilities.

Like bioretention swales, rain gardens are designed specifically for the site conditions. The permeability of the underlying native soil is critical to the design. Where soils do not drain well, the design needs to include features to ensure that the rain garden does not "pond" water for too long. Rain gardens are typically designed to drain within 72 hours of large storm events.

Rain gardens can be beautiful and effective elements for reducing flooding which simultaneously improves water quality. Due to the multiple benefits they provide in a relatively small footprint, rain gardens can be a wise investment in many urban streets (Figure 4-25).

Porous Pavement

The paved surfaces of roadways and sidewalks can work in concert with other natural system elements when they are made of porous materials. Porous paving can provide treatment of stormwater, the opportunity for stormwater infiltration, and shallow subsurface flow to swales. Porous pavements are designed for the specific situation, taking into account expected traffic volumes, the amount of stormwater flow, and soil conditions. A discharge subbase is comprised of crushed rock with limited fines, allowing the water to infiltrate over a period of time. An elevated underdrain in certain locations will allow high flows to be diverted away from the pavement section.

Porous pavements in cold climates typically have less ice build-up than standard pavement because when the ice melts, it melts into the pavement. The gravel base assists in controlling frost heaves. Aesthetically, porous pavers offer a wide range of looks and textures. The texture of porous concrete and asphalt can create an aesthetic concern for some property owners. Some "architectural concrete" mixes exist which do not have larger aggregate, resulting in a finer-grained, more appealing look. Porous pavements have been used frequently in the construction of ball fields and play courts; however, the use in the right-of-way is catching on slowly as cities obtain more data on maintenance and longevity.

CURBS, GUTTERS, AND ALTERNATIVES

Curbs are typically where drive lanes meet raised sidewalks. Curbs separate cars and pedestrians, and keep pedestrians dry by channeling water via gutters into drainage systems. The elevation of foot traffic has been seen as advantageous since antiquity—the streets of Pompeii had raised pedestrian areas along the edges of the streets, and stepping stones so that people need not walk in the water and waste that was found in the street.

Curbs provide several functions in the modern street, depending on application and streetscape design. In a streetscape where transportation modes are separated, such as arterials, curbs provide a physical barrier between pedestrians and vehicles. Curbs are often intended to restrain the movement of cars. A typical six-inch concrete curb will discourage cars from encroaching on pedestrian or landscaped zones, defining both drive lanes and parking zones.

Where vehicle and pedestrian space intersect, an apron or curb ramp is used. Aprons allow vehicle access from the street into a driveway; curb ramps direct pedestrians, wheelchairs, and strollers to crosswalks at intersections. Where driveways and pedestrian ramps provide access to or across the sidewalk and planting strip, the curb slopes down to meet the grade of the street. On pedestrian ramps, there is no lip where the ramp meets the flow line. Where driveways meet the sidewalk, a small lip between a quarter of an inch and two inches high keeps stormwater flowing into the street.

Curbs have a major visual impact on the streetscape. They can create defined edges for spaces within the right-of-way. A concrete curb adjacent to asphalt drive lanes is highly visible. Curbs are also regularly used to provide information, typically for drivers, indicating parking restrictions such as drop-off zones, bus zones, or fire lanes. Curbs are one of the elements that, perhaps unintentionally, visually signal the priority of vehicles, confining pedestrians to the space at the sides of the traffic realms.

The materials used to build curbs can vary. Curbs have traditionally been constructed from locally available materials. For instance, in New England, curbs were historically made from granite. Modern curb construction tends to be concrete that is either formed in place or with a slip-forming machine that places the curb through a continuous pour. Curb heights are generally six inches in height, but can vary from zero to seven inches. In a situation where cars will be parking along the curb, the curb should not be at a height which would prevent the doors from opening.

Curbs designed to stop vehicles are called barrier curbs. They protect pedestrians, landscaped areas, and other objects, such as hydrants or light poles. Curbs that allow some crossing motions are called mountable curbs, and have a variety of shapes. Rolled curbs have sloped faces that allow cars to move across them without damage. These are most often found in suburban settings. Sometimes straight-edged curbs that are low in height can be used where large vehicles occasionally need to make turning movements.

In Europe, there are several applications where a curb that is half-height or less is used to separate cycletracks from the sidewalk as well as the roadway. The use of this type of curb makes it difficult for bikes to access the facility from the street mid-block or for the bicycle to access a business mid-block. Gilham Road in Eugene, Oregon, used a rolled curb between the bicycle facility and the roadway to facilitate bicycles accessing the facility from the roadway. The use of the half-curb should be site-specific and may not work in every situation.

Curbs and gutters are also standard elements in urban drainage systems, directing the stormwater that flows off of the street toward the curb cut, inlet, or catch basin. Roads are often "crowned" to drain toward the edges of the street, and curbs direct water toward drains that are connected to below-grade storm sewers. Curbs and the area adjacent to the curbs are designed to handle a level of water that varies depending on local rainfall patterns. Curb and gutter drainage systems take less space than the swales or culverts that are typically found in less urbanized conditions.

When curbs are utilized in conjunction with green stormwater infrastructure, curb cuts or curb inlets can be used. This allows the stormwater to periodically pass through the curb to enter the swale or other drainage facility.

Curbs are fundamental to the paradigm of separation of uses in the street. As people reconsider the use of streets, some projects that aim to elevate pedestrian use of the street have eliminated curbs. Additionally, the ecological advantages of natural drainage systems have caused the primacy of curb and gutter solutions to be questioned.

On streets where there is a desire to blur the lines of travel areas, such as festival streets and shared-use streets, the curb can be eliminated as long as the drainage and grading is designed accordingly. When curbs are not used, access for people with limited mobility and/or vision needs to be accommodated. The Americans with Disabilities Act has greatly influenced the way in which curbs and ramps are designed. People with limited mobility must be able to move from sidewalks to crosswalks via curb ramps. In addition, people with limited vision must be able to clearly understand when they have crossed into zones where vehicles are allowed. For this reason, American cities have been installing "truncated domes" at curb ramps for several years. These tactile warnings alert the visually impaired that they are moving into a zone with vehicles. High visual contrast is called for in addition to the tactile nature of the domes, so many jurisdictions use white or canary yellow materials (Figure 4-26).

If there is a desire to indicate separation of uses, but not a desire to have a grade separation, then a textured, flush curb made of materials such as granite blocks or scored, stamped, or colored concrete can be used.

PARKING

Allocating parking in the street right-of-way, regardless of the land use, always results in a vigorous debate. In fact, the use of curb space for parking can be one of the most contentious discussions in rethinking street use. The decisions are many: How much parking is needed? Who is it for and how long can they park there? Should it be free or paid? Parallel, angled, or perpendicular? Head in, or back in? Is on-street parking really the best use of limited curb space? And that is just the tip of the iceberg. Parking policies affect land uses, air quality, retail economics, and traffic patterns. The cost of the parking infrastructure—installation, stormwater, best available use, maintenance, and replacement should all be taken into consideration when deciding where and how much parking is allocated in the right-of-way.

On-street parking provides access for retail uses and neighborhood residents and visitors. It can help provide a buffer between moving vehicles and pedestrian spaces. Parking for service vehicles, which sometimes include larger delivery vehicles, is important to the function of many businesses. However, if on-street parking is excessive, it can impact the overall quality of the streetscape. Keeping parking at the periphery of active spaces or building off-street parking facilities can provide an alter-

Figure 4-26 This curbless shared-use cul-de-sac uses materials that slow cars.

native to street parking that still accommodates cars without having them dominate the streetscape. There are also simple strategies that can make parking less obtrusive. For instance, having a cluster of landscaping on either side of a group of angled parking spaces softens the effect of parked cars. The Terry Avenue North Case Study presented in Chapter 7 illustrates this approach.

The dimensions of parking are typically dictated by the local jurisdiction and will vary depending on the type (parallel, angled back-in, angled front-in, or perpendicular). In a parallel parking situation, the width of a parking space will vary between seven and nine feet, and the length is typically twenty feet. The parking width would be coordinated with the available right-of-way area, adjacent travel lane width and if an adjacent bike lane is planned. The American Association of State Highway and Transportation Officials (AASHTO) Roadway Design Manuals provides guidance on the recommended widths.

Angled parking uses more width, depending on the angle, but also provides more spaces than parallel parking. The trend in angled parking is to move toward back-in/head-out conditions, which have multiple benefits. Visibility is much better for drivers pulling into traffic facing forward rather than backing out. This configuration also allows people to access their trunks from the sidewalk side. On one-way streets, you need to analyze the side of the street on which the parking is located. Head-in parking allows the vehicle to exit the roadway more quickly, however, when backing up the adjacent vehicles block drivers' lines of sight (Figure 4-27).

Back-in/head-out parking improves the chances that a driver, while backing into the space, is moving slowly and looking over their shoulder as they back up, making them more likely to see a bicyclist coming while they are parking. When pulling out, the driver has a direct view of the oncoming bicyclist.[13]

Signs, power poles, street lights, and trees need to be located clear of vehicle bumpers. The width of the sidewalk needs to take this bumper space into consideration so that a relatively narrow sidewalk is not made impassable by the intrusion of vehicle bumpers. Some jurisdictions use bollards to prevent the car bumpers from impacting the planting strip or sidewalk.

Through fees, time-limits, and use restrictions, parking can be actively managed. The goals of this management may be to encourage turnover in a business district, to prevent people from using the right-of-way for long-term parking, or to allow the curb lane to accommodate different functions at various times during the day—such as snow removal, early morning street-sweeping, or the demands of increased general-purpose vehicle traffic during hours of peak travel demand.

In areas with high parking demand—such as those near a public transportation stop, a hospital, or a university—parking zones can be assigned to specific users who pay a fee, making them "eligible" to park in designated spaces. Sometimes referred to as residential parking zones, these fees are typically nominal. Participants get a sticker or placard for their vehicle, and sometimes guest passes. The jurisdiction signs the on-street spaces to define the time limits that will apply in each zone. In some cases, the

13. Back-in Head-out Angle Parking, Nelson/Nygaard Consultants, 2005.

Figure 4-27 Parallel parking serves as a buffer between pedestrians and traffic and offers convenient access.

institution that has created the parking demand will pay the user fee in order to limit workers and visitors to the facilities from taking residential parking spots. This also leads to debate that people should not have to pay extra for parking near their home. Other residents, however, are happy to pay a nominal fee to have easier access to free parking near their residence.

Copenhagen, Denmark, is often recognized as one of the best pedestrian cities in the world. Copenhagen was able to transform itself by taking an incremental approach to removing parking from the denser urban areas, slowly converting that parking space into bicycle or pedestrian space. Over time, people become accustomed to the changed patterns of movement because the resulting pedestrian and bicycle space is attractive, well connected, and takes you to the places you need to go. The network of cycletracks and walking streets in Copenhagen has supported a thriving city that is a magnet for visitors who can experience the city solely on foot or by bike.

When repurposing the right-of-way, taking away parking is an emotional subject. Even when parking is not fully utilized, business owners like short-term, high-turnover parking spaces right outside their front door. In residential areas, people prefer to park in front of their residence. When adding bike lanes, transit-only lanes, widening sidewalks or completely redesigning a street to add natural drainage and other assets, available parking is often reduced or at least revised. This can lead to conflict as many people erroneously believe that the public right-of-way outside their home or business is their personal property and should be reserved for their use or the use of their guests or customers. The debate around allocation of public right-of-way space and parking often adds significant time and complexity to redesigning a streetscape and shifting the balance away from vehicles.

Chapter 5

INFLUENCES

THE KEY INFLUENCES THAT SHAPE STREET DESIGN DECISIONS are rooted in people, politics, and places. Getting a project built that pushes the envelope of local standard practices requires not just good engineering, but careful navigation among community members, design professionals, elected officials, and other stakeholder groups. Clear goals and a good set of guidance tools help the project team navigate new approaches. Strong leadership and perseverance are often the best predictors of successfully implementing innovative projects.

Figure 5-1 *Courtesy of SvR Design*

CONSIDERING CONTEXT

To begin thinking about streets in new ways, it is helpful to step back and look at the broadest context of the land that comprises the publicly owned rights-of-way. Public rights-of-way—streets, sidewalks, parking lanes, planting strips, and all the spaces that lie between the private property lines—are managed and stewarded by public agencies and funded through various taxes or tolls.

The amount of public land in street rights-of-way is significant, typically one-quarter to one-third of the land area in a city or town. For example, a city of 100 square miles with a quarter of its land as right-of-way would have 16,000 acres of public land to use for movement, connections, placemaking, and space for natural systems. These 16,000 acres are dispersed throughout a large and sometimes disconnected network that is bisected by hills and water bodies, private developments, businesses, industrial complexes, and public buildings.

As major reservoirs of public land, streets can be considered in terms of their ability to respond and contribute to the quality of the natural systems of which they are a part. Streets can offer space for recharging aquifers, slowing the flow of stormwater, reducing the heat island effect, and improving air quality. The opportunity to reconnect or improve the natural systems exists with every street design project.

Streets and the Natural Environment

All streets lie within the natural and cultural environment of a place. Consider the origins of a hypothetical typical street: At some point in the history of that place, the street was imposed on the landscape by human effort. The insertion of the street dramatically changes the environment and the place itself. Over time, the community grew around the street. Driveways were connected to it as homes were built. Sidewalks were added when the business district expanded. Paint, signs, signals, street trees, and landscaping came along as the pace of commerce grew, along with traffic volumes. Surface water was piped underground to flow swiftly away from the place where it originally contacted the ground.

With all of these incremental changes and the progression of generations of people inhabiting the community, it becomes increasingly hard to imagine the place that originally existed before the street was built. But even the most urbanized area is still part of the natural world—it lies on soils of silt, clay, loam, or rock, in the midst of a climate that includes sun, rain, and wind. It is part of a geographic region with landforms and hydrological systems.

Both climate and soils influence the functions of a street. Some climates, such as the Pacific Northwest, have numerous cloudy days with small amounts of rainfall through much of the year. Desert climates may have less annual rainfall, but it will be concentrated in a few intense storms. Cold climates with heavy snowfall place other requirements on streets—such as space adjacent to the lanes where snow can be plowed (Figure 5-1).

These local climate conditions influence what streets look like, what can or should never be done along them, and what needs to be considered in terms of long-term maintenance. For example, if you have ever visited the City of Las Vegas on a sunny day and wondered why the storm drains span nearly half a city block you will need to visit again during the flash flood season to experience the dramatic rainfall that can dump as much as three inches of rain on the street in less than two hours.

Some types of soil drain easily, allowing water to percolate through sandy or gravelly material. Other soil, which may be made up of clay or intact rock, will not drain well, and water will sheet flow off of the surface. Strategies for better handling of rainwater rely on understanding the nature of the soil, its layering, and the nature of the downstream conditions. Is the water heading toward a stream or toward a salt-water bay, or is it percolating into an aquifer? Impervious soils typically make the addition of paved surfaces more costly due to the drainage infrastructure needed to prevent surface flooding. This is true even with pervious pavement, where water detention needs to be constructed beneath the sidewalk in order to provide a receptacle for stormwater that moves through the pavement until it can infiltrate or evaporate.

Cross-Disciplinary Design

There is a growing awareness among designers, communities, and elected officials that the natural systems that host streets need to be preserved, and that it is unwise to take the health of the natural world for granted. Going even further, many people recognize that street design projects present opportunities to reconnect and heal elements of the natural environment.

Taking advantage of these opportunities is not without its challenges. The progressive street designer—the engineer or the urban designer, architect, or landscape architect—is hired by a city, a developer, or a community group to build a new street in an old place. The first step of recognizing the natural context within which the street exists is just the beginning. The influences upon the designer come from all angles: the client, the neighbors, the local business owner, elected officials, and advocacy groups. And the influences are often in tension with one another: the traffic congestion is terrible—my commute used to take 20 minutes and today it is twice that! We want this place to reflect our cultural history! That ditch on the side of the road needs to be restored to its former glory as a fish-bearing creek! We need more trees to keep this place cool in the summer and add beautiful fall foliage to our town! This route connects the school with the community center and the kids need a wide sidewalk to get them safely back and forth between the two buildings! We're lucky we got any money at all to improve this street so you need to stay within our modest budget! (See Figure 5-2.)

Figure 5-2 Cross-disciplinary discussions enrich the viewpoints on design of public spaces.

The influences can be overwhelming. To achieve success—a great transportation project that improves the community and reconnects the natural systems of that place—the "toolbox" of the progressive street designer must be expanded to include a broader set of tools that span disciplines. Beyond roadway engineering, the toolbox needs to include urban design strategies, stormwater management practices, landscape design and maintenance tools, placemaking elements, electrical engineering standards, historic preservation guidelines, financial management know-how, and community engagement skills. Despite these higher demands on designers, the many street design projects that take advantage of opportunities to reconnect, heal, and recharge are becoming the new standard. This higher standard suggests that the benefits far outweigh the drawbacks of making streets better contributors to sustainable communities.

Part of a successful cross-disciplinary effort is making sure that the right questions are being asked and the right problems are being solved. Developing an agreed-upon set of goals at the outset helps projects achieve good solutions through the complicated decision-making process that is part of every project. In creating a set of project goals, each stakeholder has the opportunity to voice their aspirations and concerns, and listen to one another. These early discussions set out the problems to be solved and the community priorities. Even the best designers benefit from the input of community members who know the details of a place. Engineers are excellent problem solvers, but they need to be asked to solve the right problems—the goal needs to be streets that support community values and objectives.

POLICY FOUNDATION—POLICIES THAT INFLUENCE STREET DESIGN

Beyond the natural environment, there is a less visible, but equally critical framework of policies that affects priorities and uses in the public rights-of-way. Policies begin by directing broad goals for land uses and transportation. The highest-level policies, often contained in a policy framework or comprehensive planning documents, consider the relationships among these broad categories or elements. *Codes* tend to address more specific issues such as open space requirements, drainage standards, and travel lane widths. *Policies* direct private sector actions on private property by setting the form, type, and scale of buildings that can be constructed, and the requirements for meeting environmental quality and addressing public health.

In recent years, many jurisdictions have made policy shifts toward walkable communities, denser urban areas, and support for public transit. Often, these philosophical changes begin at higher policy levels, and meet challenges in their implementation.

Policies are commonly moving from an emphasis on personal vehicles toward a more balanced view of transportation modes. The *Complete Streets* movement is being embraced by transportation agencies, with a new priority for accommodating all modes of movement—pedestrians, bicycles, and transit—and people of all ages and abilities. Another trend is *Context-Sensitive Design,* and the slightly broader *Context-Sensitive Solutions* approach, which looks beyond the right-of-way to include an understanding of the communities and environments that streets and roads pass through. These approaches recognize that streets are part of physical, social, and economic environments, and that these issues need to be part of mobility solutions.

These more comprehensive approaches are more complicated than simply following standard practice. More issues and more points of view are involved. The people who once made decisions about the use and design of streets had well-defined goals of throughput, efficiency, and safety. They now find that the expanded toolbox discussed earlier in this chapter needs more tools in order to accomplish the high-level policy goals that have been set out for transportation projects that now include mobility, environmental quality, economics, personal health, and strength of communities.

The Link Between Land Use and Transportation

Transportation solutions cannot be conceived without considering the land uses they support. Low-density land uses—such as large-lot, single-family neighborhoods—limit transportation alternatives because destinations are far from one another. The patterns of development over the past decades have increased reliance on private cars, and made transit expensive and inefficient. The model of compact neighborhoods with a mixture of uses and transportation options is now widely accepted. Some of the trends in land use planning need to be understood as important influences for transportation planning.

Growth Management

The idea of growth management is to locate new development where there are services available, and to limit the amount of sprawl that replaces open space with low-density development. Growth management regulations have been adopted at local, regional, and state levels. "Smart growth" is another term for the idea of compact development rather than sprawl. Compact growth supports walking, bicycling, and the use of transit.

Mixed-Use Development

Policymakers have recognized that separating land uses, with zones of only residential use and other zones with only commercial uses, has segregated the places that we live, work, shop, and play. Mixing these uses means that most aspects of life can be within walking distance. The emphasis on walkability places increased importance on the streets for pedestrians (Figure 5-3).

New Approaches to Zoning

Traditional zoning has focused on separating uses and setting upper limits for density and height. New trends are moving zoning regulations toward more mixing of units and considering parameters beyond the property line. Some cities are adopting *form-based codes* that, among other things, aim to create stronger relationships between buildings and the adjacent public spaces. Other cities have employed the *Green Factor,* which originated in Sweden and Germany and requires private developments to add urban landscaping, allowing credit for greening on both the private property and the adjacent public streets.

New Priorities for Modes

Cars and trucks are an important part of the transportation mix, but they are now seen as one of a number of modes of transportation. Challenging the dominance of private cars is still contentious, but

Figure 5-3 A mix of uses means that people can live, work, shop, and play within walking distance. *Photographer: Rick Browning*

change occurs slowly. When better facilities exist for pedestrians and bicycles, more people walk and bike. When transit is efficient and pleasant, more people use transit. From a policy standpoint, providing more options for mobility has many benefits. Many people cannot drive, because they are too young, elderly, or disabled. Others cannot afford—or choose not to afford—the hassle and expenses of car ownership, insurance, parking, and gas. Moving from transportation modes that run on fossil fuels to human-powered modes is better for the environment and for personal health. The policy priorities in any jurisdiction set the capital budgets and design standards that help drive change.

Walking Is a Transportation Mode

Both transportation and land use policies are placing increased emphasis on the amount and quality of the pedestrian environment. In a shift of thinking, walking is now seen as a viable transportation option—transportation departments are writing pedestrian plans and agencies are building more infrastructure for walking. On the land use side of the equation, some zoning codes have begun requiring

Figure 5-4 Walking is healthy for everyone.
Courtesy of SvR Design

buildings to support adjacent streets through the use of techniques such as pedestrian overlay zones or pedestrian priority streets. These overlay zones encourage designers to implement pedestrian-oriented uses at street level, adding transparency and visual interest. Some zoning codes now specify parking quantity and location to minimize impacts to walkability, making a healthy and appealing pedestrian realm a priority instead of an afterthought (Figure 5-4).

Accommodating Bicycles

Many policies are elevating the need for improved facilities for bicycles. Share the Road programs educate both cyclists and motorists about the rights and responsibilities of bicyclists. Money for bicycle infrastructure has become a higher priority in many jurisdictions, with pedestrian and cycling advocacy groups lobbying for an increased range of transportation choices. In addition to transportation policies, jurisdictions are adding incentives or requirements for private developers to include bicycle parking in commercial and residential buildings. These end-of-trip facilities are essential for supporting more use of bicycles.

Designing Communities to Support Transit

Transit has enjoyed an elevated priority in the recent planning efforts of many communities. Transit provides choices for people who are unable to drive or who choose not to drive. Where transit is highly supported, buses have their own lanes, or share a lane with carpools. High-quality pedestrian facilities also foster transit use, since every transit rider is also a pedestrian at each end of the trip. Land use planners have become very supportive of transit, since it has been increasingly recognized that higher residential densities can make transit systems viable. "Transit-oriented development" (TOD) is becoming standard planning practice—building walkable, diverse communities centered around rail and bus connections.

New Directions in Transportation Planning

Transportation planning has become increasingly complex as it is seen less in isolation and more as part of a family of multiple, mutually dependent goals. Transportation planners explore new directions that reduce the sole emphasis on providing more vehicular capacity, and look at broader solutions to creating mobility options.

Reducing Vehicle Use

High traffic volumes challenge the capacity of road networks and the quality of the pedestrian environment. Policies that aim to reduce the number of vehicles in the system, especially during times of high demand, are becoming more commonplace. Tolling can provide an incentive to driving during nonpeak times, and can reduce unnecessary trips while at the same time providing a revenue source for facility construction or maintenance. High-occupancy vehicle policies, with priority lanes for two or more people in a vehicle, encourage ride sharing where there is congestion on the unrestricted lanes. Policies that aim to reduce the volume of cars on the road have led to a number of Transportation Demand Management (TDM) programs to educate, encourage, and create incentives for people to travel by means other than driving a car. Some of these TDM programs include ride sharing, subsidized bus or rail passes, and commute trip reduction strategies. Employers or institutions may be required to create and monitor Transportation Management Plans (TMPs) to reduce traffic impacts on adjacent neighborhoods.

The Benefits of Slowing Down

Efficiency is no longer the sole goal of transportation planning. Slower speed limits and traffic calming are seen as ways of balancing the needs of drivers and communities, even along some arterials. Slowing vehicle speeds and increasing driver awareness can significantly improve safety for cyclists and pedestrians, who are more vulnerable than drivers.

Rethinking Parking Requirements and Regulations

Parking policies influence the use of streets and private property, and people's transportation choices. Until recently, it was routine for jurisdictions to require parking minimums. Now, many jurisdictions are moving toward parking maximums instead, with restrictions on surface parking lots, park-and-ride facilities, and all-day street parking. Car-sharing and fuel-efficient vehicles may be given the most convenient spaces, and some jurisdictions are developing codes that guide the placement of electric vehicle charging stations on city streets.

Integrating the Needs of Freight and Service Vehicles

Creative thinking about how to accommodate deliveries, trash pickup, load zone locations, and freight routes can elevate the quality of the pedestrian realm. Temporary parking is one simple but effective solution. Time of day delivery restrictions and freight distribution centers, such as those adopted by New York City, are a more innovative approach which deals with the large trucks used to transport goods between urban centers by interstate highway. In this distribution model, upon arriving at the edges of dense urban centers, those large trucks dispatch their loads into smaller vehicles better suited to urban-scaled streets. These smaller vehicles deliver the goods to their local urban destinations.

The Link Between Community Design and Health

Community health advocates have discovered that transportation planning is a key influence on the safety, personal health, and ecological soundness of cities. The mutual benefits of health and wellness goals broadens the constituency and resources for implementing greener, more walkable streets.

Better Ways to Handle Rainwater

Public works departments are creating policies that move away from the tight-lined drainage systems toward solutions that more closely resemble natural systems. Natural drainage systems typically require more space in the right-of-way than the "out of sight, out of mind" approaches.

Encouraging Walking

It is not only designers and engineers that have discovered the importance of the streetscape to communities. Public health professionals have become enthusiastic about the benefits of environments that encourage activity, and have become proponents of what they term Active Community Environments, where walking, cycling, and access to recreation are seen as important components of well-being. Safe Routes to School programs focus on connections between neighborhoods and schools to promote children walking to and from school (Figure 5-5).

Figure 5-5 A sign of a walkable neighborhood is the comfort of children on the sidewalk.

Cleaner Air

Vehicle emissions are significant contributors to the greenhouse gases that have an impact on environmental and community health. In some areas of the country, where the energy system is based on hydropower rather than coal, vehicle emissions are the largest contributor. In the Seattle area, for example, where the state of Washington leads the nation in the use of hydropower, vehicle emissions constitute over 60 percent of the region's greenhouse gas production. Policies that set tight targets for vehicle miles traveled (VMT) and support congestion pricing and tolling are happening in many cities to address community health and climate change concerns.

Food, Exercise, and Health

The trend toward healthier living is taking to the streets. Residential streets and underutilized urban rights-of-way offer places for local food—street-side gardening, mobile food vending, and urban agriculture. Farmer's markets spring up in streets that are temporarily closed, often on a weekly basis during growing season. For younger people moving into urban areas, there is demand for trails and loops for walking and jogging. The Active Living movement champions healthier environments that promote physical activity and healthier, more active lifestyles. This kind of shift in lifestyle is seen as particularly important for children and populations with high rates of obesity, and is directly affected by the quality of the pedestrian environment.

CODES, GUIDELINES, AND STANDARDS

Policy is a vital piece of the puzzle, but it often takes specific instructions to make policy endorsements and recommendations a reality. Where this is the case, jurisdictions have either locally developed the necessary design and construction standards, or used state or national standards as the baseline for the specific details of street design.

The American Association of State Highway and Transportation Officials' (AASHTO) publication, *A Policy on Geometric Design of Highways and Streets,* is widely used and commonly referred to as the *AASHTO Green Book. The Green Book* offers recommendations for a range of acceptable criteria for street design. Although there is flexibility in the *Green Book* recommendations, there can be a tendency to have the most conservative criteria effectively become the only design criteria. Exceptions can be allowed at the discretion of state or local officials, who may grant "design exceptions" where specific needs exist, and documentation is provided demonstrating that the solution will not cause safety problems. In 2004, AASHTO developed the *Guide for Achieving Flexibility in Highway Design,* which includes Context-Sensitive Solutions. This document assists in the discussion between highway system programming and design and sometimes competing goals of community.

COMPLETE STREETS IN SEATTLE, WASHINGTON

The development of policies often raises issues to the level of public debate necessary for change to occur. The process of actually changing the policy may take a number of attempts, but each time the effort is mounted, a few more people pay attention, education on the issues happens either directly or through media interest, and lessons are learned about tactics needed to achieve success.

A good time to implement new tactics is when other shifts in policy are occurring. Seattle, Washington, adopted a Complete Streets policy in 2007 as part of a broader effort to define funding priorities for a new transportation levy. The levy, called "Bridging the Gap," used a combination of a nine-year property tax, an ongoing increase in the commercial parking tax, along with an employee head tax (which was later repealed) to help reduce the tremendous street maintenance backlog that had accrued over many decades of shrinking transportation budgets.

The advocates for walking and cycling in the City wanted to make sure that a portion of the money raised through this levy would be dedicated to both maintenance and improvements of walking and cycling infrastructure. This group advocated that a Complete Streets policy be added to the Council Resolution defining the levy, requesting that a specific portion of the funding—18

percent of the total levy amount of $540 million—be dedicated to pedestrian and bicycle infrastructure.

The robust public discussion that followed highlighted the need for roadway maintenance and new improvements to support Complete Streets. The outcome is a long-desired source of local funding that could be dedicated to improvements on local streets: sidewalk construction, on- and off-street bicycle network implementation, pot-hole repair, street resurfacing, spot improvements for freight, striping and signage—all of which needed to meet local standards for safety, design, and quality, but do not need to compete in the arena for state and federal funds that favor congestion mitigation and safety improvements on arterial roadways and highways. In fact, projects on local roadways aren't even eligible for most state and federal transportation funding programs. Local funding measures, such as levies, tax increases, and public/private programs (e.g., Local Improvement Districts and Tax Increment Financing) are typically the only way, other than through private development, that local street improvements get accomplished.

The passage of the Bridging the Gap funding levy was a huge success story for Seattle, but the pedestrian and cycling advocates did not stop there. They wanted Complete Streets to have the

force of local law in Seattle and be adopted by Ordinance, not just formally supported by the City Council. Their zeal raised the attention and suspicions of the freight community—itself an active lobbying group. The freight mobility advocates successfully added an exemption into the ordinance for streets designated as major truck streets. Specifically, the policy language states that if a street is designated a major truck street as defined in the Seattle Transportation Strategic Plan, the movement of freight and goods in that corridor is the priority. Complete Streets improvements may be made, provided they do not impact the ability of the corridor to move freight.

The Complete Streets ordinance, which passed in 2008, is an example of a policy that creates instrumental change in how the City of Seattle conducts its transportation business. All transportation projects that are of a reasonable size and scale (over $150,000) must conduct a Complete Streets evaluation, add elements into the project that support the policy, and identify elements that should be added at a future time if funding doesn't allow them to be added with the current project. Not only does this improve the project, for example, accomplishing a road rechannelization as part of a routine paving project, but it also identifies specific needs that may be eligible for grant funding or completed in future years.

Another widely used source is the Institute of Transportation Engineers (ITE). The *Transportation Engineering Handbook* and the *Transportation Planning Handbook* provide a basis for design criteria. Similar to AASHTO, ITE developed the "Context Sensitive Solutions in Designing Major Urban Thoroughfares for Walkable Communities" providing insight into application of roadway design guidelines in communities.

Both AASHTO and ITE are shifting toward the multimodal thinking of Complete Streets, and the broader thinking of Context-Sensitive Design, but the transition is still in progress. AASHTO has newer publications with standards for bicycles and trails, but these are still separate, rather than integrated design standards.

The guidelines and recommendations in the *Green Book* or the *ITE Handbook* only become standards when adopted as such by state or local governments. Local standards tend to allow for more flexibility as they do not have to meet the needs of a statewide or federal review which includes representatives from many jurisdictions where the elected official support and public appetite for density, walkability, bicycle priority, and vehicle access may vary widely.

There are many elements in the right-of-way, and these are controlled by many different jurisdictions and agencies. Often, there is imperfect coordination among agencies, and in some cases, codes and standards may even be in conflict.

Because of the number of elements—paving, curb, sidewalk, trees, lighting, building setbacks, frontages—the design of each element, and how they work together, need to be carefully considered. For each part of the design, and for the whole to be more than the sum of those parts, the details matter.

The development of forward-thinking local standards can make an enormous difference in the ability to design streetscapes that contribute to communities. In particular, it can be helpful to have standards for:

- Minimum sidewalk widths

- Wider sidewalks tied to special districts or certain types of land uses (e.g., downtown transit streets, or blocks with light rail stations)

- Mountable curbs for trucks

- Clearances (both vertical and horizontal)

- Curb radii dimensions

- Curb-to-curb widths

- Minimum and maximum lane widths

Stormwater management is another subject for municipal policies and codes. The policy used to be simply avoiding impacts to neighbors and flooding. However, city policies that encourage environmental sustainability are leading to changes in managing stormwater and encouraging or requiring "green stormwater infrastructure" solutions. Green stormwater infrastructure is the design of streets and sites to more closely resemble natural systems.

Green stormwater infrastructure policies can be considered on three levels: site, neighborhood, and the larger municipal level. At the site level, rainwater is, to the extent possible, returned to the ground through infiltration or allowed to evaporate. The more that water is absorbed and infiltrated, the less water in the sewers, and the better the water quality for rivers, lakes, and streams. Flooding is reduced. Water may also be captured in cisterns or rain barrels and reused. Green stormwater infrastructure site features include green roofs, permeable paving, cisterns, bioretention planters with underdrains, swales, subsurface infiltration, and retaining or planting large trees.

At the neighborhood level, green stormwater infrastructure can be effective because it can work to restore drainage basins or streams. At the municipal level, policy may encourage preservation of valuable natural areas, especially of critical wetland or forested habitat. Development may be targeted to already degraded sites, such as parking lots and buildings that cannot be restored.

Street Design Concept Plans

When development along a street happens incrementally over time, and each development contributes improvements to the street frontage adjacent to their property, the result can be a hodge-podge of design elements that relate directly to the adjacent building, but do not hold together as a unified street design. In many jurisdictions, the public agency can only require improvements that are directly adjacent to the property being developed. Other streets are accomplished through a mixture of public and private investments and still others are solely designed and implemented by a public agency.

Regardless of the funding and phasing of a project, it is more the norm than the exception that street design occurs incrementally, over time through the actions of many different entities.

One tool that can be used to establish a vision for a street that is detailed enough to give a true sense of the desired end product, but not so prescriptive that it eliminates flexibility regarding frontage design for adjacent properties is the design plan. Called by various names (street master plans, street design plans, street design concept plans), these conceptual plans for street designs are a useful tool for capturing the desired future state of the street or a network of streets and making them available to future project design teams.

Some street design concept plans are initiated by private developers who may own multiple properties along the street that will be developed in a series of phases—the concept plan provides an understanding between the community (who is another common group to initiate these plans), and the public agency about the nature of the street improvements.

Concept plans are most useful when they achieve about a 3 to 5 percent level of design detail—enough to create a meaningful set of engineering plans, but still leaving some room for adaptation based on the site conditions and development program moving forward.

Development of these plans can be funded through grants, local agency funding, community group or business improvement associate dues/fees, or designed as part of one development project and then approved for use by future development projects.

To be truly useful, design concept plans need to be formerly recognized by the permitting agency so that they withstand changes in staffing, elected officials, department directors, and community groups. Additionally, the final concept plans need to be easy to find and accessible to all the groups that may find them useful in the early stages of design development. Seattle includes street design concept plans that are adopted by a joint review and approval between the planning and development agency and the transportation agency in its *Right-of-Way Improvements Manual* available on the City's website.

Private Uses in Public Space

Decisions about private uses in public space are difficult. Streets belong to the public, but might be more interesting and better used if there are cafe tables, hanging flower baskets, or retail displays. Is it okay that adjacent merchants prosper by taking up public space? Can anyone sit at the table without first buying a cup of coffee? At what point does private use become too much? These issues are particularly applicable in times when city revenues are low and local governments struggle for capital and operating funds.

The best predictor of good decisions is to be clear about goals for public space. Strong public sector policies result in the kind of actions from the private sector that achieve public goals. For example, if a community wants to have water from roofs and hard surfaces treated with natural drainage systems, the codes would be written in such a way that private developers or owners would create new natural drainage or tie into preexisting natural drainage. One incentive for developers is the ability to use the space in the right-of-way for infiltration. The jurisdiction needs to decide if infiltration of water from privately owned spaces achieves a public good, or is simply an infringement on the ability to use the space for other public priorities.

One method of retaining control of private uses in public spaces is to allow uses or elements that are not permanent, and to require permits for the use of the street. The jurisdiction can control the location of objects placed in the street, so that a sufficiently wide walk zone is retained, or visibility maintained for safety. There may be fees associated with the permits that help offset the time spent by city staff to issue permits and conduct safety inspections.

Street food is an interesting case of private uses in the street. Cities take quite different attitudes about regulating food carts or trucks. Health departments may permit foods that do not spoil easily, like popcorn, but tightly regulate foods such as poultry that can spoil. Land use codes may restrict locations. Restaurant owners may be hostile to the idea of mobile food carts on the sidewalk, and some cities require vendors to obtain signatures of nearby businesses before the mobile business is allowed to open.

Again, there is a decision to be made about what is in the best interest of the public. Vendors can add "eyes on the street" and attract people out-of-doors. Street vending is an ideal way for entrepreneurs to start businesses that can turn into "brick and mortar" restaurants if successful. Some cities

Figure 5-6 The addition of a hot dog vendor brought people and activity to a street edge near a bus stop.

have developed strong street food culture that serves the local community well, and is even a source of civic pride. New York and Philadelphia encourage competition between street chefs by offering annual awards—the Vendy Cup—to the best food carts (Figure 5-6).

The use of public space by nonprofit groups is generally less contentious. But there are still issues, such as liability or crowd control, that need to be addressed. Nonprofits can be important mechanisms that allow community groups to care for public space. "Friends of the park" organizations have long helped to advocate for and maintain public parks. There are similar organizations beginning to take on streets. The story of one, Friends of Gilman Gardens, is described in Chapter 6.

Business Improvement Districts (BIDs) are another type of private group that may take on improvements and maintenance in the right-of-way. BIDs are enabled by local laws, and collect money from property owners. They may initiate capital improvement projects, such as a streetscape project. BIDs may support maintenance or security personnel, and often take on marketing efforts for the district.

REALITY FACTORS

Culture and Behavior

The cultural influences of the people who use public space should affect the design of the space. Understanding the cultural context of a place can give a designer cues about how to integrate cultural practices, such as strolling in the evenings, design features such as a mercado or town square, and age-appropriate activities, such as space for tai chi classes for seniors or a central play area for kids.

The streets were places to people-watch and to be seen before changes in technology meant that friends could be found a phone call away. Cultures where the use of public space is widespread are vastly different than those where public space is seen as suspect. When public space is held in low regard, fewer people inhabit public space and stigmas are placed on public transit. The life of the public space can begin a downward spiral.

Cultures around the world have created streets that are well adapted to their particular circumstances. The *woonerf* or "street for living" is a Dutch cultural concept that respects the various uses and needs of people who live adjacent to residential streets. The design of a *woonerf* reflects this—signage and bollards warn that vehicles are only welcome if they are prepared to travel at speeds compatible with walking (3 to 4 mph). Paving materials typically create rich patterns in the ground plane that are not commonly found on paved surfaces used primarily for driving.

Woonerfs are designed so that through-movement is not linear or direct—trees and benches may be placed in what would normally be considered the direct path of travel, forcing vehicles to move around them, and in doing so, building a traffic-calming effect into the design. Children are comfortable playing in the street, since *woonerfs* are relatively common in Dutch culture and drivers understand the concept.

In the United States, the concept of the *woonerf* has taken root, with a number of examples cropping up throughout the country, but most American drivers are not accustomed to sharing space. Safety issues are commonly raised by jurisdictions hesitant to permit such sharing of space in the street. But the mixing of cars and pedestrians is actually very common in the quintessential American space—the large suburban parking lot. People move to and from their parking spots, walking quite comfortably through the slow-moving traffic in the parking lot. Culturally, drivers and pedestrians are so used to the situation that they don't even notice that the mixing is taking place.

In Latin culture, the concept of the *paseo* is strongly rooted. People use streets and squares as public space every day, and the cultural practice of strolling in the evenings is commonplace. Street design reflects this with streets along the waterfront or main squares coming alive in the evenings with people of all ages. Festivals and instant happenings are also frequent events.

The largest influence on travel patterns in America is land use. The relationship between buildings and the public realm, as well as the distance between destinations, influences how we travel and our daily lifestyle choices. People who choose to live in denser urban neighborhoods are able to walk to most errands, with plentiful bike and transit options available to extend their trip. Rural residents often travel long distances as a regular part of their daily routine—driving is the only option for most rural residents because destinations are spread out, parcels are large, and the nearest town may be 30 minutes or more by car.

Bicycling Culture

Cycling is very much rooted in the common culture of some places. Where cycling is widespread, the public expects high-quality, abundant bicycle facilities. In Amsterdam, cyclists can bypass traffic signals and use shortcuts through neighborhoods. Bicycle parking facilities are easy to find. The high percentages of cyclists may stem both from convenience and safety for bicycles, as well as disincentives for

Figure 5-7 People bring cultural attitudes about driving, walking, and cycling. *Photographer: Rick Browning*

driving and parking cars. In Amsterdam, vehicle parking in the center city is very restricted. Amsterdam residents appear to be using their bicycles more often than cars.[1] (See Figure 5-7.)

Bicycling culture in the United States is uniquely American. While up to 40 percent of Dutch people regularly bike to work, less than 2 percent of trips in North America are by bicycle. Americans also use bicycles more for a recreation than as a way to get to and from work or school. Commuter bicyclists favor sleek gear and a fast, direct trip while the recreational cyclist prefers a quiet street and a pleasant ride along the way. Outside of America, bicycle ridership spans the very young to the very old, while it is more typical for the American rider to be between the teen years and middle age.

---

[1] Fiets Beraad study, 2005–2007. www.worldchanging.com/archives/009450.html.

Other perspectives on bicycling range from the positive—just build the bicycle network and people will use it—to the negative—bikes are bad for business, and bikes and trucks can't share the right-of-way safely. Another cultural issue regarding bikes, especially for recent immigrants, is the challenge of overcoming the perspective that a bicycle is the form of transportation you use when you can't afford a car. Bikes, therefore, are not really part of the American Dream until you are wealthy enough to be able to choose how you travel instead of making the decision purely from a financial standpoint.

Cultures are not static. If bicycle infrastructure were better in the United States, would we begin to see increased ridership? Certainly, some currently reluctant riders would be more inclined to cycle if the trip were perceived to be less stressful. If street attire were more commonplace, and bikes were equipped with baskets, more people might find a quick bike ride a convenient way to run an errand.

The addition of new bicycle infrastructure in New York City has vastly increased the number of cyclists—the Commuter Cycling Indicator showed that regular cycling doubled between 2006 and 2010.[2] The density of New York makes traveling by car difficult and expensive, creating an opportunity to increase options for cycling that are both convenient and time-competitive.

Figure 5-8 Children can walk and bike in healthy neighborhoods. *Courtesy of SvR Design*

Health and Equity

"Where you live can make you fat." Former competitive walker and transportation consultant Mark Fenton has a straightforward assessment of the relationship between the design of communities and our health. "Wide streets with speeding traffic don't encourage you to let your child walk to school, while safe sidewalks and clearly marked crosswalks might."[3] (See Figure 5-8.)

Health and equity are becoming part of the equation for determining where projects get built and how funding gets allocated. Health data is readily available—the public health profession does an extremely thorough job of collecting data and measuring outcomes.

[2] New York City DOT, Bicycle Statistics and Reports, downloaded from www.nyc.gov/html/dot/html/bicyclists/bikestats.shtml.

[3] "Design Can Improve Health, Environment and Local Economy", Mark Fenton in Community, Municipal Advocate, Vol. 25, No 4.

Obesity in adults and kids is another factor that has strong ties to transportation. "As a species we didn't have to think about exercise until the past few decades," Fenton declares. "People know they are supposed to eat better and exercise more, but they don't do it. The message isn't sticking."[4] Creating built-in transportation options that encourage walking and bicycling means that people of all ages can easily incorporate exercise into their daily activities. Creating neighborhoods and transportation options that encourage walking have a myriad of benefits. Health advocates bring a new and powerful support group to transportation and planning policies.

The recognition of the link between health and the form of our communities has broadened advocacy for pedestrian and bicycle facilities, and for more compact and transit-friendly neighborhoods. Healthy people, healthy communities, strong local economies, environmental health and stewardship, and saving money (on gas, parking, and insurance)—are all viable messages.

Healthy lifestyles and quality communities are not as available to some groups as others. The quality of streets varies widely across neighborhoods, and the least affluent neighborhoods generally have the fewest amenities. Even so, many low-income neighborhoods use streets heavily because living conditions are dense and travel options are limited.

Equity is also tied to public process. If you use the same methods to get public input on projects, you may very well be inviting the same people with the same issues to the table time and time again. Many community members tend to be left out of policy discussions. They may be too busy, lack language skills, need child or elder care, or have not been engaged in decisions that affect their communities. Without the full range of voices, outcomes do not truly reflect the full spectrum of community ideas, wants, and needs.

Policymakers need to sort through the input from various constituencies to make sure that decisions are meeting the goals of all parties in appropriate and equitable ways. There are always some loud voices in the mix, and they should not be neglected. But the best decision-making processes seek out and balance various viewpoints for a fuller understanding of the community's needs and desires. Social media and other web-based methods of communication can offer alternatives to attending meetings, but these also can skew input toward those who are most technically savvy.

Health organizations are finding common cause with planners and designers. Routine physical activity is built into pedestrian-oriented neighborhoods. The American Health Association, American Diabetes Association, and others are creating programs and partnerships that encourage walkable communities. Hospitals, medical centers, and nonprofit organizations are also interested in healthier employees and neighborhoods. The connection of walkability and health holds promise for broad coalitions interested in healthy communities with pedestrian- and bicycle-friendly streets.

---

[4] "Waterbury Looks to Walking Expert, Mark Fenton, for Inspiration to Exercise," *The Waterbury Observer,* May 19, 2011.

Economy

Neighborhood Business Districts

People-oriented—rather than car-oriented—business districts help support local economies. The National Trust for Historic Preservation recognized the unique challenges facing small local business districts in the 1980s and 1990s, just when the suburban economic engines—shopping malls followed by the big-box retailers—captured significant portions of the local retail economy. Many of these small business districts boasted excellent examples of period architecture that were facing tremendous development pressure. The National Trust Main Street Center was founded as part of the National Trust for Historic Preservation specifically to provide funding, strategic advice, and local staffing support for local business districts along America's main streets (Figure 5-9).

Figure 5-9 Main Streets are important to walkable neighborhoods.

The concept of trip chaining—accomplishing multiple objectives by linking transportation trips together into one longer trip as opposed to a number of round trips—can reduce fuel consumption, vehicle emissions, and time spent in the car. If trip chaining can be accomplished by driving to a destination, accomplishing all of your trips on foot and then driving home, even more vehicle emissions are eliminated. If you are able to walk from your home and accomplish all of your trips by foot or with a combination of walking, bicycling and transit, then the need for a car to run most errands loses its importance. Malls can accomplish trip chaining, but at the expense of an enormous investment in land, transportation, and utility infrastructure. And this investment, while it adds to the local tax base, often comes at the great expense of damaging the existing walkable business district nearby.

A good rule of thumb is to have enough of a mix of destinations within a local business district that people can accomplish many activities in one trip. Attracting and retaining thriving local businesses does not happen by chance. Community development associations play a very significant role, as do local Chambers of Commerce and Business Improvement Associations. Owning and operating a small business is challenging, uncertain, and highly influenced by even modest changes to the local economy. Local business owners may tell you that the removal of a single parking space will contribute to putting them out of business.

Much research, analysis, and evaluation has been conducted on the mix of elements that help local business districts thrive. One of the common lessons learned is that local business districts need an intense mix of uses, a diversity of types of businesses, and well-designed public space to tie it all together. A pleasant walking environment and well-managed parking that is subservient to the primary uses are helpful to retail success. Easy access to frequent and reliable transit service is a plus. Providing plentiful, pleasant, and varied places to sit, where patrons can enjoy watching people and activities, brings people to business districts and invites them to stay.

Removal of all vehicle traffic may not be desirable. A small amount of general traffic and a little bit of on-street parking feed into the mix of activities that make a healthy business district feel bustling. Keeping a balance is challenging but important. Access has to be convenient without letting vehicle traffic dominate or overwhelm the activity on the sidewalk. Public plazas and private businesses like restaurants and cafes can have a tremendous positive impact on supporting healthy street life, but are best when buffered from the street. No one really likes to enjoy a sandwich while having to shout over noisy traffic.

There is no one formula for success. The most interesting business districts have a character and retail mix with unique aspects. Locally owned stores with locally made products are seen as increasingly attractive, while chain stores make many retail districts indistinguishable from one another. A human scale, with plenty of detail (sometimes called "granularity") makes interesting retail districts.

Well-designed streets and streetscapes offer important details, interest, and character that can make a significant contribution to neighborhoods and their commercial districts.

Attracting and Retaining Employees

High-quality street and public space improvements signal to potential employees that there are choices about how to get to work. Attracting the types of anchor tenants, such as a successful company's headquarters, is achieved through a combination of factors including tax incentives, cost of land, access to a range of housing types, and transportation access. In high-tech and professional service jobs, the quality of the commute, commute choices, and the destinations that are located within walking distance to work help attract and retain high-quality employees.

Moving Freight and People in Manufacturing and Industrial Areas

Freight movement is important for a variety of reasons, including making sure that goods get to market. There is no value in walking to a vibrant local business district if there are no goods on the shelves when you arrive. But conflicts can arise in discussions about the compatibility of walkability, bicycle facilities, and freight mobility.

In addition to moving freight around, manufacturing and industrial centers create living wage jobs, and ones that people need to get to each day. Transportation planners have been successful in reducing single-occupant vehicles for commute trips, especially with large employers who are required to meet the conditions of a Transportation Management Plan, or TMP. But the challenge of getting workers to and from manufacturing and industrial jobs in locations that have limited transit service and difficult walking and bicycling environments is much more challenging.

Using GIS analysis to identify major bus stops and the front doors of large footprint warehouses can be helpful in determining the best routes to support pedestrian or bicycle travel. Signalized crossings of high-volume, high-speed arterials are very important on these routes, as is good lighting and high-quality sidewalks. Pedestrian infrastructure does not need to be at the same level in a manufacturing and industrial area as it does in a neighborhood business district or dense residential area, but it should safely and efficiently get people from the bus stop to their job and back again. Even workers who would prefer to take transit find that it may be safer, more pleasant, and more reliable to drive if the last few blocks of their commute trip are unpleasant and uncomfortable. Incentives such as free or subsidized transit passes, charging for parking, or providing excellent end-of-trip facilities for bicyclists such as covered, secure bicycle parking, and showers and lockers can help employees with transportation options.

As described earlier in this chapter, decentralized distribution models reduce the need for very large trucks to regularly access dense, urban destinations. However, many cities do not have distribution centers and therefore have less ability to restrict local access by large trucks.

Without these distribution centers, in most cities the same trucks that do the long haul on the freeway from the container port pull up to the retailer or wholesaler—their final destination—and impose their footprint on urban streets. Even when streets are designed thoughtfully, accommodating the largest vehicles within dense urban environments and town centers affects walkability and the balance among functions in the street. Narrow lanes and tight corner radii are challenging to navigate for large trucks. Adding more lanes and wider radii has the dual effect of widening the crossing distance for pedestrians, therefore increasing their risk exposure, and making corner turns at higher speeds easier for all vehicles, again making walking less safe (Figure 5-10).

Figure 5-10 This nonarterial street is used by trucks, cars, bikes, and pedestrians.

Maintenance

Maintenance of the elements in the public rights-of-way is typically a shared responsibility among public agencies and private property owners. Where public agencies are responsible for maintenance, creative street design may be discouraged in order to keep maintenance easy. Projects that have non-standard materials and design features may be cause for concern by public agencies who see themselves as easy targets for lawsuits.

Overcoming Maintenance and Liability Concerns

The liability concerns are so far at the front of the minds of many public sector engineers that the agencies can dismiss a project, entirely or in part, because of special features. Maintenance costs and safety problems ultimately come back to the public agency to address--either through a claims settlement or the need for a costly replacement of a damaged element that is not stocked in the maintenance yard. These concerns are not unfounded. Uneven pavement, gaps created by drainage features, and slippery surfaces are high on the list of claims a city pays out each year, and therefore high on the list of potential legal hazards that a public sector engineer will look for before approving a design plan.

Managing the public rights-of-way is an inherently risky business. The American propensity to legal action is well known and feared by city staff who find themselves on a witness stand. Because thousands of people use the right-of-way every day, the likelihood of problems due to accidental mishaps or mischievous activity is a real concern.

Some jurisdictions have found success with programs that encourage adjacent property owners or business improvement districts to take on maintenance and upkeep of planted areas, street furniture signage, and other elements. Pride in place is an invaluable part of a vibrant public realm, and allows for a higher quality streetscape than most jurisdictions can support.

Materials That Last

Choosing materials that will last is an important premise of sustainability. Materials that won't have to be replaced frequently or require frequent, costly maintenance fare better in a life-cycle cost analysis than those that are initially more environmentally friendly to install, but require heavy maintenance, frequent re-application, or total replacement. This is one reason why the traditional concrete sidewalk is favored—it is straightforward to build, lasts for a long time, and does not typically require regular material maintenance. Recent modifications to the concrete mix, such as the addition of fly ash and other materials, reduce the environmental impacts of the production of concrete without significant impacts to its strength or longevity (Figure 5-11).

Figure 5-11 Good materials, such as this stone in the Sicilian town of Catania, can last for centuries.

Approval Processes

When working for or with a public agency, it is important to understand all the steps in the approval process for a project. What codes and regulations apply? Who signs off on the final design plans? What are the steps necessary to complete before final sign-off can occur?

Each piece of right-of-way has multiple layers of regulation attached to it: zoning, land use and drainage code requirements, design and construction standards, and possibly landmark designations. A variety of regulatory and advisory boards or commissions may be involved. The regulatory context and rules impact the design and schedule as projects move from concept to design to implementation.

In most cases, a project will go through a series of design reviews prior to final approval. Sometimes these reviews are standard regulatory requirements. For more complicated projects, reviews may be requested by a commission or committee, while some are merely informative for community groups or other interested parties. There is a difference between advisory bodies that have a regulatory role and those that don't. As with all good negotiations, good project proponents know the bottom line of what is necessary to make the project serve its goals and what is dispensable.

There is an art to working with review committees to make successful projects. Good design ideas start with understanding the context and the opportunities of the specific site circumstances. Good design has a clear and appropriate concept, which is then implemented with attention to detail. Listening and responding to comments, concerns, and suggestions smoothes design review processes.

Engage the Public

There is great value in working together with communities on public projects. People know their neighborhood better than anyone else, and often have useful knowledge and insights. Projects that are embraced by the community will be better used and better maintained than projects that are imposed (Figure 5-12).

Transportation agencies have become more adept at soliciting and incorporating public input. Complete Streets approaches emphasize the need for citizen involvement. If communities don't want projects, agencies may reconsider moving forward. There are particular challenges for communities along regional transportation corridors, where the needs of local and through-traffic must somehow be balanced.

Websites have made communication easier for many people who cannot or prefer not to attend public meetings. There are new ways to engage the public in addition to the important face-to-face open houses, meetings, and events that help people shape the transportation systems in their communities.

Figure 5-12 Working with the community is essential in creating support and appropriate designs. *Courtesy of SvR Design*

Leadership

Accomplishing projects in the public realm is not easy. All successful projects have leaders that have persevered through the challenges of moving an idea into reality.

Leadership—in communities, in public agencies, among elected officials, in design firms, and within the private development community—makes the difference between generating an idea and getting it built. Each of the case studies described in this book have resulted from the leadership of a group of individuals. The people who make projects happen are willing to take risks, put in extra hours, find funding, generate community support, and find ways to solve every problem that arises.

Conversely, never underestimate what can be undone by a distressed citizen, concerned elected official, or disinterested staff. Technical skill, background data, and a strong policy foundation are all vital, but simple enthusiasm is also a key ingredient in moving almost any project forward. This is especially true of projects that attempt to do something new. People at every level of the decision tree have a part to play. Decision makers need to set the stage for the actions that will follow. Looking ahead and thinking strategies through to the end are also crucial functions of project leaders.

Project managers and staff need to lay the ground work and set forth a compelling vision so that decision makers do not feel as if they are being pushed into a corner or being asked to take an undue risk if they approve the project. And if they are being asked to take a risk, what are the benefits? How does the project advance the stated goals and values of the city or the client? Perhaps the cost of the street improvement is higher than anticipated to construct, but the long-term, life-cycle costs are much lower over time, resulting in a good investment for the city and an opportunity for the decision maker to demonstrate strategic fiscal thinking.

Many hard-working staff, in both the public and private sectors, have taken a risk and not been backed up by their leaders. The gun-shy staff member can also hamstring a project. A deceptively simple point, perhaps, but backing a junior staffer on a project may be just what is needed to keep their creative juices flowing and move the next project to an even higher level of resolution.

It is wise to be honest about the good, the bad, and the ugly of a project, and to be grateful for advocacy from an engaged and thoughtful community group. Even if the process is slower, community groups should be challenged to come forward with good ideas and creative solutions. Bringing information to community groups early and often, asking for their opinions, and building a case for change can turn nay-sayers into advocates and create a better project for all involved.

If you have managed to complete a successful project in your community, make the key factors that led to your success known by others so they can try to apply some of the lessons learned in their own area. Certain cities and towns have a reputation for being out ahead of others. This can occur for

Figure 5-13 Collaboration across disciplines and learning from one another will move forward the design of public spaces, and help solve issues that are common to decision making in the public right-of-way.

a variety of reasons, but if an innovative project is ripe to move forward in your area, you can bet that eventually, the factors that led to change in your community will happen elsewhere. When that time is right, it is invaluable to have good examples from which to draw.

The adage that replicating a great idea is the sincerest form of flattery applies here. Help set the ball rolling for change elsewhere—it is one of the great benefits of being an early adopter. Early-adopting cities are often those places where the density has outpaced the ability to add open space. People put pressure on leaders to make change. Pilot projects can then test the waters. It is also true that early adopters can "hit the wall" at some point. Push-back—moving too many innovations forward too quickly—makes the pace of change uncomfortable and this cycle starts over again (Figure 5-13).

Don't dismiss the small victories. Building a new partnership across disciplines—like the strong relationship that has been forged over the past decade between public health professionals and transportation and land use professionals—is a dramatic example of a victory. Street design is typically an incremental process of change. And in an incremental world, the small victories are not to be minimized. Small victories can result in big changes. Getting a cross-disciplinary team of engineers, planners, landscape architects, and specification writers to agree on a new standard for porous concrete for one project is a small victory. Getting that standard approved for general use by public and private sector projects is an even bigger victory and one that can eventually lead to systemic change. We all have a great deal to learn from one another.

Chapter 6
TYPOLOGIES

TYPOLOGIES OVERVIEW

STREETS HAVE A WIDE RANGE OF FUNC-
TIONS AND CHARACTERS. They have typically been classified by their transportation
functions as arterials, collectors, and local
streets. Some cities have been moving to
street classifications that draw on both
transportation function and land use context. Denver, Colorado, for instance, classifies streets as residential streets, main
streets, mixed-use streets, commercial
streets, and industrial streets. They also
include a category of "landmark" street
(Figure 6-1).

For the purposes of this book, we
are looking at several kinds of streets as
typologies in order to better understand
the opportunities that they hold to create
stronger communities. This is not intended
to be a rigid classification system, but to
be helpful in terms of recognizing patterns
and possibilities.

Figure 6-1

The descriptions used here for the typologies are:

- Residential Streets

  Residential streets are part of the neighborhood. People feel ownership of these streets, and take their use and quality personally. With low volumes of traffic and slower speeds, residential streets have many opportunities for community activities, bicycle networks, increased landscaping, and natural drainage systems.

- Green Streets

  Green streets are designed to take advantage of space within the right-of-way for trees, landscaping, and natural drainage. They tend to be urban streets, intended to invite people to walk between destinations, and to provide open space opportunities within the city.

- Alleys

  Often underutilized, alleys can provide space for many different needs. They typically function as service and utility corridors, but they can serve a wider array of functions. They can provide opportunities for improving water quality and reducing flooding. Alleys can provide space for backyard meeting places, lively concentrated retail space or entertainment activities.

- Main Streets

  Traditional centers for community activities and identity, Main Streets are the economic engines of many towns and neighborhoods. Successful Main Streets make walkable, desirable communities. Street strategies can support them with well-balanced configurations of hardscape, greenery, and parking.

- Thoroughfares

  Thoroughfares are the workhorses of the roadway system. They move large volumes of traffic long distances. Successful examples of thoroughfares exist where high volume roadways support or even enhance neighborhoods. Multiway boulevards that incorporate lower speed frontage roads nearest to the sidewalk and include green medians separating the travel lanes are achieving success in many cities.

- Festival Streets

  Festival Streets are roadways that can easily be converted to other uses for short periods of time. Temporary uses—parades, marathons, street fairs, cycling days, farmers' markets—are well-accepted uses that do not require physical changes to the street. Some cities have increased activity in the street either on a one-time or recurring basis. Temporary "pilot" projects allow experimentation with low budgets and little risk.

- Shared Space Streets

  The shared-space, or *woonerf* concept (introduced in Chapter 5), is increasingly being incorporated into cities across the world. Mixing uses, under the right circumstances, creates safe and lively people-oriented spaces.

RESIDENTIAL STREETS

Streets in suburban and low-density neighborhoods make up a large percentage of land within urbanized areas. Many of these streets have low volumes of traffic and low vehicle speeds. Often oversized when originally built, there are many opportunities for reclaiming excess paved areas for a range of uses including natural drainage, gardens, bicycle routes, or community space.

Simple Improvements

The simplest greening projects can be done by residents who have median strips or tree pits in the publicly owned right-of-way adjacent to their homes. Individuals have transformed portions of right-of-way into gardens and small pea-patches, sometimes inspiring their neighbors to do the same (Figures 6-2 and 6-3).

Local jurisdictions have taken different approaches to these small interventions in the public right-of-way. Vancouver, British Columbia, at one time discouraged citizens from creating "boulevard gardens," for several reasons. Because utility corridors may be located anywhere in the right-of-way, digging was deemed to be potentially dangerous. These strips of space between the curb and the sidewalk are also used by pedestrians moving to and from their parked cars.

Despite the City's concerns, people kept inquiring about using the unpaved space in the right-of-way, or simply starting in on projects without permission. As a result, Vancouver's Planning Department began a demonstration project on boulevard gardening in 2001. A set of planning guidelines resulted from the demonstration project, addressing the City's concerns for access, visibility, and coordination with other elements in the right-of-way, such as fire hydrants. The City also included suggestions for drought-tolerant plantings and information on water-wise gardening (Figure 6-3).

The City of Minneapolis developed a program called Blooming Boulevards, instigated by a council member inspired by Vancouver's boulevard gardens. The program evolved into the nonprofit organization, Metro Blooms. Once focused on beautification, Metro Blooms has been moving toward educating citizens about stormwater management, offering classes and web-based resources. Even so, Minneapolis does not currently allow rain gardens in the boulevard strip. Only shallow swales are permitted in the center of boulevard gardens.

Figure 6-2 Grassy medians are excellent places for neighbors to turn into gardens.

Figure 6-3 Well-tended streetscape and landscape that provides a buffer from the road make pleasant and safe places to walk.

The Twin Cities Boulevard Gardening guide assists Minneapolis and St. Paul gardeners in understanding the pitfalls of working in the right-of-way. Planting gardens in front yards and the street can offer several advantages over traditional backyard spaces—more sun, more space, and the opportunity to share gardens with neighbors. However, boulevard gardeners must be careful to protect street trees and their roots, avoid digging near utility lines, retain street visibility for safety, and keep away from designs with berms that can cause runoff.

The initiatives of Vancouver and the Twin Cities offer good advice for property owners interested in gardening in the median: Call the local utility companies to make sure that you don't disturb underground utilities. Make sure that tall plantings do not create unsafe conditions for pedestrians or drivers, and find out if your jurisdiction has a height limit for plantings in the median. Consider soils and drainage so that the garden improves the local drainage conditions, and use plant materials that can hold up under the sometimes harsh conditions adjacent to the street.

Block or Neighborhood Scale

On a slightly larger scale, neighbors can work together to turn underutilized space in the right-of-way into green space, or to lobby for traffic-calming measures. Other neighborhoods have been temporarily closed off for block parties, games, or music events. These efforts can make a difference in local communities by improving drainage problems, beautifying neighborhoods, making safer places to walk, and strengthening social networks.

Residents of Portland, Oregon, have initiated grassroots changes in residential streets that have become national models. Using a temporary structure built by a local resident in the spring of 1996, people in Portland's Sellwood neighborhood began gathering for tea and conversation. Because the structure, the "T-Hows," was built without a permit, the local building department insisted that it be removed. But by that time, the T-Hows had become a cherished institution, and the Bureau of Buildings was faced with a sea of protest. The T-Hows remained.

For their next project, the neighbors asked for permission from the City of Portland to paint the asphalt in the center of their intersection. The Bureau of Transportation (PDOT) rejected the idea. In September of 1996, the neighborhood obtained a permit for a block party, closed off the streets around the intersection of SE 9th Avenue and Sherrett Street, and painted a colorful design in the intersection. "Share-It-Square" was born (Figure 6-4).

PDOT directed that the painting be removed, threatening to fine the neighborhood. But conversations began between the Sellwood residents, PDOT, and the City Council. The residents surveyed the effect of the installation on the behavior at the intersection, and found that the vast majority of people who responded to the survey reported increases in safety and neighborhood interaction, and decreases in traffic speeds and crime. In fact, the changes in the neighborhood were meeting the City's goals for livability without using any public funds.

Since that time, the T-Hows has been rebuilt with more permanent materials, and other structures added. The artwork in the intersection has been redesigned and repainted numerous times. A nonprofit organization, the City Repair Project, is an outgrowth of Share-It Square, and in 2001 painting and building structures in the right-of-way was legalized in Portland. A petition of support from each adjacent neighbor and support from 80 percent of the residents along the project street frontage is required to assure public support. Drawings need to be submitted to PDOT to show that traffic safety will be maintained. In addition to painted intersections, other neighborhoods have added kiosks, ponds with solar-powered pumps, benches, and a poetry garden. PDOT now has an official liaison to City Repair who assists with permitting and makes sure designs meet City standards.

The "intersection repair" projects have inspired other communities in Los Angeles and Oakland, California; Eugene, Oregon; Boulder, Colorado; Ocean City, New Jersey; Minneapolis and St. Paul, Minnesota; and Ottawa, Ontario. In Ocean City, New Jersey, the painted intersection is along the "sharrow" lane where cyclists are welcomed into the car lane. The Ocean City Police were pleased by the community efforts, and attended the intersection painting to express support for incorporating art into traffic calming. Several municipalities now have official permission forms for community intersection repair based on Portland's model, making it easier for neighborhoods to know the rules in advance and achieve city support for such projects (Figure 6-5).

Community Gardens

Community gardens are another way to repurpose medians for greener neighborhoods. The median strip in Seattle's Gilman Drive West was neglected and unattractive before Charlie Hoselton took the lead on organizing his neighborhood in the creation of Gilman Gardens. When he moved into the neighborhood, he missed having a garden. He couldn't help but notice the opportunity in the nearby right-of-way.

Hoselton organized interested neighbors and designed a 2,450-square-foot garden with 32 assigned plots of organic growing space. With vegetables, flowers, a picnic table, and a basket for sharing, it's clearly a place that is loved.

Figure 6-4 The Sellwood community's painted intersection. *Photographer: Miriam Sytsma*

Figure 6-5 A neighborhood resident painting the street in St. Paul, Minnesota, with Paint the Pavement. *Paint the Pavement, Photographer: Jun-Li Wang*

Figure 6-6 Gilman Street medians before the gardens.

Figure 6-7 Gilman Gardens transformed into a neighbor-hood garden and gathering place.

So how do you turn an unneeded piece of the street into a community garden? Hoselton's advice for other community organizers is to make sure you know how to get the permit first. The City required drawings indicating sight distances for drivers at the intersections and a planting plan for the new trees. And to make sure that they are not liable for anything that would go awry, they asked for insurance. So that meant organizing, nonprofit status, and a bank account.

The newly created Friends of Gilman Urban Gardens broke ground in March of 2010, with work parties of local volunteers. By summer, the gardens were in full bloom, with table and chairs for relaxing, and a basket to hold extra produce for the neighbors. In the spring of 2011, Gilman Gardens expanded into the adjacent median, with another 20 plots and native plant restoration.

The success of Gilman Gardens offers lessons for other neighborhoods. Its sunny location, adjacent to a road that has fairly low traffic volumes, is well suited to a neighborhood with multifamily housing nearby. A user agreement, signed by garden participants, clarifies expectations and rules.

Water has been the biggest issue. Gardeners must either cart water from their homes or from the nearby Interbay neighborhood pea-patch. But there is plenty of water in a spring just up the hill, eroding the neighbor's driveway. If the Gilman Gardeners can figure out how to get it to the garden, they'll have the water they need. But that's what their project is about—turning problems in their neighborhood into great assets (Figures 6-6 and 6-7).

San Francisco, California, has been proactive in transforming unused right-of-way into community gardens. Their Street Parks program is a partnership between their Department of Public Works (DPW) and the nonprofit San Francisco Parks Trust (SFPT). The goal of the Street Parks program is to transform unused public right-of-way into community-managed gardens.

The process requires a Steward interested in taking on the responsibility for planting and maintaining a space for at least three years. The Steward meets onsite with DPW and SFPT representatives to confirm the suitability of the space. The next step is a community meeting to which all residents and property owners who would be affected by the project are invited. The Steward or Street Parks group is responsible for raising funds, which often includes grants as well as donations of time and money. The City helps identify potential grants, offers information on where to find free materials, and allows Street Parks' members to borrow tools for work days. Water meters and bibs can be installed by the City's Public Utilities Commission, but the installation costs the project several thousand dollars. Once the water meter is in place, the City will pay for the water. Since the program began in 2004, 100 community gardens have been successfully created, and more are in progress.

A number of cities are partnering with nonprofit groups to actively encourage citizens, organizations, and businesses to "adopt" and care for spaces in the right-of-way. For example, the City of Indianapolis partners with the nonprofit Keep Indianapolis Beautiful (KIB) with an Adopt-a-Median program. While "unadopted" medians in Indianapolis are maintained by the City, a variety of organizations and individuals have taken on landscaping and caring for the strips of land in the center of streets. These are touted as advertising opportunities for businesses, indicators of civic pride, and an opportunity for citizens to help reduce City expenditures.

The City tries to keep the process simple. Applicants identify the median that they would like to adopt and contact KIB. The applicant submits a landscape and maintenance plan and signs an annual agreement to maintain the median and a signed agreement form.

As of 2010, about half of the City's 650 medians have been adopted. Keep Indiana Beautiful sponsored the "Drive for 500" to get 500 adopted medians ready before the 2010 Indianapolis 500 Race. Each June, a competition rewards the most beautiful median. But Keep Indianapolis Beautiful aims for more than simply increasing the number of attractive medians in Indianapolis. The program also helps to improve air and water quality and reduces erosion, runoff, and pollution. "Participating in the Adopt-A-Median program is a great way for people to become involved with your community and beautify the neighborhood in which you work and live," according to Mayor Greg Ballard.[1] Newark, New Jersey; Dallas, Texas; and Boulder, Colorado have created similar programs.

Incorporating Natural Systems

Residential streets are increasingly being seen as important opportunities for improving stormwater management. Cities across the country have started implementing "green streets" that not only improve the way that stormwater is handled, but may also improve water quality, replenish groundwater, create more attractive streets and neighborhoods, provide wildlife habitat, make better places to walk, and help bring communities together.

1. http://www.kibi.org/news/drive_for_500_the_race_to_adopt_500_medians

Portland, Oregon, has played a leadership role in the design and implementation of green residential streets. The success of its program comes from leadership within the City, a concerted effort to coordinate the multiple agencies (bureaus) within the City government that are affected by work in the right-of-way, and a multilevel strategy to maximize the incorporation of green approaches to street design. Portland's ground-breaking work identified and solved some of the barriers to new, sustainable models for street design, making it easier for other municipalities to move toward greener streets.

One of the award-winning designs for a residential street in Portland is the Siskiyou Street curb extension project. Part of the appeal of this project is that it is effective, simple to construct, attractive, and relatively inexpensive. Some 590 square feet of paving in the parking lanes on residential Siskiyou Street was replaced with shallow landscaped basins just above the storm drain inlets. Stormwater flows into the landscaped areas, where it slows down and soaks into the ground, while native wetland plants filter pollutants. During the most intense storm events, excess water continues into the storm drain inlets. The two curb extensions drain an area of more than 9,000 square feet.

Water flows along the curb, entering the curb extensions via an 18-inch curb cut. A series of small dams, called checkdams, hold the water for most rainfall. In heavier rains the water cascades into the next cell, until plants and soil absorb the water, or the system reaches capacity. The low-growing, evergreen plants are mostly native to the Pacific Northwest, low-maintenance, and selected for their ability to cleanse the water of pollutants. In the spring, iris and daffodil bring color to the neighborhood (Figure 6-8).

Figure 6-8 Siskiyou Street's curb extensions with spring flowers. ©*Environmental Services, City of Portland, Oregon*

Despite its simplicity, the project is very effective. According to testing done by the City of Portland, the planters have the capacity to manage the water for their Water Quality Design Storm criteria of 0.83 inches of rain in 24 hours, meaning that there is no overflow for a storm of that size. Results would vary for similar projects, depending on the type of soil and its ability to drain, the type of vegetation used, and sediment loads.

The City designed and constructed the project in 2003 for less than $20,000. The costs were kept low by leaving the existing curb intact, and avoiding modifications to the existing stormwater collection system. Decisions were made with the neighborhood, especially regarding the amount of parking that could be removed and maintenance issues.

In learning from the project results, the City found that there was some difficulty with bypassing, meaning that some of the water continues to flow down the curb instead of taking the 90-degree angle into the planters. Gutter depressions and beveled edges could help guide the water, and with this in mind gutter dams were used in a subsequent project at SW 12th Street. Another unexpected aspect of the project was that water from a larger drainage area than assumed was directed into the planters because the upstream inlets were often clogged. Because of the added load, silt needed to be removed from the planters more often than originally expected.

While this project fits well into its specific context, there are many sites on residential streets that could be treated similarly. Suitable sites would be low-traffic residential streets without conflicting underground utilities. Slopes should be enough to drain; at Siskiyou Street they are 2 percent. Soils, such as the well-drained Multnomah soils in the Portland project, need to be able to infiltrate well.

Designer Kevin Robert Perry won honor awards from the American Society of Landscape Architects (ASLA) for the Siskiyou Green Street project, and for other rain garden projects in Portland—the Mount Tabor Middle School Rain Gardens and the SW 12th Avenue Green Street project.

> Short, sweet, and simple, this is a great example of stormwater management in residential settings. It gains a lot of environmental mileage for very little and sets a prototype for designers, policy makers, and neighborhoods. It works on every level, even traffic calming, and it even looks great with the existing landscape.
>
> *—2007 Professional Awards Jury Comments on Siskiyou Green Street*

Who Makes Decisions in the Right-of-Way?

One of the benefits of citizen-led efforts to design and care for their local rights-of-way is the potential variety that can give character to particular places. But any private effort in public space raises the question of the decision-making process. Who gets to decide what happens on public property? An interesting case in Albuquerque, New Mexico, arose when movie prop master Ben Lowney took on a 12-foot by 100-foot median outside his converted warehouse live/work space. In a middle-of-the-night guerrilla planting session, Lowney put in xeriscape plantings that stayed for five years without any official notice. He later added steel pyramids made from materials left over from a movie project. But when the City's Municipal Development Department was scheduled to "beautify" ten medians in the vicinity, they gave Lowney 24 hours to remove his plantings and sculptures before the bulldozers arrived.

Albuquerque's Municipal Development Department planned to install a high-efficiency irrigation system for low-water plants and trees. The City meets with community members before beginning projects, offering alternate prototypes, including a xeriscaped version that does not use water. Michael Riordan, director of the Municipal Development Department, noted that neighborhoods typically have never preferred a xeriscaped option. Local City Councilor Isaac Benton favors adding trees that provide shading.[2]

Figure 6-9 Ben Lowney added xeriscape plantings and sculpture to the median. *Photographer: Benjamin Lowney*

The Municipal Development Department prefers that people leave the work in the medians to the professionals because of safety concerns and visibility rules for materials in the right-of way. The department estimates that the cost of the median improvements averages $500,000 per mile for installation alone. Lowney, who once was hired by the City of Albuquerque for a public art sculpture near the Los Altos Skate Park, disparages the uniformity of design in the street. "Why does everything have to look so generic?" he asks. The City dug up Lowney's plants and suggested that he apply to the adopt-a-median program.

Clearly, jurisdictions vary in their attitude toward citizens' efforts to green local streets. But the issues are similar, and the most progressive jurisdictions have found ways to solve those issues. They can serve as models for communities looking for support from less supportive local officials (Figure 6-9).

---

[2] Newscity News/Opinion, City Uproots DIY Median Project, by Marisa Demarco. June 24, 2010; accessed at http://alibi.com/news/32750/City-Uproots-DIY-Median-Project.html

GREEN STREETS

Many opportunities can move streets from gray—asphalt and concrete—to green. Some of these opportunities are small moves, instigated by property owners or required of developers. The most exciting opportunities for green streets develop them into complete green systems. Within a larger-scale plan, localized efforts using low-impact development strategies or green infrastructure can manage stormwater; keep rivers, bays, and lakes clean; and return green, living materials to the urban environment. As an interconnected network of public land, streets are able to play a unique role in inviting nature and natural systems back into the city.

Greening projects are instigated by a range of people and groups, from individuals to community organizations, businesses, and local governments. As green streets have become more common, there have been lessons learned regarding new approaches to drainage and increased landscaping in the street. The next steps are to move from pilot projects to new standards, and from individual projects to networks of green that support habitat, recharge soils, produce local food, and create walkable neighborhoods (Figure 6-10).

The Portland Model

The City of Portland, Oregon, is an innovator in creating green streets. Its climate and soils are both well-suited to strategies that infiltrate rainwater, and the local culture is highly supportive of efforts to improve environmental quality. One of Portland's greatest successes is the policy framework that underlies not only the green street program, but the broader understanding of the many factors that create healthy environments and healthy cities.

In 2005, Portland created a watershed management program that recognizes the breadth of issues that affect the health of the environment. "Each component of a watershed affects every other component, and the whole watershed system is connected through the hydrologic cycle," the Plan states. "Rather than focusing separately on single issues such as flooding, combined sewer overflows, or contaminated sediments, the Portland Watershed Management Plan considers all activities that affect watershed conditions including issues like transportation, redevelopment, and open space needs."[3] Accomplishing this holistic approach requires coordinated planning

Figure 6-10 © *The Pollinator Pathway, Photographer: Robin Ginac*

---
[3] Portland Watershed Management Plan, p. 17.

Figure 6-11 The meeting of land and water is visible throughout Portland, Oregon. *Photo courtesy of Travel Portland*

and action across bureaus and departments, and integrating work by businesses, nonprofits, and private citizens. Public outreach and engagement is understood to be a key component of achieving a healthier city (Figure 6-11).

In Portland, land and water are elemental, the very icons of the city. The rain, our region's rivers, and our land—the watersheds that gather, feed, and protect them—are our identity, the essence of who we are and where we've come from.

—Actions for Watershed Health, 2005 Portland Watershed Management Plan

---

Green Streets are one of a number of actions that work together toward goals for each watershed's particular needs. Green streets are taken seriously as an important part of the infrastructure required to manage stormwater runoff, to improve the health of the watershed, and to conserve the capacity of the sewer system.

Green Streets exemplify the objective of simultaneously meeting multiple objectives. Catherine Ciarlo, the Mayor of Portland's Transportation Policy Director, discusses the value of three curb extensions built in 2008 at the intersection of SE 12th and SE Clay Street on video for the Mayor's Office. She points to benefits for traffic, for pedestrians, and for water management. By expanding the curbs into the street, they shrink the intersection and clarify movement for vehicles. The curbs shorten the crossing distance for pedestrians. Water-loving plantings in the swale treat the stormwater onsite, rather than sending stormwater down the drain. "It makes things better for everyone who uses the intersection," she says.[4]

---

[4] http://bikeportland.org/2010/03/18/mayors-office-releases-new-video-on-green-streets-30952.

Who Instigates Green Streets?

Green Streets have been instigated by the City of Portland as demonstration projects. Because the right-of-way is controlled by the City, Green Streets are relatively easy to implement. These demonstration projects allowed the City to test and monitor the designs and incorporate lessons learned into future Best Management Practice for projects in both the public and private sectors. "Best Management Practice (BMP)" is a term commonly used in environmental management, and refers to the most effective means to achieving an objective, such as reducing pollutants in stormwater discharge.

Portland took a multidisciplinary approach to the design and review of the demonstration projects, which helped broaden the engagement in the program and create better outcomes. City staff took care to consult with the neighboring property owners for input on landscape materials and to make sure the intent and benefits of the project were understood. The demonstration projects provided an opportunity to show both the environmental benefits and the contribution that could be made to a more beautiful street. Portland has set a high bar not only for functional green streets, but beautiful designs. The much-photographed SW 12th Avenue Green Street Project, by Kevin Robert Perry, ASLA, won the ASLA 2006 General Design Award of Honor, which the jury found to be "the best executed example of this type of work we've ever seen."[5] Perry's Mount Tabor Middle School Rain Garden won the General Design Award of Honor the following year (Figure 6-12).

[5]www.asla.org/awards/2006/06winners/341.html.

Figure 6-12 SW 12th Avenue Green Street. ©*Environmental Services, City of Portland, Oregon*

Citizens may also request green facilities, and the City has received many requests because people want attractive and environmentally friendly neighborhoods. Funds to create green streets are limited, and the City prioritizes requests according to target areas where there are problems with sewer capacity or water quality.

The Durham and Dekum Green Street is an example of design solutions with multiple benefits. Portland Bureau of Environmental Services is working with the Bureau of Transportation and the Regional Arts and Culture Council to combine new curb-extension green street areas with a sheltered bike rack that incorporates art, a green roof, and conveyance of roof water from the adjacent building to the rain garden. Artist Buster Simpson's design, with the carcass of a car atop the green roof, provokes varied opinions on the future of urban car culture.

The "found space" in the right-of-way, like so many, is partly due to the irregular geometries of the street grid. The policy basis comes from not only the watershed management work, but also from the neighborhood's 2008 Woodlawn Triangle Master Plan, which recommended additional bicycle parking.

Who Pays?

The City of Portland pays for their Green Street projects. The Green Streets are seen as a cost-effective infrastructure investment—so much so that when various sewer projects came in under budget in 2010, the City invested $20 million into building additional planted curb extensions and roadside drainage swales.[6] The money invested in Green Streets prevents the need for expanding the sewer system, and is a long-term approach to improving water quality.

Portland's Tabor to the River Program is a major infrastructure project designed to control flooding in a 2.3 square mile area in southeast Portland. The cost estimate for repairing and replacing the sewer lines was $144 million in the original traditional design approach. The redesign of the project, incorporating Best Management Practices including green streets, tree planting, rain gardens, and green roofs had an estimated cost of $86 million, or some 40 percent less than the traditional design.[7]

Another City of Portland program, called GreenBucks, gives sewer customers the opportunity to contribute small donations per billing period to help public schools maintain green stormwater facilities on school property. Sewer bills include a GreenBucks box on their bills, and the donations are distributed at the end of the City's fiscal year to help schools maintain rain gardens, swales, pervious pavement, and ecoroofs. City administrative costs are supported by 5 percent of the funds received, while the remainder goes to the schools.

---

[6] Portland's Mayor's office www.ci.portland.or.us/mayor/index.cfm?c=49521&a=303099.
[7] Tabor to the River Factsheet 2009, www.portlandonline.com/bes/index.cfm?c=50500&.

Who Maintains?

Because the Green Streets are part of the municipal infrastructure, the City of Portland is responsible for maintenance in order to ensure that the system is fully functional. City landscape crews water the plants during the first two years in order to establish the plantings. Long-term maintenance includes removing sediment and clearing curb openings to ensure proper functioning of the system. The crews weed, trim plantings, and remove trash.

In an effort to engage residents and to leverage City maintenance funds, the Bureau of Environment Services has a Green Street Steward program. Citizens volunteer to adopt a Green Street and help keep it functional and attractive. The Green Street Steward Maintenance Guide explains the function of green infrastructure, and divides maintenance into a two-year establishment phase and a long-term maintenance phase. City crews or professional landscapers on contract to developers take on more tasks during the establishment phase.

Green Street Stewards assist with removing trash and debris and watering during dry spells. After the plants have matured, Stewards also remove weed species identified in the Maintenance Guide. The City offers training courses for the Green Street Stewards, and has safety guidelines to emphasize the importance of caution when working next to passing bicycles and cars. The City requires all Green Street Stewards to agree to a statement regarding safety issues, with a disclaimer so that the City of Portland is not held responsible for any damages or injury.

For capital projects the Contractor is responsible for maintenance during a two-year warranty period which provides a consistent level of effort for initial establishment. The City takes on the long-term maintenance.

Seattle's Green Grids

Seattle's public utilities department initiated a series of projects to test using natural drainage systems (NDS) in an urban residential neighborhood. These projects, ranging in size and context, provide valuable insights into how NDS can be incorporated into existing neighborhoods and in new development in order to reconstruct urban infrastructure.

SEA Street

Seattle built its earliest green stormwater infrastructure project, called SEA Street (Street Edge Alternatives), in early 2001. SEA Street combined the idea of retrofitting an existing street with a new model: a street that would succeed as a pedestrian-friendly neighborhood street while simultaneously implementing state-of-the-art low-impact development stormwater solutions. A location for the project was selected where natural drainage would bring the most value to an urban watershed with inadequate in-

Figure 6-13 SEA Street narrowed and shaped the drive lane.

frastructure for drainage: The 660-foot-long block of Seattle's 2nd Avenue NW, part of the Piper's Creek watershed. The single-family neighborhood had some history of flooded basements, and an incomplete network of sidewalks. The new right-of-way design replaced the ditch and culvert system, or informal drainage, typical of this creek watershed (Figure 6-13).

The new design for the 60-foot right-of-way narrowed the street to 14 feet of asphalt bordered by 2-foot-wide drivable concrete "flat curbs" on either side. This narrowing reduces the amount of impervious surface by 11 percent from standard design, but still allows two fire trucks to pass one another as required by the City's fire safety code. Parking for residents and visitors is provided in several asphalt-paved clusters of angled parking. A pedestrian path is located between the planted swale and the property line. The narrower drive lane, and its gentle curves, slows cars on the street.

Swales catch water from the roadway and adjacent properties, and were sized to handle a 2-year, 24-hour storm event. The swales are planted with a variety of trees and shrubs that are primarily native to the region, and are selected for their ability to tolerate water, to filter pollutants, and to create an attractive landscape. Residents are expected to maintain the plantings in the right-of-way in front of their homes, which includes weeding, mulching, and sometimes mowing.[8]

The project has been monitored by a group affiliated with the University of Washington's Center for Urban Water Resources Management. With two years of monitoring, their report found that during the dry season, the NDS has prevented all discharge flow, and during the wet season, 98 percent of discharge is prevented. Baseline studies had shown that monitoring of the previous condition, mostly done in the dry season, resulted in discharge.[9] (See Figure 6-14.)

Cascades and Green Grids

Seattle Public Utilities (SPU) took the lessons learned from the SEA Street project and applied them to a neighborhood-scale Green Grid program, also in the Pipers Creek watershed. For Seattle's 110th Cascade project, in 2003 and 2004, a series of pools was constructed along a steeper east-west street with a 21-acre catchment area. The previous system of ditches and culverts brought water too quickly into the creek during storm events, eroding the banks of the streams and degrading water quality. The new system creates a series of weir walls and swale cells that slow and infiltrate water. Sediments settle to the bottom of the catch basins at the ends of the swales. Because of the challenging topography, the swale cells have fairly steep walls. These were built with fabric-wrapped clay soil bricks that allow plants to grow on the side slopes.

Broadview Green Grid, completed in 2005, covers 15 city blocks and handles the stormwater from 32 acres. The north-south streets were done in a similar way to the SEA Street, with reduced roadway width and planted swales for stormwater conveyance and retention. The road section includes a 10-foot drive lane, an 8-foot parking lane, a 2-foot-wide flat concrete edge on one side, and a 5-foot concrete sidewalk on the other side. The sidewalk is raised 2 inches above the asphalt drive surface.

---

[8] Hydrologic Monitoring of the Seattle Ultra-Urban Stormwater Management Projects, Richard R. Horner, Heungkook Lim, Stephen J. Burges; Department of Civil and Environmental Engineering, University of Washington; Water Resources Series Technical Report No. 170, November, 2002.

[9] Horner, 2002.

Figure 6-14 The sidewalk is between landscaped zones on the SEA Street.

Figure 6-15 Weir at the Broadway Green Grid.

Figure 6-16 Rock wall at Broadway Green Grid.

A cascade system for 107th Street drew on the lessons learned on 110th Street. The design incorporated large swale cells, divided by weirs with flow control notches, and used engineered soils to increase absorption and infiltration. There were more weirs on the 107th Street cascade, and stone walls to provide stability (Figures 6-15 and 6-16).

The monitoring of the project found that stormwater discharge decreased significantly with the natural drainage system, and that the Green Grid is protecting Piper's Creek from elevated discharges during the largest storms and wettest conditions when risk to the channel and habitat are greatest.[10]

10. Broadview Green Grid Natural Drainage System Performance Monitoring, Prepared for Seattle Public Utilities, by Richard R. Horner and Jennifer Reiners, Department of Civil and Environmental Engineering, University of Washington, Revised May 2009.

Tough Lessons from the Ballard Roadside Rain Gardens

Following the successes of the experiments in the Piper's Creek watershed and other projects, including the High Point neighborhood discussed in Chapter 7, SPU embarked on a series of rain gardens in Seattle's Ballard neighborhood. Replacing planting strips with over 90 rain gardens in the right-of-way on 10 blocks in the neighborhood was intended to reduce stormwater runoff and combined sewer overflows into Salmon Bay. The pilot project was awarded money from the Federal Recovery Act, which was looking for "shovel ready" infrastructure projects. Neighborhood residents were supportive of the project and the need to reduce overflow into the sewer during heavy rainfall.

After the project was completed in the summer of 2010, residents were surprised to find that the new rain gardens did not look or seem to function like the ones they had seen in the photos of examples at the presentation. The rain gardens were deep and many were not draining. Unhappy residents organized and brought concerns to the City about the lack of function, safety, and aesthetics. Rain gardens are meant to infiltrate elements, draining water within 72 hours of a storm event. The neighbors argue that because these are not draining, they are not rain gardens, but are really bioretention ponds. What happened?

Seattle was formed by glaciers, and the soils left as the glaciers receded are tricky. The Vashon Till found in the Ballard neighborhood originated as poorly sorted pebbles, sand, silt, and boulders that was hardened by the weight of glacial ice. Locals call it "hardpan." Perhaps in a rush to apply for federal funding, the project was fast-tracked. Test pits were done during the dry season, without the winter monitoring critical to understand the site-specific patterns of water movement with saturated soil. It appears that some of the rain gardens have connected to unexpected shallow groundwater. The fast-track process also shortchanged the typical neighborhood outreach that can bring in the site-specific knowledge from residents.

Green solutions need to be part of the healthier future of cities, but site-specific design is critical. The earlier pilot projects have made it look easy—lush plantings, walkable streets, and healthier water. But green design is harder than it looks.

Curtis Hinman directs Washington State University's Low Impact Development Research Program. "They are tough soils," he told journalist Lisa Stiffler. "But we have (rain garden) systems that are working well on tough soils."[11] The lessons learned have included the danger of cutting corners and the importance of aesthetics to neighborhood residents. As green infrastructure has become more common, it is still extremely site-specific. The neighbors felt that the design was utilitarian, and the black and yellow signs to warn drivers of the curb extensions grated on the residents, especially given the lack of greenery resulting from the initial plantings. If the adjacent property owners are the caretakers, green infrastructure needs to add to the quality of the neighborhood.

---

[11] Seattle Post, Intelligencer, "Ballard's rain gardens: A green experiment gone wrong," Lisa Stiffler, Investigate West, April 22, 2011.

Edmonston, Maryland

Portland and Seattle are well-known for their embrace of natural drainage systems. But green infrastructure is being put in place by cities, towns, and neighborhoods of all types and sizes. Edmonston, Maryland, has some 1,400 residents. "We're a teeny tiny town," says Mayor Adam Ortiz, relaying Edmonston's story at the National Building Museum's Smart Growth lecture series.[12]

The town is bisected by the northeast branch of the Anacostia River, and is situated on low land with a history of flooding. The Anacostia is one of the most polluted in the country, and much of the problem comes from stormwater. In Edmonston, measures have been taken over the years to prevent the flooding. But decades of urbanization in the Anacostia watershed took their toll, and from 2003 to 2007 flooding ruined many of the town's homes.

It wasn't so much the river that caused Edmonston's problems, but the overtaxing of the town's retention pond, which couldn't handle the volume of runoff. The town spent $7 million to build the infrastructure to move overflow water from the retention system to the river. This enormous investment raised questions about how to best replace the aging infrastructure in the town. The responsible thing to do, the decision makers agreed, was not more of the same kind of solutions, but to make the most environmentally sound infrastructure possible.

Edmonston decided to transform their main street, Decatur Street, into a fully environmentally responsible street. A $25,000 grant from the Chesapeake Bay Trust got the town moving forward with the Low Impact Development (LID) Center Inc., to redesign Decatur Street.

The narrowness of Decatur Street's right-of-way, 50-feet, presented the challenge of fitting in everything the town wanted to include. Narrowing the asphalt surface of Decatur Street accomplished several goals at once—calming traffic speeds, reducing impervious surface, and shortening the distance for pedestrians crossing the street. Planting strips approximately eight feet wide were located on one side of the street, alternating sides on each block for LID elements and trees. The bioretention cells are designed so that when they are filled to capacity, the stormwater will bypass the bioretention and flow to the storm sewer inlet via the gutter. Large, native species of street trees will be planted where there is no bioretention. The design details are all "open source" documents that can be accessed from the town's website, and Mayor Ortiz challenges other communities to make use of them. "Steal our ideas," he says, "and improve on them."[13] (See Figures 6-17 and 6-18.)

Decatur Street now has bike lanes made of permeable pavement and six-foot-wide, ADA-compliant sidewalks. The new configuration of the street slows traffic, and captures 90 percent of the stormwater onsite. Large, native tree canopies will provide shade and habitat. The streetlights run on efficient LED ballasts, and the town council voted to purchase green power from Clean Currents, which uses 100 percent wind energy, to power the streetlights.

---

[12]The EPA's Smart Growth Speaker Series, http://itunes.apple.com/us/podcast/national-building-museum-audio/id385989112.

Figure 6-17 Decatur Street before renovation. *Photo courtesy of Town of Edmonston, 5005 52nd Avenue, Edmonston, MD 20781*

Figure 6-18 Decatur Street with curb bulbs, natural drainage improvements, sidewalks, and bike lane. *Photo courtesy of Town of Edmonston, 5005 52nd Avenue, Edmonston, MD 20781*

Figure 6-19 New curb with cut to bring in stormwater.
Photographer: Bryon White, City of Laurel, MD

Funding came from the town's budget, with help from the Chesapeake Bay Trust, the EPA, and the Low Impact Development Center. The timing of the project was fortunate in that it was "shovel ready" when federal stimulus money was being released, and the project received $1.3 million for construction. This infusion of funding will allow more projects to be built with the money the town had set aside. Fifty or more new jobs were created, and now local people have green job skills.

Mayor Ortiz stresses that if his little town can build green streets, then anybody can. "We are moving from 'this is what we should do' to 'this is what we do,'" he says. "We all have to assume that leadership."[14] (See Figure 6-19.)

Pollinator Pathways

Green streets, designed with particular thoughtfulness and knowledge, can help wildlife thrive. Inspired by the colony collapse problems for honeybees, environmental designer Sarah Bergmann decided to do something to support habitat for native pollinators and the plant species that depend on them. It's not just the honeybee that keeps life going by transferring pollen. Butterflies, bumblebees, hummingbirds, flies, ants, moths, and orchard mason bees all contribute. But loss of habitat, pollution, and pesticides have taken their toll on all the pollinators. The typical grass median found in many streets is as sterile as a desert to most pollinators.

Bergmann came up with the idea of a "Pollinator Pathway," a link for garden-friendly creatures to move through an urban neighborhood. The mile-long pathway runs from the organic gardens on the Seattle University campus to Nora's Woods park. Connecting the two gardens means that they are more than just islands for wildlife. Biodiversity needs connections.

[14]The EPA's Smart Growth Speaker Series, http://itunes.apple.com/us/podcast/national-building-museum-audio/id385989112.

With a $6,000 grant from the City of Seattle, Bergmann and dozens of residents along Columbia Street dug up the grass in the median strips and planted pollinator-friendly native plantings. The planting began in 2008, and today 18 gardens are in place, tended by volunteer residents.

The plans and plant selections for the rest of the Pathway are ready to be put into action. Most, but not all of the plants are native. Plant types are placed in groups and swaths because the pollinators prefer it that way, and the design is meant to please them. The bees like blue, the butterflies like flat flowers, and the hummingbirds like tubular flowers.

The idea has begun to spread. The Wild Ones Niagara Falls and River Region chapter is working on their own Pollinator Pathway along 10th Street in the north end of Niagara Falls, New York. Urban Abundance, a community group in Vancouver, Washington, just received grant funding for developing pollinator pathways in its communities. The Pollinator Pathway website offers landscape plans and resources for others who would like to make their own pollinator-friendly gardens or pathways[15] (Figure 6-20).

[15] www.polinatorpathway.com/.

Figure 6-20 Pollinator Pathway installation with community volunteers. © *The Pollinator Pathway* , *Photographer: Jenny McIntosh*

Malmo, Sweden

Malmo is a city of over 600,000 people, and lies on the southern tip of Sweden. It was one of the first jurisdictions to make bold moves toward sustainable systems. Malmo began building ponds and wetlands to manage their stormwater in the late 1980s, and based on the lessons they have learned since that time, Malmo has created multifunctioning ecocorridors that function on a regional basis. Malmo is leading the way not only in testing the boldest approaches to stormwater management, but incorporating new philosophical approaches to the interaction of energy, waste, and water in an urbanized setting.

Historically the site of some of the world's largest shipyards, the ship-building industry began a serious decline in the early part of the 1990s. Malmo's mayor at the time, architect Ilmar Reepalu, recognized that the era of heavy industry in Malmo was coming to an end and a bold vision for the future of the area was a necessity. Planning for the future took on a formal process, and the "City of Tomorrow" project began in 1997.

At that time, Malmo had already acquired some experience in sustainable urban drainage. In the late 1980s, when the idea of sustainable practices were just beginning to emerge, Malmo Water company began looking for alternative ways of handling peak flows of water from new developments. New development was overloading the downstream systems during heavy rainfall, and solutions were expensive.

In 1988, a new development of nearly 150 acres was planned on the outskirts of the City. The existing system would not handle the needed capacity. Malmo Water and the department of Parks & City Environment jointly developed the idea of a wetland that could simultaneously solve the stormwater problem with an open pond, create a park for the community, and create a diverse habitat. The success of this project, the Toftanas Wetland Park, led to more projects that provided natural drainage solutions with multiple benefits.

Constructed in 1999, 11 years after the Toftanas Wetland Park, the Vanasgaten Swale is an example of onsite drainage alongside drive lanes. The combined sewer system in a southwest sector of the City was overloaded, and Malmo Water found that disconnecting surface runoff from the streets would help to solve the problem. Vanasgatan, a local residential street, was an excellent candidate for natural drainage because of an existing buffer strip on one side of the street. That buffer strip had been planted with willow trees, whose roots were invading the sewer pipes below, causing failures in the piped system and flooded basements.

The Water and Parks Department's solution created a swale in the existing 15-foot-wide buffer that would accept water from the street. The willows were replaced with plantings with less aggressive roots to protect the pipes. Because the swale needed to collect water from both sides of the street, a means of conveyance was necessary from the other side of the street. The Department of Street and Traffic was, at the same time, looking into ways to calm traffic on Vanasgatan. "Concave" speed bumps, depressed rather than raised, served both as conveyance devices and as traffic-calming elements.

Peter Stahre, who was the deputy managing director of Malmo Water & Wastewater Works, told the story of 18 sustainable design projects in his book, Blue-Green Fingerprints in the City of Malmo, Sweden, Malmo's Way Toward a Sustainable Urban Drainage. "The transition from a traditional urban drainage towards a more sustainable drainage concept is a long process," he wrote. "When you enter the path of sustainable urban drainage it will soon become obvious that the institutional barriers between the different stakeholders involved in the planning and implementation of the facilities often are unexpectedly high."[16] (See Figures 6-21 and 6-22.)

[16]Blue-Green Fingerprints in the City of Malmo, Sweden, Malmo's Way Toward a Sustainable Urban Drainage, p. 95.

Figure 6-21 Detail of drainage in Malmo's Western Harbor neighborhood..

Figure 6-22 Natural drainage systems at Ekostaden Augustenborg, outside of Malmo, Sweden.
Photographer: Mueller Images, J.C. Mueller

Figure 6-23 The "boulders" in the runnel in Augustenbourg, Sweden are a design feature suggested by a resident of this community to capture leaves and other objects that could block the runnel or various drains throughout this green infrastructure system.

The work of Stahre and his colleagues, and others who have taken the risks to implement new ideas, have helped open the way for others. The projects in Malmo, Edmonston, Portland, and Seattle are both testing new ideas and proving that they are—with refinement— feasible. It is now a much easier task to bring nay-sayers around with the body of work that has already been successfully accomplished.

Low-impact development (LID) and natural drainage systems are moving from the realm of experiments to that of established standard practice. The resources that follow are some of many efforts with lessons learned that inform the next generation of sustainable practices in and beyond the right-of-way (Figure 6-23).

ALLEYS

Alleys were intended for the unsightly things. In earlier eras, these included the stabling of horses, coal delivery, and trash and privies, leaving the grander frontage along the street free from undesirable sights and smells. "To skulk through an American alley is to step back into time, downward on the social ladder," wrote Grady Clay in his book, *Alleys: A Hidden Resource*, "and quickly to confront the world of trash collectors, garbage-pickers, weekend car mechanics and children. Refugees all of them, from the wide-open world of the big street and the Out Front."[17] (See Figure 6-24.)

[17] *Alleys: A Hidden Resource*, Grady Clay, Louisville, Grady Clay and Company, 1978.

Figure 6-24

Historically, poorer urban residents have turned to alleys for places to live. The burgeoning city populations in the later 1800s included freed slaves, immigrants, and transients, and back alleys provided cheap, often squalid, living accommodations.

The Library of Congress and The Washington Revels describe life in the alleys in their publication *The Alley Communities of the Nation's Capital.* "People built their dwellings with whatever scraps they could find: timber and cloth scavenged from local building sites or former army camps. There was no indoor plumbing, no electricity, and infant death rates were high because of the unsanitary conditions."[18]

Urban reformers and city planners targeted alleys as unhealthy and threatening to acceptable morality. By World War I, alleys were rarely found in new plats. Cars moved around to the front of houses. Omitting alleys from land plats meant more property to sell. The Urban Land Institute's 1960 *Community Builder's Handbook* proclaimed that "The disappearance of the alley is one of the advances which has been made in land planning during the motor age."[19]

Figure 6-25 The living spaces over the garage add people who can keep an eye on the alleys.

As suburbia matured, houses were almost taken over by garages and driveways, accommodating two, three, or more cars in the front of the house. Front yards tended more toward an unused showpiece, with rear yards as the living space.

But as trends swing back toward walkable, compact communities, alleys have made a comeback. They provide a place for garages and driveways that are away from the front of houses along the main street. The New Urbanist movement, in particular, has returned alleys to favor in new developments, recognizing the value of the more fine-grained grid to increase connectivity. The alleys might once again be a place where cars are sparse enough for neighborhood children to be able to play (Figure 6-25).

Another force leading toward rediscovery of the potential of existing alleys is the reinvigoration of urban living. Alleys are often underutilized space within denser districts where space for movement, commerce, and respite are at a premium. This has long been the case in dense urban areas, such as those of Asia, where people and commerce fill the narrow streets and alleys (Figure 6-26).

[18]The Alley Communities of the Nation's Capital, The Library of Congress and The Washington Revels.

[19] *The Community Builder's Handbook*, prepared by The Community Builder's Council of the Urban Land Institute, The Executive Edition, 1960, Urban Land Institute: Washington, D.C., p. 135.

Cities differ in terms of the number and types of alleys. Since alleys have gone in and out of vogue over time, the presence and type of alley within cities and towns depends on the philosophy toward them when neighborhoods were platted or developed. For instance, in Chicago, almost every block has alleys; the City has a total of nearly 2,000 miles of alleys and small service streets.[20]

Portland, Oregon, took a different approach to platting, with a grid of blocks that are 200 feet on each side. The small block size eliminated the need for alleys, because the shallower lot depth did not require alleys for light and access. Alley networks reflect the unique historical pattens of urban development, and each city has its own particular opportunities for reuse of alley networks.

How do alleys differ from streets? First, alleys are about connectivity rather than mobility. That means that though they serve important functions, there are few vehicles that use them, and those vehicles are traveling at relatively low speeds. Cars accessing parking garages, garbage trucks, and utility vehicles account for most of the traffic.

As spaces with low traffic volumes and speeds, alleys are perfect candidates for shared use with pedestrians. But the typical uses in alleys—garage entries, garbage storage, utility connections, and service doors—result in few pedestrians and few activities.

Alleys have different spatial qualities than streets. Their narrow width gives them a volumetric quality and a human scale that is often missing in multilane streets. Alleys often have a physical configuration that makes for an ideal "outdoor room." Some commercial alleys have furthered the feeling of a room by using lighting, vegetation, or other elements to create the perception of a ceiling in the outdoor space (Figure 6-27).

Figure 6-26 An alley in Tokyo is filled with activity and people. *Photographer: Daniel Toole, recipient of AIA Seattle Emerging Professional Travel Scholarship 2010*

Figure 6-27 The small streets and alleys of older cities feel like intimate, human-scale spaces.

---

[20]"Miles of Alleys, Chicago Finds Its Next Environmental Frontier," *New York Times*, Susan Saulny, November 26, 2007.

Figure 6-28   Even narrow streets can make room for simple greening, lighting, and signage.

When alleys are lined with active uses, they can become some of a city's most lively urban spaces. With cheaper rent than the street front, alleys can serve as incubators for small retailers, artists, or craftspeople. For example, the narrow, winding streets of older sections of Asian cities like Singapore, Hong Kong, and Tokyo count among the best urban spaces in the world.

The constricted space of alleys can concentrate energy and activities. People attract people, and a critical mass of people out walking and using urban spaces make the spaces themselves more interesting. Great alleys worldwide often feel like they are overflowing with merchandise, signage, and seating.

The narrow, winding streets of Europe's historic towns and cities have proportions, a level of detail, and a human scale that attract people from across the world. Built in a carless time when cities needed to be walkable, these narrow streets and alleys contain lessons for modern neighborhoods (Figure 6-28).

Revitalizing a Network of Alleys

Melbourne, Australia, made a concerted effort to revitalize their alleys, referred to as laneways. In a purposeful initiative to improve public spaces, the City of Melbourne brought in Gehl Architects from Denmark to study opportunities for public life. The laneways were seen as important opportunities to expand pedestrian connections and to create a 24-hour city.

One of the techniques used in Melbourne to encourage entertainment uses in the laneways was to reduce the cost of liquor licenses for establishments in the alleys. Buildings were encouraged to front onto the laneways.

The laneways offer a distinctly different experience than the main streets. The emphasis is on human scale and a walking speed. The laneways have more intimate proportions than the streets, and the shops and businesses tend to be small and unique. There is a sense of discovery and variety. Frequented by both locals and tourists, Melbourne's laneways have become part of the identity of the City and its public realm. Melbourne has become a model and an inspiration for other cities looking for ways to make more active, pedestrian-friendly downtowns (Figures 6-29 and 6-30).

Figure 6-29 Melbourne's revitalized laneways offer alternatives to pedestrians. *Photographer: Daniel Toole, recipient of AIA Seattle Emerging Professional Travel Scholarship 2010*

Figure 6-30 Each laneway has different character. *Photographer: Daniel Toole, recipient of AIA Seattle Emerging Professional Travel Scholarship 2010*

Figure 6-31 Taking the dumpsters away and adding presence of "ambassadors" help make alleys feel safe.

Cleaning Alleys

One of the common difficulties in reclaiming alleys is the presence of trash and garbage containers. Seattle found a way around this problem by changing the way garbage is handled. The Clear Alleys Program, started in 2009, bans dumpsters from the City's commercial core, replacing them with color-coded bags that separate waste into recycling, compost, and trash. Pickup is frequent—mostly three times a day.

A detailed study to monitor the results was done after the Clear Alleys Program had been in place for a year, with surveys and stakeholder interviews. Shifting from dumpsters in the alleys to a more frequent bag pickup was considered an improvement by most respondents, even with fee increases for many users. Because rates are designed to favor recycling, there was a modest decrease in the amount of waste generated and a modest increase in the amount of recycling. People felt that the alleys were cleaner, with better access, better sight lines, and less odor. The alleys felt safer. Negative responses included bags being ripped by birds or scavengers, and this problem has been resolved by using thicker bags. Businesses have been given flexibility so that food wastes can be stored in locked "totes" instead of the bags.[21]

At the time of the survey, only one alley had seriously begun to take advantage of the cleaner alleys to change how the space was being used (see the Nord Alley case study in Chapter 7). Since that time, other property owners have begun to pursue public uses in adjacent alleys. Other neighborhoods would like to be included in the program, which is certainly a measure of success. Today, clean alley advocates in Seattle's Pike Pine neighborhood and its Chinatown/International District, where some alleys already have retail uses, are pushing to bring Clear Alley Programs to their neighborhoods (Figure 6-31).

Naming Alleys

Some cities have found success giving names to alleys. Because most alleys are unnamed, there is no need to remove an existing designation, and

[21] Seattle's Clear Alleys Program (CAP): Evaluation, Findings, and Recommendations, Submitted to Seattle Public Utilities. Submitted by Lisa A. Skumatz, PhD and Juri Freeman, Skumatz Economic Research Associates, Boulder, Colorado, April 2010.

there isn't the same need for a logical wayfinding system that many cities employ through numerical or alphabetized street names. Naming alleys can help tell the stories of the city, and highlight intriguing history. There is more myth than truth to some of the most colorful alley names such as Blood Alley in Vancouver, British Columbia, or Pirate Alley in New Orleans, Louisiana.

Names also give a sense of legitimacy. In Columbia City, Missouri, the City Council has been interested in naming alleys not only to give them validity as places in themselves, but also because without names, businesses may not be established with their only entrance off of an alley. Storefronts are required to have street addresses, and nameless alleys do not qualify for addresses.

One thing leads to another. If alleys are named, some council members asked, shouldn't they be cleaned up? What about places to park? Should they have design standards? The particular names proposed for the alleys stirred controversy. One suggestion, Sharp Alley, caused concern because of its origin in the knife and razor fights in the alley's wilder days. The name chosen for Columbia City's first named alley was simply Alley A. Kampai Sushi Bar & Restaurant became the first business establishment to locate in the City's alleys, and the owners hope to attract the students from nearby Stephens College and the University of Missouri to the terrace that overlooks the alley.

Art in the Alleys

Naming alleys can be part of fostering an identity. Mangum, Oklahoma, renamed its West Court Street Artist's Alley in 2007 at the request of a group of local artists. Mangum, a town of about 3,000 people in western Oklahoma, made use of the National Trust for Historic Preservation's Main Street program to revitalize their downtown, and found that bringing together a core group of artists to create Artist's Alley has infused the town with the arts and has brought new businesses, tourism, and investment.

Artist's Alley is now fully occupied, and artists have begun opening studios in nearby spaces. Twenty-four new businesses have come to the town. According to the National Trust Main Street Center, "It just goes to show that one alley can transform an entire downtown."[22] (See Figure 6-32.)

Art also found its way into the alleys of urban Baltimore. Maryland Institute College of Art (MICA) professor Sarah Doherty saw opportunity in the largely vacant alleys of her neighborhood. She lays out the mission of the project: "Axis Alley seeks through creative engagement to utilize the backyards of vacant properties and vacant lots as a canvas for creative works that transform, activate, and revitalize the overlooked, under-attended areas of Baltimore's back alleys."[23]

The three blocks behind 22nd Street were largely vacant and forbidding. In 2009, Doherty and the Axis Alley team coordinated with the Baltimore Housing Authority, the Mayor's City Council, and the

Figure 6-32 Magnum, Oklahoma's Artists Alley helped bring new life into the town. *Photographer: Will Sanders*

---

[22] Main Street News, The Monthly Journal of the National Trust Main Street Center, No. 266, December 2009.
[23] Axis Alley website, http://axisalley.wordpress.com/.

Figure 6-33 This art piece by the artist Sarah Doherty, titled *Drowning*, graced a Baltimore alley through the Axis Alley project. *Artist: Sarah Doherty, Title: Drowning. Photo courtesy of the artist.*

Old Goucher Community Association to clean up the alleys and fill them with art. The task of cleaning up the alleys was so daunting that she hired homeless men to help out. Finally, 22 art pieces were installed, with efforts from neighbors, artists, students, architects, and dancers. The project resulted in many successes—neighbors met neighbors, art walks drew people to visit the alleys, and the project received grants and won awards.[24]

The Axis Alley project finished in the summer of 2010. The project, and the art, was intended to be ephemeral, but without the infusion of art and energy, the alleys began to collect trash again. Although the project had great benefits for the community, it did not solve the social and economic problems of the alleys. Individual projects, no matter how engaging they are when launched, need care and nurturing to actually accomplish long-term changes to social and economic problems (Figure 6-33).

Greening Alleys

Municipalities and citizen groups are using alleys as a resource for making greener cities. Chicago has been on the forefront of this movement, and an inspiration to cities across the country. Rich in alleys, Chicago saw their network of alleys as a resource for green infrastructure and a way to reduce existing problems with drainage. Because many of the City's alleys were built without connections to the stormwater system, flooding was a chronic problem. Chicago's Green Alley program, started in 2006, was an extension of an existing program for improving alleys, but placed a new focus on environmentally sound design and materials. Instead of building expensive new connections into the sewer system, the Green Alley program replaces hard surfaces with permeable pavement and open bottom catch basins to infiltrate stormwater where soils drain well. Natural detention areas, rain gardens, and swales are other techniques that are suggested for improving drainage and natural systems.

Other environmental improvements in the alleys include the use of light-colored pavements. Lighter-colored (high albedo) pavement reflects more light and absorbs less heat, reducing the "urban heat island" effect which makes cities several degrees warmer than less developed rural areas. New light fixtures are "dark-sky compliant," directing light toward the ground and reducing light pollution. Recycled material, such as concrete aggregate and rubber tires, is encouraged.

Because the City funds the alley improvements, green alleys have proliferated. Since the program began, over a hundred green alleys have been installed.[25] The price of the construction, according to the Chicago Department of Transportation (CDOT), is offset by what it

[24] Axis Alley website, http://axisalley.wordpress.com/.
[25] City of Chicago, www.cityofchicago.org/city/en/depts/cdot/provdrs/alley/svcs/green_alleys.html.

would have cost to connect the alleys to the sewer system. The money is better spent fixing the drainage problems with environmentally sound solutions. Those environmental benefits tie in to Chicago's agenda to be a greener city, and as an unexpected benefit, the program has created a local market for permeable concrete. Costs of the material have come down since the concrete plants began producing permeable material at the beginning of the program.

The award-winning illustrative booklet *The Chicago Green Alley Handbook*[26] made the purpose and the elements of the project clear and understandable to the public. Janet Attarian, of CDOT's green alley program, says that the program has transformed her department, and given them the confidence to broaden their ability to try sustainable solutions. Now CDOT is testing permeable materials in parking lanes and parking lots, and using a variety of recycled materials.

Community Greens

Nonprofit groups have also helped instigate alley greening programs. Community Greens is an initiative of Ashoka, an association of social entrepreneurs that promote sustainable, replicable solutions for social change. , Community Greens supports citizen efforts to "transform alleys from blighted spaces to community places, and give life to vacant lots in a manner that is sustainable and systems-changing."[27]

Community Greens founder Bill Drayton was inspired by what he calls the "secret gardens" of New York. As a prime example, he cites the MacDougal-Sullivan Gardens Historic District in Greenwich Village. A model of shared space on the interior of a full city block, MacDougal-Sullivan Gardens was renovated in 1921 with the intent of creating attractive housing for middle-class residents. The central private community garden is vital to the neighborhood's spirit of community, with a low-walled garden for each residence, adjacent to a common green where children play and community events take place.[28] Community Greens calls these spaces Backyard Commons—multifunctional spaces shared by urban residents that offer social, economic, and environmental benefits

The Backyard Commons model turns out to be very applicable to alley-served residential neighborhoods. Community Greens set out to apply this model in Baltimore, where hundreds of miles of alleys were often crime-ridden, rat-infested, and strewn with garbage. The issue of safety could not be ignored in the transformation of the urban alleys. In a downward cycle, neighboring properties fenced off their backyards and turned away from the alleys, which became increasingly neglected and abused spaces.

---

[26] *The Chicago Green Alley Handbook, An Action Guide to Create a Greener, Environmentally Sustainable Chicago*, Chicago Department of Transportation.

[27] www.communitygreens.org/history, Community Greens website, History and Mission.

[28] William Drayton, "Secret Gardens", Atlantic Monthly, June 2000, accessed at http://www.theatlantic.com/past/docs/issues/2000/06/drayton.htm.

In order to gate the alleys to create shared space for the adjoining residents, Community Greens, citizens, and City staff put together new legal mechanisms. In 2004, the Maryland General Assembly passed the enabling legislation that would allow the City to permit gating the alleys. The City of Baltimore followed up in 2007 with the Alley Gating and Greening Ordinance.

Under the new law, 80 percent of the people living adjacent to the alley need to approve of the plan to gate and green the alley; if the alley is closed to traffic, 100 percent of the neighborhood must agree to the plan. The high bar for approval is challenging, and it only takes one nay-sayer to reduce the scope of the project. Some residents are unwilling to give up the ability to park in the rear of their property, and some blocks were unable to come to an agreement.

Even with the full complement of signatures, City agencies must agree to the gating. The Fire Department, Utilities, and Police can veto the plan. Even with agency support of the program and its safety benefits, the access component of the alley needed to be solved. The departments agreed that with keys in "Knox boxes" outside the gates, access would be acceptable for the pilot alley-gating projects.

Community Greens worked with residents of Baltimore's Patterson Park neighborhood to test the potential of alley gating and greening. The "before" and "after" pictures show how neglected spaces have become active common space, like extended back yards where children can play and neighbors can meet. (See Figures 6-34, 6-35a, and 6-35b.)

Figure 6-34 This alley in Chicago has pavers to allow stormwater infiltration. *Photo courtesy of the City of Chicago*

Figure 6-35a and 6-35b Luzerne/Glover alley in Baltimore's Patterson Park neighborhood is shown before and after the Community Greens projects. *Photo credits to Kate Herrod/Ashoka*

Funding is always a challenge in community-based projects. The removal and replacement of concrete is expensive, and raises issues such as drainage and the ability of emergency vehicles to drive on softer surfaces. So plans are scaled-back, or enacted in increments. Because gating the alley is the first move, it is a necessity. For one of the alleys, two students from the Maryland Institute College of Art offered to design and construct the gates. These artistic entries to the new community space help keep the space friendly, even if it is inaccessible to the broader public.

The Backyard Commons is an interesting contrast with the Axis Alley project. These two projects, focusing on alleys in Baltimore, took very different approaches to common space. Axis Alley brought art and creative expression into the neglected spaces of the neighborhood, and showed, if briefly, what they could become. But permanent changes need ongoing advocates and stewards.

With all the benefits of the alley as Backyard Commons, the privatization of a public space is a model that gives pause. Where crime is less of a problem, and where residences have not turned their back on the alleys, these spaces can still flourish without gating. Grady Clay has sympathy for the gates. "Since most alleys reach into the intimate spaces of family life, they should be made distant if not inaccessible to the public at large."[29] Is it possible to adequately have "eyes on the street" in both the front and rear? As with reconsidering any street or alley, the solution must work physically and culturally for its context, to meet the needs of the place and its people.

Alley Housing

Housing in various forms has activated alleys. The idea of "mews" housing, originally where horses were stabled, is a well-loved urban typology. Washington, D.C.'s Gessford Court and New York City's Washington Mews are beautiful examples of urban mews. Similarly, carriage houses atop stables (or the modern equivalent, the garage) can be quiet, attractive living spaces that have surveillance over alley space.

Some jurisdictions are removing regulatory barriers to creating housing that fronts on an alley. In 2009 Vancouver, British Columbia, began to permit laneway housing as a mechanism to increase density in urban neighborhoods as part of its EcoDensity Charter. Vancouver found that laneway housing would also accomplish its goal for adding affordable and rental housing options across the City. The guidelines for laneway housing focus windows and balconies toward the lanes. Lots with laneway houses must have at least one onsite parking space, which can be used by either the primary or laneway house. Laneway house permits are reviewed for tree retention. New trees need to be planted if a tree is removed to construct the laneway unit. In community discussions, reducing crime or activating the laneways were not brought up as issues—neighbors' concerns related primarily to neighborhood scale and shading.

In newly platted communities, alleys have come back into favor so that garages can be eliminated from the street frontage. Without the multicar garages along the street, room is available for porches and stoops. These semi-private porches, stoops, and small gardens allow residents to personalize and occupy the spaces adjacent to the street, encouraging interaction among neighbors. With alleys in the rear, there is an additional alternative zone that may be suitable for children to play or neighbors across the alley to meet (Figure 6-36).

Recreational Space in the Alleys: Los Angeles

Los Angeles, California, is another city that is rediscovering its alleys. They total up to over 900 linear miles, according to Jennifer Wolch, formerly of the University of Southern California's Center for Sus-

Figure 6-36 A residential alley with new construction and a renovated historic building. ©*Michael Burns, Seattle*

[29] *Alleys: A Hidden Resource*, Grady Clay, Louisville: Grady Clay and Company, 1978, p. 56.

tainable Cities (USC). USC's research found that Los Angeles's alleys are very underutilized—without any activity 80 percent of the time.[30] Many of the alleys are in Los Angeles's tougher neighborhoods, where park space is rare, and alleys have been considered problematic spaces.

Los Angeles had a program for gating alleys, the Nuisance Alley Closure Program. Residents who complained about crime, drug-dealing, and illegal dumping were allowed to pay for gates if they agreed to maintain the alleys. However, without any money to make improvements in the alleys themselves, most languished. Gating came to an end after the California Supreme Court ruled that rights of ingress and egress needed to be maintained for public rights-of-way.

USC's Center for Sustainable Cities began its efforts to better utilize Los Angeles's alleys in 2006. Drawing on lessons learned from other North American cities, the aspiration for Los Angeles was to have a comprehensive program that accomplished multiple goals for environmental improvements, and strengthened communities by meeting needs specific to the City and its neighborhoods.

Alleys could provide much-needed recreational space. Los Angeles has one of the lowest percentages of open space of any U.S. city, with less than 8 percent of its land area devoted to parks and open space.[31] Alleys could become good places to walk in neighborhoods, as an alternative to streets with heavy traffic. Alleys could incorporate new trees and green infrastructure, such as bioswales or permeable paving, to reduce stormwater runoff and recharge groundwater. New lighting and more people using the alleys could reduce criminal activity. Walkable alleys with green spaces and play spaces could bring neighbors together.

One of the keys to transforming the alleys will be funding and community support. Because there are multiple and varied benefits in improving the alleys, a number of agencies and organizations are working to bring the vision to life. The Trust for Public Land, working with the City of Los Angeles Community Redevelopment Agency, received grant money to develop a South Los Angeles Green Alley Master Plan. Los Angeles's Jefferson High School received funding from State Farm Insurance's Environmental Grant program to support students to work with engineering students from California State University of Los Angeles on studies that will be given to the City's Green Streets Committee. Through Los Angeles County's Department of Health, the Los Angeles Community Redevelopment Agency won a $16 million grant in federal stimulus funds for increasing access to healthy food and exercise in Los Angeles.

The greening of alleys in Los Angeles drew on the experiences of Chicago, Seattle, Baltimore, and Vancouver, British Columbia. Thanks to lessons learned in these cities' pioneering efforts, Los Angeles is crafting a program that meets the specific needs of its unique urban patterns, culture, climate, and hydrology. The successes of one place can raise the level of knowledge for communities and jurisdictions everywhere.

---

[30] Transforming Alleys into Green Infrastructure for Los Angeles, USC Center for Sustainable Cities, June 2008, Arly Cassidy, Josh Newell, and Jennifer Wolch.

[31] Transforming Alleys into Green Infrastructure for Los Angeles, USC Center for Sustainable Cities, June 2008, Arly Cassidy, Josh Newell, and Jennifer Wolch, page 1.

ALLEYS: CHALLENGES AND POTENTIAL BENEFITS

Alley Challenges

Designing for Stormwater

When improving alleys, the design needs to take drainage into account to make sure that flooding does not become a problem, and that changes in the alleys do not impact adjacent properties and structures. When funding is available to properly design and construct a better stormwater system, alleys can become valuable resources for a city.

Emergency Access

Alleys are sometimes used to provide adequate access by fire departments, especially on deeper lots where fire access is needed in the front and rear of lots. When that is the case, the alleys need to be open and designed to accommodate the size and weight of fire trucks. Most fire departments ask for 20 feet of width in order to have space for the outriggers that stabilize the pumper trucks when fighting a fire. Police departments may also have requirements for emergency access in alleys.

Utilities

Because alleys have been built as service zones, new solutions may be needed for garbage storage and pickup, parking, and other delivery or service needs. Sometimes only part of an alley is available for more people-oriented uses.

Some alleys are used as routes for overhead power lines and connections, or underground pipes for water or sewer. Overhead wires may limit tree planting. Because of access requirements from utilities, underground pipes may mean restrictions on elements that can be built in the alley.

Some cities have found alternative ways of dealing with trash. A number of European cities are using automated waste collection systems that use below-grade pneumatic tubes to carry waste to a centralized processing facility. Seattle's shift away from dumpsters to more frequent pickup has opened up alleys for reuse. In

Melbourne, Australia, most businesses cannot store waste bins permanently on the laneways of the central city, but bring them out after business hours, and need to put them away promptly. Limiting the allowable times for trash and service activities allows active uses during daytime and evening hours.

Snow Removal

In cold climates, snow removal can be challenging in alleys because they may be too narrow for equipment, and there is no place to put the extra snow. Buildings adjacent to the alley are sometimes less sturdy than those along the street—garages may have minimal footings and be susceptible to damage. These issues are present whether the alleys are "people-places" or not. Alleys are generally lower priority for city snow removal efforts and if they are used for parking, cars can get stuck after snowstorms.

Lighting

Safety is critical when people are invited to more fully use alleys. If alleys are going to be used as a public place, they need to be designed and treated with the respect of a public place, with particular emphasis on elements necessary for a safe environment. Lighting requires money for installation, and ongoing maintenance, but it is essential for a public space. Like so many elements in the right-of-way, it is important to know who is responsible for that maintenance over the long term. Chicago is using its Green Alley program to move toward more environmentally friendly lighting, using dark-sky compliant fixtures to reduce light pollution.

Governance, Maintenance, and Liability

Who gets to decide what happens in the alley? Citizen-led efforts need to have the buy-in of neighbors. Local governments, including city departments, need to have all of their regulations and concerns met. The mechanisms for allowing changes in the alleys need to exist, whether it is partial closure to the public or temporary uses that are at stake. A community-based organization is very useful in solving all of these problems, and for helping to attract funding (Figure 6-37).

Potential Alley Benefits

Reduced Crime

In some places, making alleys safer is the primary motivation behind the improvements. Neighbors who use and care for a space make a real difference in safety. Gating, or not gating, alleys is a tricky question in areas where crime is a problem. There are legal issues specific to states and localities, but the broader question of privatization of public property always raises vigorous debates.

Increased Community Cohesion

The effort needed to improve local alleys requires that neighbors communicate and work together. Where spaces are shared and enjoyed, neighbors get to know one another. While anecdotal evidence supports this notion, organizations such as Community Greens are initiating studies to measure the social impacts on residents with shared green spaces.

Environmental Benefits

Alleys can serve a variety of functions that improve environmental quality. Where there is sufficient space to add trees and landscaping, alleys can make cities greener. Where alleys need to remain as hardscape, they can be redone with permeable paving if soil types permit.

More Walkable Neighborhoods

Alleys offer alternative connections for walking and biking. With little traffic, alleys have the potential to allow safer connections between the home and schools, parks, and friends and neighbors.

Health Benefits

The crucial link between walking and health is now recognized, and brings new opportunities to support reuse of alleys for recreation, green space, and safe pathways. For that reason, organizations such as Community Health Council are supporting the changes to alleys in Los Angeles.

Space for Recreation
When alleys are made safe and traffic is minimal, they can become places for play or recreation. It is relatively simple to close an alley from cars for short periods, allowing children to ride bikes or play games.

Economic Benefits
Better alleys make better neighborhoods, and this can increase property values. In commercial districts, alleys can offer new business opportunities. The most dramatic examples, such as Melbourne, Australia, have created exciting new districts.

Figure 6-37 Green Garage brought a community of people together to revitalize an alley in Detroit. *Photographer: Daniel Toole, recipient of AIA Seattle Emerging Professional Travel Scholarship 2010*

MAIN STREETS

Figure 6-38

Main Streets are the traditional hearts of communities. Shops, the bank, theater, post office, and town hall might be found along a classic Main Street. Traditionally the social and institutional center of towns and neighborhoods, Main Streets embody local history and culture. Businesses are often owned and run by people from the town, and business owners and customers know one another. Main Streets are not only part of small towns, but are also found at the center of neighborhoods within larger cities.

Development patterns after World War II were not kind to Main Street. New roads connected to new large chain stores, surrounded by spacious parking lots. Shopping malls pulled the energy away from Main Street. Some Main Streets, in efforts to compete with the new auto-dominated paradigm, were widened and redesigned to accommodate higher vehicle speeds.

But despite those blows, the value of traditional Main Streets is clear, and many communities have worked hard to reinvigorate them. The National Trust for Historic Preservation has been active for many years in providing assistance to communities trying to improve their commercial districts. Over 1,600 communities in America have worked to save historic buildings, strengthen local economies, and revitalize the character and charm of their original commercial districts.[32]

Main Streets and town centers are key to walkable communities. They can and should be the "strolling streets" that bring communities together. Because having quality destinations is the most important predictor of walking, the quality of Main Street–style retail environments can go a long way to encouraging walkable, healthy communities.

Retail streets need additional space for people to linger and enjoy spending time. Places for the interactions of public life offer more than simply room for people to walk. "Eddies" of space, alongside

[32]From the article "What Happened to America's Main Streets?" National Trust for Historic Preservation, www.preservationnation.org/main-street/about-main-street/getting-started/what-happened-to-main-street.html.

movement zones, provide room for small group conversation, resting, or people-watching. Quality public spaces become destinations in their own right. When communities have attractive public spaces such as Main Streets, people choose to spend time in them—walking, shopping, dining, or pursuing recreational activities. These optional activities support businesses, community events, and interaction between community members (Figure 6-38).

Edges and Eddies

Great Main Streets are full of people and activities. Ideally, many of the people using Main Street live nearby and can walk or bike to the place that serves as a neighborhood center. All the efforts within the Main Street district, including those involving the right-of-way, need to focus on attracting and supporting the people and activities of the place.

These "people spaces" need to be as varied as the types of activities that occur on Main Street. These spaces will draw on, and take advantage of, the strengths and quirks of the particular place. Oakland, California's Fruitdale Street is a successful example of an active Main Street that reflects the rich cultural identity of its neighborhood. Fruitdale's transformation began with facade improvement grants and support for the merchants in the Latino-based community. It has since grown with a transit-oriented village adjacent to the BART station. Other Main Streets have found identities tied to the arts, entertainment, history, or adjacent institutions such as colleges. Being "known" for something gives an identity as a destination to the region and beyond (Figure 6-39).

Figure 6-39 Solana Beach's South Cedros Avenue is the spine of the Design District. *Photographer: Joe Iano*

Figure 6-40 Pasadena's Old Town uses connections to parking as "eddy" spaces. *Photographer: Paul Iano*

The particularities of connections and movement create opportunities for placemaking. Street corners can be highly visible locations, and people waiting to cross the street gather at intersections while waiting to cross. The active nature of the street corner has advantages for some purposes, but where traffic is heavy, quieter locations along the street may make better spaces for seating. Opportunities for quieter eddy spaces can be found along pedestrian-friendly connections between Main Streets and parking areas. Pasadena, California's Old Town district was laid out with many smaller alleyways that give the area a distinct character and scale. These quieter connecting spaces make excellent locations for outdoor seating (Figure 6-40).

Figure 6-41 Buildings that open up to the street create interaction between outdoor and indoor spaces. *©Michael Burns, Seattle*

The Public/Private Edge

The edge between the public space and the adjacent uses is a critical juncture. Ownership, maintenance, and the regulatory environment shift at that line, but interaction between the public side and the private side is fundamental to a successful public realm. Facades that fully open to the sidewalk enliven the street, and create interest for people on both sides. Bringing cafe seating or street vending out into the sidewalk adds interest for people walking by and economic advantage for shop and restaurant owners (Figure 6-41).

How can both sides of the public/private edge work together? Private developers can open up their buildings to the street, but what is the mechanism for the building owners to connect their activities to the adjacent sidewalk? Where do you draw the line between activating the sidewalk in a way that is healthy for the community, and private "take-over" of the street by private business? Permission from the city or town may include a permit to use the street for signs, retail display, or tables and chairs. Where cooking or serving food is involved, permission may be required from a health department. Some jurisdictions have additional requirements for serving liquor.

Figure 6-42 The entry to transit offers generous space, good materials, shade, and activities.

More permanent improvements bring up new sets of issues. If better materials are installed by developers in public property, how will they be maintained? Carefully designed integral color concrete may end up patched with standard concrete after utility repairs. If property owners add plantings, how can the city make sure they stay healthy?

Local governments interested in better streets often find themselves in a quandary. Their policies call for better streets, but their budgets are inadequate. They need to both encourage and to regulate property owners. The solutions are found when jurisdictions are clear about their concerns, and work with property owners to ensure safety, maintenance, and public benefit for uses and materials in the right-of-way.

Public Space and Transit

Main Street areas adjacent to a major transit connection need space associated with movement of people to and from the station and any waiting areas where transit is at-grade. Wide sidewalks or plaza space is very important near busy transit links (Figure 6-42).

Transit areas offer interesting design opportunities that can make the use of transit more appealing and can result in well-activated spaces and successful businesses. Some cities ask for amenities on the buildings adjacent to transit stops, such as weather protection, seating, or leaning rails. Transit riders then tend to congregate near the building, and property owners may resist their building edge being used as a gathering space.

Another approach is to have people wait near the curb, which is possible if there is sufficient circulation space between the transit shelter and the building face. Transit amenities need to be designed so that transit patrons are assets to adjacent businesses. Adequate circulation space and visibility of building entries, safety, and lighting are issues that need to be considered near urban transit stops.

Outside of dense urban areas, transit stops are opportunities for simple amenities that can be enjoyed by anyone. A place to sit, perhaps to stay dry, and pleasant landscaping add to the walkability of the neighborhood as well as making transit use attractive.

Climate and Comfort

Spaces need to be designed for year-round comfort. Weather protection from harsh sun or persistent rain encourages walking in a variety of climates. Cities in colder climates cannot dismiss half the year as unsuitable for public space, and many have found ways to celebrate winter with special lighting, winter carnivals, and holiday markets. "Warmth features," such as fireplaces or glazed winter garden spaces, entice people to enjoy public spaces (Figure 6-43).

Thoughtful urban design makes a real difference in the attractiveness of public spaces in hot climates. There are many time-tested design solutions for providing shade, including trees and arcades. Trees have the added benefit of cooling the air with evapotranspiration. Using lighter-colored materials that retain less heat can significantly change the comfort level of a space. Water features cool spaces, and are often used as iconic design elements.

Public Space and Diversity

Public spaces should have something for everyone. Places to sit should be frequent enough to make people of all ages and abilities comfortable. Older

Figure 6-43 Coffee shops have created "warmth" features with seating along the street.

Figure 6-44   Integrating places for skateboarders offer activity for skaters and viewers. *Designer: van der Zalm + Associates, Inc., Photographer: Jaqueline Lowe, BCSLA*

people and families with children will be more inclined to walk and spend time out-of-doors where seating is available and convenient.

Places to play broaden the diversity of people drawn to the public realm. Even the simplest water features delight children and the adults who watch them. Outdoor ice skating enlivens many civic downtowns in colder climates, including the ice rink along North Michigan Avenue in Chicago's Millennium Park. Skateparks are beginning to be designed as active urban parks and plazas. Places to play not only appeal to the active participants, but draw people to watch. For tired parents, a place to play with adjacent seating can be a godsend. An active, diverse crowd in turn can make places safer and more pleasant, fueling a positive cycle of use (Figure 6-44).

Ways for the Public Sector to Help Main Streets

Local governments have been active participants in the Main Streets that have thrived or been revitalized. Government entities are involved in decisions in the zones under public control, including streets, and are often the key to whether or not innovative uses and designs are possible. The public sector can help Main Streets by looking for flexibility in regulations and standards where good ideas have merit. Sometimes, projects can be allowed dispensation if they are considered pilot projects. Local governments can have processes in place to allow use of the street, especially temporary uses such as events or vending carts.

City staff can assist businesses and community groups in finding funds. Some cities have their own funds available for grants, and often staff members are familiar with grant possibilities from other government sources or nonprofit groups. Facade improvement grants have used relatively small amounts of funding to make significant improvements to Main Streets. Portland, Maine, is one of several cities that have used a facade improvement program to invigorate a Main Street. Their program offered funds for a portion of Congress Street, contributing to design assistance and construction, so long as there was a private matching fund equal to or greater than the grant. Money for the Façade Improvement Program came through the City's Community Development Block Grant (CDBG) funds.[33]

Streetscape improvements are often instigated by local government in order to bring vitality to commercial districts. Well-designed streetscapes are one part of a complex set of variables that make successful Main Streets. While the amenities and materials can be helpful in supporting desired activities on Main Streets, streetscape alone will not attract people.

---

[33] http://www.ci.portland.me.us/citymanagers/facade.asp.

However, good streetscape shows that a place is valued and cared for. Priorities vary depending on the existing conditions and opportunities of each place. For some, street trees may be the highest priority, given the many benefits they bring to commercial districts. Pedestrian lighting can make a major difference in the attractiveness and the perception of safety for Main Streets. Some places lack enough space along the sidewalk, and need to look at options for increasing the amount of space available in the public realm.

Streetscape design should aspire to bring out the special characteristics of a place. For historic districts with masonry facades, brick in the streetscape can amplify the character. Other places have used streetscape design palettes that draw on sustainability and local materials. For Director's Park in Portland, Oregon, Landscape architect firm Olin used a modern palette of stone, wood, and glass in a downtown park and shared-use street The modern style and a high canopy for weather protection fit well with the local climate and culture (Figure 6-45).

Figure 6-45 Director's Park's distinctive furnishings.

Another way that the public sector can encourage Main Streets is by making it easy to attain permits for activities in the right-of-way. Street fairs, farmers' markets, and other celebrations can be central to the identity of Main Street communities, and the city needs to work with community groups in order to make these events happen. Street-use permits for cafes and outdoor vending should be simple enough to encourage businesses to activate public spaces.

City, county, and state agencies can help Main Streets with support for public transit. Agencies may be able to fund seating, lighting, and weather protection at transit stops. Many transit agencies incorporate art into their facilities, helping to strengthen the identity of the station area. These kinds of improvements benefit Main Street districts and transit riders, and can increase ridership for transit agencies.

Local governments can assist in finding funds for Main Street improvements through a variety of sources. Because healthy streets touch on so many aspects of community life, sources of funds may be found through diverse sources including economic development, public safety, historic preservation, sustainability, and public health.

Rethinking the Street in Main Street

One of the many challenges to the health of Main Streets over the past decades has been the treatment of the street itself. Where traffic has increased and roads have been widened, the character and the pedestrian experience of Main Streets have deteriorated.

In many towns, Main Street is also a state highway. In order to move more cars more efficiently, state highway departments have widened Main Streets and raised the speed limits. As the pedestrian realm suffered, the stores suffered. In other towns, the highway bypassed Main Street, and car-oriented businesses on new highways replaced the smaller local establishments in the old part of town.

The local impact of turning a Main Street into a faster, wider road has been recognized by a number of state highway departments. Several state highway departments have published very useful documents illustrating ways to balance local needs and values with the need for safety and regional mobility. California, Maryland, Oregon, and New Jersey have led the way with design manuals that offer more design flexibility for state highways that run through neighborhoods and towns.

Some of the ways to improve the street zone of a Main Street include the following strategies.

Reducing Posted Traffic Speeds

Pedestrian comfort is related to the speed of travel on the adjacent streets. Main Streets fare best with speed limits between 15 to 30 miles per hour, with speeds on the lower end of that range preferable. For drivers traveling through a retail district at 30 miles per hour, the storefronts and signage go by in a blur. For pedestrians, higher-speed traffic can cause discomfort, noise, and splashing water from cars driving along the curb in the rain. A balance between the regional mobility, local access, and the quality of the experience of Main Street need to be weighed for every particular instance.

Although it may seem counterintuitive, increased speed does not always increase road capacity. Faster-moving traffic needs to maintain larger distances between vehicles. Lower speeds make turning movements easier, as drivers look for gaps in the traffic flow. Most importantly, lower speeds result in safer environments for pedestrians.

For Main Streets designated as state routes, the reduction in speed may be difficult when there is a mismatch between state requirements and the priorities of the community. One solution is declassifying the street as part of the state system, or to swap Main Street for another through-route.

Maplewood, New Jersey, is an example of the state transferring ownership to the Township. Maplewood, New Jersey, was part of State Route 124, which ran from Newark west through Essex County. The Township has worked since 1997 on the economic development of its business district along Springfield Avenue. The street itself, with some 17,000 cars a day, detracted from the potential for a pedestrian-friendly Main Street district. The Springfield Avenue Partnership and the Township asked the New Jersey Department of Transportation (NJDOT) about reconfiguring the four-lane arterial to one travel lane in each direction, a center left-turn lane, and parking on both sides. NJDOT considered the request, even though Springfield Avenue was part of both State Route 124 and the National Highway System. Temporary markings and cones were used to test the reconfiguration. Level of service remained adequate, and the reconfiguration was made permanent.[34]

State Route 124 had historically been a major long-distance route running southwest from Newark. Interstate 78 took over much of the through-connection, and the State was able to shift control of Springfield Avenue to the Township. With that transfer, in 2002, came a $1.5 million grant for improvements to the roadway. NJDOT Transportation Commissioner Jamie Fox said at the time, "We are here to turn over control of this roadway to the Township so they can turn Springfield into a destination, not just a thoroughfare. Time has proven that when we invest in our downtowns, commerce and opportunity follow."[35]

---

[34] Flexible Design of New Jersey's Main Streets, prepared by the Voorhees Transportation Policy Institute, Edward J. Bloustein School of Planning and Public Policy, Rutgers, The State University of New Jersey, for the New Jersey Department of Transportation. Chapter 3.2.1. Accessed at http://contextsensitivesolutions.org/content/reading/flexible-design-new-jersey/resources/flexible-design-new-jersey/

[35] NJDOT News Release, October 30, 2002, www.state.nj.us/transportation/about/press/2002/103002b.shtm.

Traffic Calming

Tactile and visual clues can change the behavior of drivers. There are many ways to calm traffic, and the best traffic-calming elements offer multiple benefits. Trees, on-street parking, curb bulbs, landscaping, narrower lane widths, and entry markers slow cars down, and at the same time, contribute to making a better place.

With landscaped zones in the right-of-way, motorists have both drive lanes and landscaping within their field of vision instead of "wide open spaces" of asphalt that encourage speeding. Roundabouts, curb bulbs, medians, and chicanes include natural elements into the mix. These elements are especially important where speeds are reduced at the entry to Main Street zones.

Curb bulbs are one of the best streetscape investments. Bringing pedestrian space out into the intersection is relatively easy to do, especially when there is on-street parking. Curb extensions define and protect parking areas, and keep cars from using parking lanes as additional travel lanes when no parked cars are present. Curb bulbs add space at intersections, where people wait to cross the street. Curb bulbs shorten the length of the street crossing, which can make a significant difference for pedestrians on wider streets (Figure 6-46).

Landscaped medians break down the scale of streets, and when planted with trees, can support full tree canopies. Medians also serve as refuge areas for pedestrians crossing the street, allowing people to cross one direction of traffic at a time. Where medians are used as pedestrian refuges on multilane streets, they should be wide enough—about six feet—for a person with a bicycle or stroller to stand within the width of the median.

A median can replace a lane or can be added, resulting in increased overall width of the right-of-way. Replacing a lane with a median can also help manage traffic speeds and limit some turning movements across travel lanes. Managing access is an issue raised by both local businesses who don't like any restrictions placed on access to their businesses, as well as emergency responders who have concerns about moving police and fire trucks past stopped traffic in emergencies.

Curb Radii and Intersections

The intersection is the place where pedestrians and vehicle zones meet. The design details at intersections are key for safe crossing. The details also give many visual cues about the priorities between pedestrians and vehicles.

A curb radius defines the dimension of a corner curb return. Urban designers argue for tight curb radii on Main Streets for aesthetic reasons, to slow turning vehicles, and to shorten crossing distances for pedestrians. The American Association of State Highway and Transportation Officials (AASHTO) calls for an inside turning radius of 14.4 feet for a passenger vehicle, and 28.3 feet for a single-unit truck. According to the Voorhees Transportation Policy Institute, corner radii of 10 to 15 feet are common in cities, and do not appear to cause problems, possibly because drivers are more cautious when conditions are constrained.[36] Trucks and other large vehicles argue for wide curb radii that are much easier for them to maneuver. This debate is vigorous and often solved on a case-by-case basis.

For Main Street curb radii, practical minimums will favor pedestrians, especially where "free" right turns are allowed. In order to keep curb radii tight and to allow bulbing of the curb, it is helpful to be strategic about which curb radii of the four at each intersection needs to be wider to support truck turn movements and which can remain tighter. In some cases curbs can be designed to be

[36] Flexible Design of New Jersey's Main Streets, prepared by the Voorhees Transportation Policy Institute, Edward J. Bloustein School of Planning and Public Policy, Rutgers, The State University of New Jersey, for the New Jersey Department of Transportation. Chapter 2. Accessed at http://contextsensitivesolutions.org/content/reading/flexible-design-new-jersey/resources/flexible-design-new-jersey/

Figure 6-46 A "kink" in the street slows cars and discourages through-traffic.

Figure 6-47 Curb bulbs add landscape and improve the pedestrian realm.

mountable by trucks or emergency vehicles. Sometimes, alternate routes for trucks can be found. By reducing height or using sloped faces, mountable curbs allow vehicles to encroach on them without damaging tires or wheels Mountable curbs need to be used with caution because they also enable vehicles to enter the edge of the pedestrian space and could put people standing on the corner at risk (Figure 6-47).

Converting from One-Way Streets to Two-Way Streets

Converting streets from one-way to two-way has proven successful in some Main Street districts, reducing traffic speeds and supporting better pedestrian space. Businesses have more visibility to passing vehicles and better access. Conversion to two-way has been shown to increase economic activity in a survey of 25 towns and cities across the United States. All of the jurisdictions in the survey found positive results from the change. Pedestrian safety improved. People drove more slowly, and many communities found that private investment in the retail district rose and vacancies went down.[37]

Yet converting to two-way streets is not always the right answer. A number of characteristics need to be considered for each context. What is the amount and type of traffic, including the level of truck traffic and the amount of turning movements? How does the street fit in to the local and the regional network? Are there plenty of alternate routes on a grid system, or few optional routes? Which jurisdiction—city, county, state—is responsible for the street? Would the adjacent use benefit?

Changing Traffic Patterns

Rerouting traffic requires careful consideration in order to have a positive impact on the "people places" of a town or neighborhood. Pedestrian-friendly commercial districts need to balance visibility and accessibility with the impact of through-traffic. Reducing traffic by providing alternate routes for freight or commuters can make a safer and quieter Main Street, but rural bypasses that created alternate, higher-speed routes have drained the life out of Main Streets in many communities.

Under the right circumstances, a reduction in the volume of traffic on Main Street may allow for increased sidewalk space, parking, and access for bikes. The key is making the street work for the uses that make a healthy community—vibrant businesses with sufficient visibility and easy access, and high-quality spaces for people to linger and enjoy the Main Street environment.

Reducing the Number of Lanes

When Main Streets need additional space for pedestrians, bicycles, and landscaping, it is sometimes possible to reduce the number of travel lanes. Sometimes called a "road diet," the most common way to reduce lanes is to go from a four-lane configuration to a three-lane section, with one lane in each direction and a dedicated turn lane in the middle. This strategy is discussed further in the thoroughfares typology section of this chapter. For Main Streets, reducing the number of lanes and adding on-street parking and/or extra sidewalk space can be a very effective change.

Reducing Lane Widths

Another strategy for calming Main Street is to retain the number of lanes, but to reduce lane widths. Some streets have low-enough traffic levels to allow a reduction in the number of lanes. If there is excess roadway, this space can be reallocated to widened sidewalks, or to more parking to increase access to shops, bicycle lanes, or other uses.

---

[37] "Converting One-way Streets to Two-way: Managing Traffic on Main Street," by John D. Edwards, Main Street News, June 2002, p. 3.

Especially when Main Streets transition from higher-speed rural roads to downtowns, lane widths may be reduced in zones with lower speeds for vehicles. Reduced lane width itself helps to slow traffic, but additional traffic-calming measures are useful in slowing traffic entering the heart of the community. If lane widths are reduced, the road must still be safe for larger vehicles such as trucks, buses, recreational vehicles, and fire trucks.

Narrower lane width can allow space for other uses in the zone between curbs, such as bicycle lanes, parking zones, or planted medians. Reduced lane width can offer additional space for pedestrians if the curbs are relocated. Moving the curb line adds costs because changes to the drainage are usually required, and utilities may also be affected. Standards typically call for 12-foot lane minimums, but some jurisdictions have a process that allows some flexibility. For instance, the California Department of Transportation may approve lane widths below 12 feet, but only after review on a case-by-case basis (Figure 6-48).

Figure 6-48 The planted median makes crossing safer and more pleasant for pedestrians.

Parking on Main Street

The amount, location, and management of parking can be very contentious. Parking, like the streets themselves, supports successful land uses. But it is important to remember that people come to Main Streets to shop and to enjoy a mix of activities and destinations, not just because parking is available.

In considering Main Streets and the ways that the right-of-way can contribute to the success of these districts, the availability of on-street parking and the quality of the walking environment are key (Figure 6-49).

Figure 6-49 Where streets are wide enough, angled parking provides more spaces than parallel parking.

Figure 6-50 Lake Oswego, Oregon, created curbless parking adjacent to the pedestrian space.

On-street parking provides access to businesses and other uses, and at the same time serves as a buffer between moving traffic and the pedestrian zone. On-street parking also reduces the amount of parking needed outside of the right-of-way.

Parallel parking uses a fairly narrow width, usually eight feet, and is often found on both sides of the street. Angled parking requires more width, depending on the angle and the design vehicle, but if the width is available, it generates more parking spaces. Back-in/head-out angled parking allows easier turning movements than parallel parking and better visibility when leaving than head-in/back-out parking.

On-street parking works well with curb bulbs to define parking areas, and to bring landscaping out toward the center of the street. When adding landscape near on-street parking, it is important to make sure that visibility is adequate for drivers moving in and out of parking spaces.

On-street parking should be as effective as possible for patrons of Main Street or downtown. Enforcing time restrictions prevents employees from storing their cars in the most convenient spaces for the duration of business hours. Another simple way to better use on-street space is to limit time restrictions for loading and unloading zones. Many restricted zones need not be limited after normal work hours, opening up spaces for restaurant patrons in the evening.

Parking availability is also related to the distance that people are willing to walk from parking to their destinations. When the walking environment is comfortable, people are more inclined to park several blocks away from where they are going.

Main Streets thrive when people go there not just out of necessity, but by choice. When an entire commercial district is in itself a destination of choice, there is less need to circle the block to get the most convenient parking spot.

The transportation-land use connection, as always, is part of the parking equation. When plenty of people live within walking distance, and transit is convenient, Main Streets are less dependent on providing parking for every patron (Figure 6-50).

THOROUGHFARES

A thoroughfare is the powerhouse of the roadway network. Urban arterials, regional corridors, turnpikes, and interstate routes all fall within this category. Thoroughfares are critically important components of the transportation system, moving large amounts of traffic over long distances, while also serving local uses (Figure 6-51).

Thoroughfares structure the pattern of the city, becoming part of the "mental map" for tens of thousands of drivers each day. They share many common characteristics among their type—they are often limited access roadways which feed vehicle traffic to local roadways and destinations. Engineers tend to follow certain rules of thumb when designing thoroughfares, especially pertaining to their spacing within the street grid and their design features. Many thoroughfares are grand and majestic civic spaces such as the Champes-Elysees in Paris, France, and the Benjamin Franklin Parkway in Philadelphia, Pennsylvania.

The more typical example, however, is neither grand nor glorious. These roadways are often inhospitable for people who are not in a vehicle. Major arterials can be nearly as problematic for the cars, buses, freight, service, and emergency vehicles that use them because heavy congestion, multiple turning movements, and high speeds can impact travel times and driver safety.

Limited-access thoroughfares are generally designed to support speeds of 30 miles per hour or above—with some states opting for speeds as high as 70 or 80 mph along certain stretches. Thoroughfares must accommodate oversized vehicles—buses and trucks that need wider lanes, more gentle curves, and few mandatory stops along the way. Some restrict pedestrian and bicycle access. Others carry so many vehicles that for walkers and bicyclists, they are unpleasant and sometimes even unsafe.

Major arterials that move large volumes of traffic and need to serve adjacent land uses present particular challenges for creating better mobility and higher-quality urban places. As land use patterns moved from rural lands punctuated by denser towns and urban areas to more suburban

Figure 6-51

models, the distances between destinations expanded. Long stretches of roadway were widened, and became strewn with isolated buildings, expanses of parking lots, and competing signs.

Businesses tend to locate along thoroughfares, aiming to attract customers with large signs, oversized parking lots, and multiple curb cuts for driveway access. No one wants to walk across the parking lot, much less between stores.

As businesses and residences are located along these routes, vehicles turning from the main route into driveways and local roads create friction for through-traffic that can easily create traffic congestion. The combination of sprawl, wide roadways that are difficult to cross, and the noise and exhaust from traffic turns these roads into real eyesores, even though they are major routes for people traveling through and to destinations along them.

Many thoroughfares, including state routes, bisect residential neighborhoods and historic downtowns. Others are heavily used transit corridors where buses discharge people who might be eager to access nearby destinations on foot or by bike if the roadway was not such a barrier. When getting to the transit stop along these routes, waiting for the bus, and crossing the street are all uncomfortable, then people will only use transit if they have no other alternative, and will choose to drive for more trips.

Many thoroughfares have grown far beyond their original capacity, reaching out to expanding suburbs and exurbs. Roadway widening, increased traffic volumes, and higher speeds create roadways that can be unsightly and undesirable, especially for local residents.

There is a growing friction between highway engineers and local communities who are eager to reclaim and retrofit thoroughfares to be more friendly to modes other than cars. Retrofitting a heavily traveled thoroughfare from a strip-retail environment into a pedestrian and bicycle-friendly place doesn't happen overnight. Improvements may focus on nodes, rather than the length of a thoroughfare. Although taming the thoroughfare has its challenges, there are several models that not only function well, but have turned thoroughfares into valued spaces.

Thoroughfares can be made better by increasing their functionality and the placemaking elements alongside them, but keeping the general use of the street the same. For example, scenic highways incorporate a number of green features into the design of the right-of-way including trees, landscaping, scenic overlooks, iconic architecture, and other points of interest to create a pleasant driving experience for the recreational traveler. These are all excellent improvements for long-haul corridors. The National Scenic Byway Program, part of the U.S. Department of Transportation, has designated some 150 diverse roads beautiful routes that deserve preservation and enhancement. Some of the notable scenic byways include the California coast's Route 1 Big Sur Highway, Arizona's Coronado Trail Byway, and Vermont's Connecticut River Byway.

Thoroughfares as Places

An urban thoroughfare has the dual challenge of moving vehicles and supporting relatively dense adjacent land uses. Pedestrians and cyclists have often been lost in the equation. .

There are a number of improvements that can support walking and bicycling. Sidewalks are essential to pedestrian safety, and balancing the timing of traffic lights to reduce pedestrian wait times at key locations improves crossing the arterial. Access management solutions, such as consolidating driveways and adding medians to better manage turning movements, helps both drivers and pedestrians. Landscaping and street trees improve the character and potentially the comfort and environmental quality of the road. Transit stops can be made safer and more comfortable, with ample space, seating, weather protection, and good lighting. These improvements can make better, if not drastically different, thoroughfares.

The City of Shoreline, Washington, won multiple awards for their Aurora Corridor project. When the City incorporated in 1995, they declared Aurora to be their "Main Street," despite its inhospitable nature. The three-mile stretch of Aurora Avenue North, also known as State Highway 99, carries over 40,000 cars per day, has a major transit route, and a variety of auto-oriented land uses. Redoing this important and regional arterial to live up to the vision of the community's Main Street became a key priority for the new city.

Historically, the Shoreline area was a rural location, yet still easily accessible to Seattle's jobs and activities. The Seattle-Everett Interurban line served as the main connection between these two destinations from its construction in 1906 to its closure in 1939. Meanwhile, traffic grew along Highway 99—the major north-south route connecting the region to the Canadian border. Residential development boomed in the postwar years, and automobile-oriented commercial uses sprang up along the corridor.

The Aurora Corridor exemplified the challenges of taming arterials. The transportation function is very important both regionally and locally. Auto-oriented development needed access, but the number of driveways and turning movements caused problems for both vehicles and pedestrians. The pedestrian environment was an unpleasant and uncomfortable environment for people to walk to and from transit, and to wait for the bus.

Safety was becoming a significant issue. According to the Washington State Department of Transportation (WSDOT), this section of Aurora in Shoreline has ranked as one of the state's most hazardous urban arterial highways. Within a 5-year period, 42 pedestrian and vehicle accidents occurred in Shoreline's segment of the Highway 99 corridor. Fatal and disabling accidents in this stretch of highway were twice as common as the statewide average for similar conditions.[38]

---

[38] From WSDOT project page, www.wsdot.wa.gov/projects/sr99/shoreline_ncthov/.

Figure 6-52 Aurora, before reconstruction, is typical of older auto-oriented strip development. *Photo courtesy of City of Shoreline*

Figure 6-53 Aurora now has good sidewalks, crosswalks, lighting, and landscaping. *Photo courtesy of City of Shoreline*

The City, working with consulting engineers CH2M HILL, used a context-sensitive solutions approach to the corridor redesign, with community participation at the heart of the process. The public was invited to dozens of public meetings, open houses, and presentations. A Citizen Advisory Task Force included a range of community and business interests, and an interagency team brought together stakeholders and decision makers from the various agencies at State, City, and County levels (Figures 6-52 and 6-53).

The redesign resulted in a typical seven-lane section within a flexible 110-foot right-of-way, with two general-purpose lanes in each direction, a median/turn lane, and outside lanes that are reserved for transit and right-turning traffic. The engineers, in an effort to best accommodate throughput and the local needs for access, devised a new type of managed lane referred to as a "BAT" lane—business access and transit. The BAT lanes are reserved for right-turning vehicles or for vehicles that are entering traffic from adjacent driveways. Segregating buses and other vehicles making turning movements is intended to increase efficiency for through-traffic. Reserving these lanes for turning vehicles also helps provide access to the adjoining businesses.

Shoreline's Aurora Corridor is part of Community Transit's 17-mile bus rapid transit (BRT) line, called Swift—Washington State's first BRT service, and one of the longest BRT routes yet built in the country. Buses run every ten minutes on weekdays, and have seven miles of dedicated lanes, with signal priority for much of the route. New transit shelters are well-lit, with seating, iconic markers, weather protection, and real-time monitors so that transit patrons know when the next bus will arrive (Figure 6-54).

The corridor is safer for people walking, with well-defined pedestrian zones including sidewalks, a pedestrian bridge, and better crossings at intersections with pedestrian-activated signals and median refuges. It is safer for drivers with clarified channelization and turning movements. Bicycles are accommodated on the nearby Interurban Trail. It is still a thoroughfare, carrying tens of thousands of vehicles, but it is safer, greener, and more functional for all modes of transportation. These improvements set the stage for land use changes that will create pedestrian-friendly nodes over time.

Figure 6-54 The business access and transit lane has slower-moving traffic along the curb.
Photo courtesy of City of Shoreline

Boulevards and Parkways

Before freeways and highways became common-place, boulevards carried large traffic volumes and, at the same time, served as significant civic spaces. Boulevards originated on the ramparts of the walled cities of Europe. Later, when no longer needed as fortifications, these bulwarks were planted with trees and used as promenades. The famous boulevards of Paris, constructed in the mid-1800s under Emperor Napoleon III, reinvented the structure of the city. Wide and formal civic spaces, these boulevards became signature streets that define urban form and serve as iconic spaces in themselves. They were built not only in European cities, but also around the world in the British and French colonies (Figure 6-55).

Figure 6-55 Lucca, Italy, is an example of the tree-lined ramparts of old European cities. *Photographer: Kirk McKinley*

Figure 6-56 Ocean Parkway in New York is an example of a multiway boulevard, with local access lanes on either side of through-lanes. *Photographer: Paul Iano*

Boulevards became popular in the United States in the latter half of the nineteenth century, and remained in vogue through the City Beautiful era during the early part of the twentieth century. In a famous American example, Frederick Law Olmsted and his partner Calvert Vaux conceived of a series of connections between Central Park and Brooklyn's new Prospect Park. The Americanized approach, a parkway, was less urban than the European models. The parkway was a green connection, bringing the romanticized version of natural landscape outward from parks and through communities (Figure 6-56).

Boulevard design is a topic in itself. Allan B. Jacobs and his coauthors have written a seminal book—*The Boulevard Book*—focusing on the multiway boulevard in particular. The multiway boulevards and other types of boulevards are models for integrating movement and placemaking that merit new attention.

Jacobs classifies boulevards into three types. The simplest type, a street boulevard, is a heavily landscaped arterial with large trees defining the edges. The second has a central median separating the lanes in each direction. A third type, the multiway boulevard, has central through-lanes, flanked by planted medians, and side streets to carry local traffic.

Multiway boulevards are interesting in that they separate out the functions of access and mobility, centering through-traffic in the right-of-way, and separating access functions at the periphery. Multiway boulevards are signature streets in Europe. In the middle of the nineteenth century, French civic planner Baron Haussmann carved boulevards, including multiway boulevards, through the tangled web of the streets of Paris. They remain an essential part of the iconic fabric and structure of the City. The generous width required for these boulevards is part of their grandeur, and the allées of trees define important places in the City for both motorists and pedestrians.

In the United States, grand boulevards were built in the late 1800s and early 1900s as part of the City Beautiful movement. Philadelphia's Benjamin Franklin Parkway is an excellent example, with the portion between Logan Circle and the Philadelphia Museum of Art designed as a multiway boulevard. The Fairmount Park Commission adopted Jacques Greber's plan in 1917, with the Parkway cutting a diagonal through the City grid, connecting civic institutions and creating an entry to Fairmount Park. The middle lanes provide through-access, with quiet side lanes providing access for institutions such as the Rodin Museum (Figure 6-57).

Figure 6-57 Benjamin Franklin Parkway in Philadelphia frames City Hall. It accommodates both arterial traffic and pedestrians along its edges. ©*Andreas Metz*

The Parkway is a highly intentional insertion into the fabric of the City, with framed vistas of the grandest institutions highlighting the beginning and end, just as the Arc d'Triomphe does in the Champs Elysees. One of the four famous park squares in William Penn's plan for Philadelphia, Logan Square, was reconfigured into a large circle around the heroic Swann Memorial Fountain, designed by Alexander Calder in 1924.

The Parkway design beautifully accomplishes several functions—creating a civic space, structuring the urban pattern, carrying large volumes of traffic, and creating good pedestrian space that serves the uses along the Parkway. The Parkway right-of-way is very wide, and allows space for all these functions. Six central lanes (three in each direction) carry the through-traffic between Logan Circle and the Museum of Art. Pedestrian space within a double colonnade of oak trees separates the through-lanes from the side lanes. The slower side lanes have one lane with parallel parking serving the adjacent uses.

Benjamin Franklin Parkway is a grand volumetric space. Framed views of civic monuments are in scale with the width of the automobile-scaled six-lane space. The large trees and buffer space make pedestrian space comfortable. The City Beautiful movement fell out of favor not long after the completion of the Parkway, with efficiency of movement trumping the idea of civic-scale urban placemaking.

Road Diets

Not every thoroughfare can be turned into a grand civic space. Sometimes thoroughfares can be tamed by reducing the number of lanes. Fewer lanes may be sufficient, depending on how many cars use the road (measured in ADT, or Average Daily Traffic), the number of turning movements, the way in which transit is handled, space for bicycles, parking configuration, safety issues, and particular needs of adjacent land uses.

The most common way to reduce lanes, sometimes called a "road diet," is to go from a four-lane configuration to a three-lane section, with one lane in each direction and a dedicated turn lane in the middle. Generally, this approach to rechannelization works for ADT of 20,000 or below. The advantages of a road diet are counterintuitive and often result in robust debate among roadway users. Since traffic capacity is managed at the intersections, which still need to be designed to manage the anticipated roadway capacity, the actual impacts to travel times and overall congestion are minimal if they occur at all.

Road diets can reallocate space within the roadway for other purposes, such as on-street parking, median plantings (where there are no left turns), and bicycle lanes. However, the main benefit from a road diet is improving pedestrian safety. A three-lane section largely eliminates the potential for the most common type of collision involving pedestrians—the multiple-lane threat. This scenario occurs on a roadway with four or more lanes, when the car in the lane nearest to the curb stops to let a pedestrian cross at an unsignalized crosswalk. The car in the center lane, with the driver's view of the pedestrian blocked by the car that is stopped, does not see the pedestrian and does not stop. These collisions often occur at higher speeds and frequently result in injury or death for the pedestrian who is hit. Many cities and towns across the country are rechannelizing roadways and finding safety benefit as a result.

The three-lane street can also result in better pedestrian comfort as curb bulbs or short medians can often be added to reduce the crossing distance and provide better visibility between the pedestrian and the driver. Additionally, there is an increased buffer from traffic lanes when bike lanes or on-street parking is added. The benefits also accrue to the driver as left-turning traffic is taken out of a moving lane, resulting in fewer rear-end collisions. Because fewer cars swerve to avoid left-turning traffic, sideswipe collisions are reduced. Left turns are easier because turning drivers only need to cross one lane of traffic.

Rechannelizations can also be one of the most affordable tools in the designer's toolbox. These projects are most affordable when existing road profiles, curbs, and drainage are in place and the restriping can be accomplished in tandem with maintenance schedules for repaving.

Seattle, Washington's first road diet, along North 45th Street in the central Wallingford neighborhood, was completed in 1972. Since then, the City has rechannelized 30 arterial roadways including South Columbian Way in the Beacon Hill neighborhood. As part of a routine paving project in 2010, the design for South Columbian Way was informed by Seattle's Complete Streets principles—looking to make improvements for pedestrian, bicycle, and transit use while improving safety for all users whenever a major roadway project is accomplished (Figure 6-58).

Figure 6-58 South Columbian Way before the project.
Courtesy City of Seattle

The existing roadway was in serious need of repaving—the outside lanes needed full reconstruction. The original cross-section had four lanes—two in each direction, with an unimproved roadway edge and informal on-street parking. The roadway was rechannelized to three lanes—one lane in each direction with a center turn lane. Curbs, curb ramps, sidewalks, and bike lanes were added for the first time and helped to define the street edge and protect pedestrians from moving vehicles. The new curbs also helped manage a surface flooding situation by raising the elevation of the new sidewalk to better direct stormwater into the storm drainage collection system. The local community pitched in and volunteered their time to plant nearly 100 new trees—future assurance of new canopy coverage—and a new dedicated right-turn lane was added into the busy campus of a major medical center (Figures 6-59 and 6-60).

Moving Toward Walkable, Mixed-Use Zones

After years of suburbanization, decision makers are working to create denser, pedestrian-oriented places. Thoroughfares were part of the automobile-related structure that supported suburb development patterns, and will continue to play a significant role in regional mobility. It is unrealistic to think that they will become multiple miles of "Main Streets." But there are circumstances where portions of strip arterials can be transformed into nodes of walkable zones, especially as new or better transit facilities are added.

Another opportunity to make a more people-friendly thoroughfare is where strong retail centers already exist. Not long ago, the centerpiece of the rapidly growing city of Bellevue, Washington, was a large indoor shopping mall that once completely turned its back on the street. As part of years of effort to create a more walkable urban downtown, new stores and reconfigured storefronts have brought pedestrians to Bellevue Way, the City's central five-lane arterial. Sidewalks have been widened and new windows and retail entries have opened up to them. Plentiful parking below-grade serves the shops, restaurants, and theaters of this regional destination. Traffic moves slowly, and even comes to a standstill during weekends and the holiday shopping season, but the congestion might be seen as a symptom of success of the area's desirability.

Figure 6-59 South Columbian Way just after construction, with a turn lane, bike lane, sidewalk, and landscaping. *Courtesy City of Seattle*

Figure 6-60 A wide sidewalk, a good buffer, and street activity have changed what once was an automobile-dominated corridor into an active downtown streetscape.

SHARED-USE STREETS

Figure 6-61 *Photographer: Dave Knight*

The concept of mixing modes and zones within the right-of-way—forcing pedestrians, bicycles, and vehicles to share space—slows the pace of the street and makes room for different types of events to occur. Kids playing, neighbors meeting for a coffee and a game of chess at an outdoor table on a sunny day, a small grove of trees casting shade on the pavement—shared-use streets can reclaim for these activities while still enabling vehicles to pass through (Figures 6-61 and 6-62).

Figure 6-62 This landscaped plaza serves as a through-route for pedestrians, a drop-off, and short-term parking.

Shared-use streets result from a different way of thinking about how streets are used by pedestrians, cyclists, and vehicles. Conventional engineering focuses on distinct separation of modes. Signage, striping, and traffic lights direct behavior. This approach creates safe environments for high vehicle speeds, but when all modes are moving at a similar speed, people can rely on eye contact and environmental clues to travel safely. The absence of signage and blurring of zones means that drivers need to be more aware of other drivers, cyclists, and pedestrians.

Figure 6-63 Streets were once safe enough for children to play, and some are becoming so again. *Complete release per Wikimedia.*

The pioneering work of British architect Ben Hamilton-Baillie and the late Dutch traffic engineer Hans Monderman indicates that when transportation modes are all moving at the same speed—that of the pedestrian—people pay more attention, use eye contact, and behave in a more civil fashion. It may even prove safer than standard road design under certain circumstances.[39]

Considering drivers as a second priority on streets in U.S. cities is still a strange concept to many people. But these shared-use spaces are more common than most people think. Pedestrians and slow-moving cars commonly coexist in parking lots. Four-way stops require that drivers are aware of who moves next. Many college campuses mix service vehicles in pedestrian zones. Hotel drop-off zones easily accommodate taxis and people moving in and out (Figure 6-63).

Low volumes of cars and slow speeds make shared-use streets possible. Land uses that generate foot traffic make shared-use streets successful, because it is in part the presence of pedestrians that causes drivers to slow down. As in so many cases, the land uses and the right-of-way need to work together to create successful public spaces. When traffic is calmed, people are more comfortable, and the presence of people keeps traffic speeds low and driver awareness higher.

Shared-use streets run the spectrum from almost pedestrian-only to supporting a full mix of modes. At the most pedestrian-dominated end of the spectrum, cars are rare, streets are curbless and have high-quality materials and numerous amenities. They may even be designed to encourage children's play. On the other end of the spectrum, streets may be close to standard, but incorporate traffic-calming measures and possibly higher-quality materials.

Shared-use streets can be in residential neighborhoods where the primary users are the residents of the block. This is often the case with the Dutch *woonerf* or the "home zone" street found in England. It can also be in a commercial or mixed-use area, such as Winthrop Street in Cambridge, Massachusetts, or the network of streets within Malmo, Sweden's Western Harbor neighborhood. In commercial areas, shared-use streets are often enlivened by outdoor cafes, public art, trees and landscaping, vendors, play structures, and places to sit and people-watch.

---

[39] For more information on Monderman, see Project for Public Spaces, www.pps.org/articles/hans-monderman/.

Residential Shared-Use Streets

Woonerfs, loosely translated as "streets for living," originated in the Netherlands in the late 1960s in residential areas where space was at a premium and increased traffic was affecting community life. The living environment, rather than the transportation role of the street, is prioritized in a *woonerf*. By 1976, the Dutch government had laws on the books regulating traffic in *woonerfs*. The idea of people, bicycles, and cars sharing the street spread to other countries.

England embraced the concept with home zones, described as a residential street or group of streets where space for people is prioritized over its use by vehicles. The United Kingdom's Department for Transport created official policies in their 2006 Manual for Streets. In designated home zones, regulators work with the residents to describe the specific uses allowed in the street, and the permitted speed for vehicles. Even with the designated speed, which may be as low as 10 miles per hour, the design of the space is critical in affecting driver behavior. Paving texture and diversions in the vehicle path effectively reduce speeds and increase driver awareness. Regulations for home zones prioritize safety, but allow flexibility to meet the specific need of the residents, and create a strong sense of local identity.

Figure 6-64 A residential home zone in Copenhagen.
Photo by Chris Brunn

In the United States, people are becoming aware of this new concept, but streets designed as shared-use streets are still rare in practice. The United States Federal Highway Administration only recognized the home zone concept as a design tool for pedestrian facilities in 2002. Some streets actually function unofficially as *woonerfs*, but that is more a result of the way the space is used rather than an intentional design. For instance, it is still not uncommon to find children playing in streets that have very few cars, such as low-density neighborhoods with cul-de-sacs. Sometimes people will informally block off the street when children are playing. Residential alleys may also have low enough traffic volumes to become preferred walking routes or play areas. These streets might be thought of as natural *woonerfs*, rather than designed and permitted shared-use streets (Figure 6-64).

Some of the earliest examples of residential *woonerfs* in the United States, deliberately designed and permitted as shared-use streets, were built in Boulder, Colorado, in the 1980s. The Wonderland Development Company was experimenting with building developments with a priority on pedestrians and the shared facilities that strengthen communities. Two Boulder developments, the Cottages and Bridge-walk, have provided some lessons since their implementation:

- The residential shared-use streets have proved to be safe.

- The streets have not necessarily been used in the same frequency as the Dutch model. When homes are built with the typical American rear yards and other open spaces, the street space is less likely to be used for walking and play. Without pedestrians using the street, drivers are less likely to slow down.

- The developers noted that local jurisdictions need to allow for flexibility in order for more progressive kinds of streets to be built.

Some jurisdictions are beginning to integrate the idea of *woonerfs* into their regulatory process. Snohomish County, Washington, has adopted a standard for *woonerfs*, intended as residential recreational space. They allow a maximum of 15 dwellings to have access from a 12-foot-wide *woonerf*. The maximum speed is set at 10 miles per hour. North Bend, Washington, also has provisions for building *woonerfs* to provide access to homes when adjacent to a park or common open space.

Despite the reluctance to fully embrace the high bar of fully shared-use, traffic-calming measures have become incorporated in many American neighborhoods where residents are concerned about speeding, noise, and other safety concerns. On local streets, traffic-calming elements such as traffic circles and islands, speed bumps, diverters, and chicanes discourage cut-through traffic, and slow down local drivers. Calm traffic is a prerequisite for a shared-use street.

Shared-Use Streets in Commercial or Mixed-Use Neighborhoods

The concept of shared-use streets can also be successfully applied to town centers or commercial streets. In addition to improving walking conditions, many of these areas have turned common business areas into thriving tourist attractions. The Priority Pedestrian Zones in Switzerland have been used to improve complicated intersections and create better public spaces. In 1996, the town of Burgdorf, Switzerland, created a pilot project in its town center to create a traffic zone for strolling. There are four basic principles of these zones:

1. Cars must travel no faster than 20 km/h (just over 12 mph).

2. Pedestrians have the priority.

3. Pedestrians may not interfere with car traffic.

4. Cars may only park in designated area. Cars are not restricted in these zones, but they must travel at slow speeds and they do not have a direct path of travel.

These streets are known as "zones where people come into contact" and the activity of both pedestrians and drivers creates a certain amount of chaos that forces everyone to look out for one another. These areas not only put pedestrians first, but also help create a lively and thriving business environment where people stroll, shop, and meet their friends.[40]

The city of St. Gallen, Switzerland, created an unusual shared-use zone, organizing a design competition to enliven its banking district. The jury for the design competition was intrigued with the idea of a "city lounge" proposed by architect Carlos Martinez and artist Pipilotti Rist. The designers played with the idea of inside versus outside, and the district was covered with a bright red "carpet" of rubber surfacing, similar to the material used in sports fields. The streets of the district allow cars, but the "carpeted" pavement feels more like a living room than a street—with modular street furniture, curves and twists for cars to navigate. As with all priority pedestrian zones, car parking is restricted except in designated areas. St. Gallen's example shows that, with imagination and good technical problem-solving, it is possible to use a wider range of materials in civic spaces than is generally recognized.

There are a few examples of shared-use streets in the United States. Asheville, North Carolina's Wall Street is an early example of a street that functions as a *woonerf*. It was a service alley until the 1980s, when it was redeveloped as part of the pedestrianization movement of the time. The facades were redone to be front doors instead of rear doors. Slow traffic mixes with pedestrians. Wall Street is physically well suited to be a shared-use street—it is narrow, curves gently, and has pavers on the road surface. The quality, scale, and mix of adjacent uses are critical to the street's success because they generate large amounts of foot traffic. Asheville's example demonstrates that shared-use streets can function well in American cities, as safe and very popular destinations.

Similarly, Pike Place is the shared-use street that runs through the middle of Seattle's Pike Place Market. Benefitting from historic brick pavers and mid-twentieth-century public market architecture, Pike Place is given over to pedestrians during most of the day and into the evening. It is not typically closed to vehicles—vendors unload and park in spaces adjacent to the market stalls during the business day, and through-traffic continues to traverse the area. However, the large crowds on foot and the pedestrian-scaled street design cause cars to move slowly enough that pedestrians feel comfortable crossing the street in the most direct path, or walking in the street if the sidewalk becomes too crowded. Market stalls spill out onto the sidewalk on the east side of the street, further extending the

---

[40]Pedestrian Mobility: Swiss Pedestrian Association from www.walkinginfo.org/videos/pubdetail.cfm?picid=6.

Figure 6-65 At Pike Place Market, cars move slowly through crowds of pedestrians.

low-level chaos into the right-of-way and signaling to drivers that this space has pedestrian priority. For festivals, Pike Place is closed to traffic, allowing access only to vendors and emergency vehicles (Figure 6-65).

The City of Vancouver, British Columbia, boasts another public market, Granville Island, which also has shared-use streets. In addition to the public market, this community has an arts college, marina, artists' studios, hotels, a community center, a theater, and numerous shops and restaurants. The main streets are used by slow-moving vehicles, and are comfortable for walking. The streets are also routinely shared by heavy, industrial vehicles that serve a working machine shop and a concrete plant onsite.

Shared-use streets that have evolved over time in mixed-use neighborhoods are typically in places where the land uses create so much activity and foot traffic that people naturally begin to encroach on the vehicle zone. These could be called natural shared-use streets. It is much more challenging to design and implement newly created shared-use streets (Figure 6-66).

Liability is a major obstacle for most jurisdictions. Even though there is an increasing body of evidence that under the right circumstances, shared-use streets are safe, the idea of blurring pedestrian and vehicle zones flies in the face of conventional engineering practice and decades of case law. How careless a driver must you design for? When you consider a road that carries 10,000 cars every day, even the worst 1 percent of drivers means 100 poorly driven cars.

Figure 6-66 This example of a shared-use street was created in right-of-way between retail uses and parking. It doubles as emergency access.

Figure 6-67 This shared-use street was built as part of Vancouver, B.C.'s 2010 Olympic Village.

Figure 6-68 Bicycles, cars, and pedestrians can mix in this downtown street.

Blurring the distinction between pedestrian and vehicle zones is also challenging in terms of accommodating those with limited vision. This has been the biggest source of complaint in the European shared-use streets. In the United States, the Americans with Disabilities Act (ADA) calls for tactile warning strips with a 60 percent visual contrast between pedestrian-only areas and zones where vehicles are allowed. The commonly seen white or canary yellow strips with "truncated domes" at curb ramps are a result of this provision in the ADA. This issue is discussed in more detail as part of the Terry Avenue Case study presented in Chapter 7 (Figures 6-67 and 6-68).

DESIGNING RESIDENTIAL *WOONERFS*

Allow Vehicles, But Design for Driver Alertness

Design to ensure low volumes and speeds. Allow places for vehicles to pass one another.

Involve the Community

Solicit community input in both concept design and the details. It is the community's space, and they need to play a major role in the decision to create a *woonerf* and the way it is designed, used, and maintained.

Consider Density

Residential *woonerfs* work best when there is a need for open space. Where residents have large homes and backyards, there will not likely be the desire or need to use the street as open space. Without people using the street as open space, drivers will not be on the lookout for pedestrians.

Design for Emergency Vehicles

Use minimum requirements and accommodate them discretely.

Blur the Distinction Between Drive Space and Pedestrian Space

Removing the distinction heightens awareness on the part of drivers, pedestrians, and cyclists. Much as this is a departure from recent design practice, the ambiguity is key to slowing speeds.

Design for Amenity

Residential front yards provide a buffer between home and street. In *woonerf* design, the buffer is not so important. A small planting zone can personalize homes. Landscaped areas or other hardscape features in the *woonerf* zone shorten drivers' sight lines, but must be designed so that drivers can see people using the road, especially children.

Consider Lighting

Keep it pedestrian-scaled. Use building-mounted light when possible to reduce poles. Illuminate any obstacles in the roadway (chicanes, landscape zones, etc.).

Create Safe Conditions in Play Zones

Protect areas for play by using bollards, raised landscaped areas, carefully sited seating, or hardscape elements. Fences can be provided for the youngest children. Consider noise from children's activities.

Parking

Make accommodations for needed spaces adjacent to the *woonerf* or offsite.

Designing for Accessibility

Incorporate accommodations for people with mobility and visual impairments.

Signage

Minimize signage in general, but make sure drivers know when they are entering a *woonerf* zone. Well-designed entry features can add identity and increase driver awareness and caution.

Intersections

Consider "squareabouts" (like roundabouts, but with orthogonal geometry) or raised tables that bring the street level up to sidewalk level.

Drainage

Use natural drainage whenever possible.

Maintenance

Set up a mechanism to ensure ongoing maintenance. This may be a homeowners group or community nonprofit.

The Broader Context

Consider the effect of creating a *woonerf* on the larger neighborhood context, so that traffic reductions on one street do not create unintended problems on adjacent streets.

FESTIVAL STREETS

Figure 6-69 *Designers: Gustafson Guthrie Nichol*

One way to address the changing landscape of streets is to use them differently during limited time periods. It is easy to imagine using a street differently in the middle of a Sunday than during commute hours, and some streets lend themselves well to temporary community-based events. These festival streets take many different forms—some are permanently closed to support ongoing festival market places, while others have design features that make it easy to close the street for events. Still others have no distinguishing features other than a location that provides a successful venue for community events, large or small (Figure 6-69).

When a street is designated a festival street, the placement of the street within the neighborhood and its function within the grid are key to making it successful. A street within a local business district may work well because it has lots of foot traffic. The main street in a town can be more challenging for either a permanent or temporary festival street, especially when local transit service would need to be rerouted or local parking restricted. Side streets tend to be a little quieter—a little off the beaten path and energized by an injection of local activity. Businesses that are on the back side of a main street may be allies in putting the event together because festival days will bring more potential customers strolling by their shop windows.

In addition to the location and the level of design features that support events, festival streets can benefit from a few clearly defined guidelines, such as the maximum number of people that can be safely handled, hours of operation, and requirements for emergency access. Organizers also need to know what it takes to have a festival at the location. Designating a street a festival street recognizes, for both the community and the local jurisdiction, that this section of street is a good candidate for a temporary, one-time or regularly occurring community-based event.

Streets with Festivals

Many communities simply close their streets off for a day to have a party. Temporary seating, such as the lawn chairs New York City first used at its inaugural summer streets festival on Broadway, can suffice to make places for people. Street vendors, parades, fun-runs, roving performers, people on foot and wheels of all varieties gather together—typically in the nice weather—to enjoy the day on a street that is closed.

For these streets, it is much less about the permanent design features and much more about the event, although some streets work better than others. Similar to festival streets, those pieces of the grid that already have good foot traffic and can add vibrancy to a local business district are a good choice. Complexity is added when the street chosen for a festival is a transit route—requiring cumbersome and often costly reroutes of existing transit lines. This can be accomplished, but can make the process more challenging (Figure 6-70).

Street festivals can be large, like Austin, Texas's Pecan Street Festival. Twenty-four blocks of 6th Street are filled with artists, musicians, jugglers, dancers, and food. The Pecan Festival has continued for 33 years, and brings together some 300,000 people per year.[41] Festivals such as these become important events that people look forward to long ahead of time. They bring boosts to the local economy, and most of all, are a chance for people to share a good time.

---

[41] www.oldpecanstreetfestival.com.

Figure 6-70 Farmers' markets can make use of streets that are temporarily closed.

Street festivals can also be small, such as a block party that requires nothing more than notice to the local agency, a few street closure signs, and a group of neighbors who enjoy meeting in the street for food and fun. Farmers' markets are another type of street festival that also requires advanced planning and coordination, but can become a much anticipated weekly celebration of local food and farmers on streets which are usually inhabited by cars.

Figure 6-71 Streets can be used for special events—even as temporary dining rooms.

Most jurisdictions have a number of requirements linked to temporary street closure. Permits are typically required for closing the street. For larger events, police officers may be needed for traffic control and fire access. Vending permits may be required, from city agencies including the Health Department. Some of these permits and requirements are free or very inexpensive, and some are much more costly and time consuming, requiring advanced planning and coordination among multiple parties (Figure 6-71).

Streets Designed for Festivals

Much less formal than the festival market place, the festival street is designed as a travelway for all modes that is also easily converted to a venue for community festivals or events. Examples of festival street design features include traffic-calming measures at the entrances to the streets, curbless designs that place the street plane at the same level as the sidewalk, street furniture, pedestrian-scaled street lighting, trees and landscaping, and artwork that attracts both pedestrians and slows traffic. Unique paving colors or textures that enliven the ground plane can create a street environment which looks more like it should host people on their feet, rather than in their cars, and can be another useful feature for festival streets. Other very useful elements to include in the design of a festival street are access to power and water hookups, trash and recycling bins, and signage that indicates the special function the street plays in the neighborhood.

A key difference between a festival market place and a festival street is that the street can be used as a travelway most of the time, but can easily be closed off for pedestrian-only use during events. Removable bollards are handy features to ensure that no traffic enters the street when events are occurring—especially if closure of the street is infrequent, or will cause traffic patterns in the area to change in ways that may be unexpected to a driver unaware of the festival.

Davis Street

In Portland, Oregon's Chinatown District, two festival streets were built as part of a larger improvement project for the Old Town/Chinatown neighborhood. The project was a partnership between Portland Development Commission (PDC), Portland Office of Transportation, and Old Town/Chinatown community. But like most well-executed streetscape projects, this is about much more than redesigning the right-of-way.

Figure 6-72 Davis Festival Street is built without curbs.

Old Town/Chinatown has had its problems over the years, trying to balance the need for economic revitalization with fears of gentrification. Asian family businesses had been leaving the neighborhood, relocating further from downtown, while the nearby Pearl District was booming with new upscale high-rise development. The Old Town/Chinatown community needed to be reinvigorated, but still keep its multicultural history and fine-grained scale.

The project design team, including Lloyd D. Lindsay, ASLA, Nevue Ngan Associates, and Suenn Ho, worked with a multiconstituency steering committee and input from the public. One of their findings was a need for open space in the area. Having the street double as open space for community festivals would be a way to invite people to celebrate in the neighborhood (Figure 6-72).

Figure 6-73 The landscaped planter at the entry to the Festival Street notes a shift in the type of street.

"Dragons, phoenix, the pagoda roof, that is not the essence of the place," says Suenn Ho, who was a designer and liaison for the project. "It's the people. If you don't have that, you don't have Chinatown."[42] She should know. A Hong Kong native, she studied the five largest Chinatowns in America with a National Endowment for the Arts grant. Ho was able to engage people who otherwise have cultural and language barriers. The goal is a diverse neighborhood, but if the Asian roots of the neighborhood are lost, it will be a loss for everyone.

42 Portland Tribune, Gang of one takes on Chinatown, Kristina Brenneman, updated October 30, 2009.

So the streetscape improvements aimed to create places to gather. The festival streets on NW Davis and NW Flander Street were an experiment for the City of Portland. They allow traffic, but can be easily closed for neighborhood and city-wide festivals. Gateway elements draw on the landscape in the nearby classical Chinese garden and mark the zone as different from a normal street.

The project opened in 2006 with the Under the Autumn Moon Festival. Over 35,000 people came to celebrate.[43] The Under the Autumn Moon Festival has become an important annual event. Ellen Vanderslice, AIA, of Portland's Office of Transportation, explains, "this place is about more than just the concrete and the granite and the beautiful design that we have. It's really about finding a way to create community."[44] (See Figure 6-73.)

Lander Street

Although Seattle has used traffic-calming elements on streets since the mid-1970s, the Lander Festival Street in the Beacon Hill neighborhood is the first intentionally designed festival street in the city. Lander Street is adjacent to the Sound Transit light rail station, and a segment of the street was closed while the station was under construction. The community realized that the closed segment of Lander was not really needed for cars. The result was a partnership between an engaged neighborhood group and a few city agencies. The festival street project was envisioned in 2007, with funding secured through the City's Neighborhood Street Fund community grant program in 2008 and construction completed in 2009.

South Lander Street between 16th Avenue South and 17th Avenue South serves as an extension of the light rail station plaza. It creates a transition from the low-density residential neighborhood at the east end of the street to the center of the neighborhood business district on the west end of the street. Although the festival street is only one block in length, it is ideally located for community festivals. Removable bollards are unlocked and moved to locations at the entry points to the street when vehicle access is restricted. Keys for the bollards are held by both City staff and the community group that programs the festivals and events.

The street improvements include:

- A new roadway with decorative pavers at the same level as the existing sidewalks to create a "curbless" street
- Bollards and other side treatments to delineate the roadway surface when the street is open to vehicles, and to provide a traffic-calming function as well as attractive features for pedestrians
- Pedestrian-scale lighting

[43] Streetfilms, Portland, Ore. Festival Streets, Clarence Eckerson, Jr., January 31, 2007.
[44] Old Town Chinatown Newsletter, Winter 2006.

Figure 6-74 Lander Festival Street is adjacent to the new light rail station and a community center.

A major issue in designing curbless streets is meeting the pavement contrast and texture requirements of the Americans with Disabilities Act. To denote the zone where vehicles are allowed, the color contrast is met by adding lampblack in the concrete to create a dark band along the edge of the travel way, along with a linear strip of tactile warning panels. This transition enables people with visual impairments to discern—either through the contrast in pavement color or through the textured strip—the pedestrian area from the vehicle area when the road is open to vehicles (Figure 6-74).

Drainage also requires a different approach in a curbless street. Designer Curtis LaPierre of OTAK used a ribbon of low-slope concrete channels to convey water. The de-

Figure 6-75 Because it is curbless, Lander Street's design needed to take care in addressing drainage and separation of pedestrians and the drive zone.

sign team was eager to include more sustainable elements to reduce runoff, but the tight budget for construction limited their options.

The creation of the festival street has elicited new ideas from the community about how to use it. Beacon Rocks is now hosting summer concerts. "We are excited about our new community meeting place, Lander Festival Street," reads their website. "Among the seemingly endless possible uses, Beacon Hill Music wants neighborhood musicians to perform there for you, their neighbors."[45] (See Figure 6-75.)

The Festival Market Place

On a larger scale, many cities have festival market places that serve as a destination for residents and tourists alike—attracting millions of visitors annually. Many of these festival market places were developed in the 1970s and 1980s as part of efforts to revitalize downtown districts, and have retained their popularity over the decades since. Often renovated historic markets or meeting places, some of the best known large examples include Boston's Faneuil Hall and Quincy Market, Baltimore's Inner Harbor, New York City's South Street Seaport and Pier 17, San Francisco's Fisherman's Wharf, and Chicago's Navy Pier.

Although each one of these differs in size, scale, character, and function, they are similar in that each includes:

- Historic centers, a marketplace, or waterfront
- Community-driven efforts to save and restore the buildings and the functions
- Redevelopment efforts that have added museums, housing, offices, shops and/or galleries to support the vibrancy of the area
- Historic character of the streets and the buildings
- Pedestrian zones or pedestrian streets with limited vehicle access
- Conscious effort to unify design character through building and paving materials, plantings and lighting fixture styles, signage, and street furniture
- Management organizations, either a public development authority or other private entity

Festival market places typically have enticing streets for walking. The pleasant atmosphere and dense mix of retail uses, restaurants, and bars attract tourists and locals. They often take advantage of an asset, such as the waterfront, which people may otherwise not be able to enjoy.

They are in no way temporary, but are often the heart of neighborhoods that have grown up around them. For example, Seattle's Pike Place Market hosts a farm and craft market with rotating and per-

[45] www.rockitspace.org/beacon-rocks.html.

Figure 6-76 Pike Place allows vehicles, but with so many people, the street also becomes a pedestrian zone.

manent vendors, restaurants, and shops, both low-income and high-end market-rate housing, a senior center and community health clinic, and a child care center, as well as office buildings. This intense mix of land uses creates a neighborhood around Pike Place—the street in the center of it all—that is active night and day. The street life is bustling and although Pike Place does not typically restrict vehicle access, any driver knows that if you travel along Pike Place in a car, you will be traveling at the pace of someone walking, as pedestrians clearly rule the space. Common to most festival market places, street artists have a healthy trade, and unexpected performances and happenings are delightfully common (Figure 6-76).

Ciclovías

Closing streets for bicycle riding is a trend that has been growing in cities across the world. Begun in Bogotá, Colombia, in 1976, Ciclovía—which means "bike path" in Spanish, is a weekly event that draws more than 1.5 million people to walk, bike, skate, and enjoy more than 70 miles of streets opened to people—and closed to automobile traffic. Nearly 20 percent of this City's population turns out every Sunday and holiday to participate in the 7 a.m. to 2 p.m. closures, which include unparalleled free recreation and social opportunities, including dance and yoga lessons in the City's streets and local parks. Bogotá has been careful in expanding their Sunday event, choosing routes that connect neighborhoods.[46]

The ciclovía movement also has a presence in North America dating back over 25 years. Among the oldest, started in 1983, is Wayne County, Michigan's "Saturday in the Park," in which a six-mile stretch of the Edward Hines Parkway is closed to motorized traffic every Saturday from May through September. By the late 2000s, the concept had spread to a number of U.S. cities including Cleveland, Ohio; Philadelphia, Pennsylvania; New York City, New York; and Portland, Oregon. Today, ciclovía-style events take place in over 30 communities around the United States and Canada (Figure 6-77).

Major Events as Opportunities

Festivals are ideal testing grounds for what is possible in the street. Cape Town, South Africa's Fan Walk is a success story that used a major event to create a shift in thinking about walking in their Central City. In 2004, South Africa was selected as the host country for soccer's 2010 World Cup, which brings together the best soccer teams and the rapt attention of hundreds of millions of fans from nations around the world once every four years. Planning began for infrastructure improvements to accommodate hundreds of thousands of visitors. One of these improvements, the Host City Cape Town Fan

[46] www.atlantastreetsalive.com/about/the-ciclovia-movement/.

Figure 6-77 Ciclovía in Mexico City. *Photography by atelierjones*

Figure 6-78 Fan Walk in Cape Town, South Africa. *Photograph by Damien du Toit*

Walk, created a signature pedestrian corridor along the mile and a half route from the train station to the stadium.

Cape Town is a car-oriented city. But the crowds coming for the World Cup would need to have another way of getting to the stadium. The City of Cape Town and the nonprofit Cape Town Partnership drew on the route that the annual New Year's Ministrel Carnival took to Green Point Stadium. The idea of a major pedestrian route for World Cup soccer fans became a centerpiece of an integrated transportation system for Cape Town.

The route begins at Exchange Place, across from the train station, and moves through historic St. George's Mall, which has been a pedestrian-only street since 1992. It follows Waterkant Street, crosses a major Central City arterial with a new pedestrian bridge leading to St. Andrew's Square. At the end of the route, a pedestrian underpass connects to the new stadium. The length of the route was improved, with new pedestrian-priority areas, cycle lanes, lighting, outdoor furniture, trees, and signage.

The Fan Walk had a precedent in Berlin's successful "Fan-Mile" for the 2006 World Cup. Cape Town's Fan Walk surprised organizers by exceeding even the vast crowds of Berlin's Fan Mile, filling Cape Town's Fan Walk with many times the number of people expected. At its peak, over 150,000 people filled the route. This number was roughly ten times the amount that planners originally expected. The Fan Walk had become much more than an exciting part of the experience of moving to the stadium. It became a destination in itself (Figure 6-78).

Entertainment and vending along the route were part of its success. Organizers auditioned new and emerging artists to perform along the route, and a wide variety of performers enlivened Fan Walk—jazz bands, rappers, opera singers, poets, minstrels, drummers, and dancers. Vending kiosks added to the options for food along the route. Street sculptures, murals, flags, and artistic lighting enlivened the route.

Fan Walk was a Cape Town City initiative managed by the nonprofit Cape Town Partnership. A great deal of thought, effort, and collaboration was required to make the World Cup a success, and to create a legacy of projects that will make a better city. The details of the creation and management of the Fan Walk were documented by the Cape Town Partnership, and are available on their website.[47]

A primary goal of the Cape Town Partnership was not only physical changes, but to activate the citizenry. According to the organization's summary of the outcome of Fan Walk, "above all else, the Fan Walk has created an important venue for social cohesion."[48] Fan Walk drew people in and created a place for celebration. It leaves behind a permanent legacy of the new pedestrian and bicycle improvements, landscape, and art. There is another equally important legacy of cooperation and the confidence of well-earned successes.

One of the interesting aspects to festival streets is that they can test the suitability of a street as a pedestrian place. Cape Town not only proved that the Central City could attract and accommodate many thousands of people, but, as the Fan Walk has been used for events ever since, that it could achieve a lasting legacy to the City. A lesson to take away from the Fan Walk is that it provided a real alternative to driving. It was easier than driving and much more fun. That works.

---

[47] See http://www.capetownpartnership.co.za/fan-walk-central-city-2010/#more-5478.

[48] Host City Cape Town Fan Walk, Executive Summary of the Report to the City of Cape Town & the Cape Town Partnership, September 2010, Carola Koblitz, 2010 Project Coordinator, Cape Town Partnership & Project Manager, Host City Cape Town Fan Walk.

Chapter 7
CASE STUDIES

EVERY GREAT PLACE HAS A STORY TO TELL. These case studies illustrate opportunities that people have recognized for using streets in creative ways. In each case study, there was an opportunity. Sometimes these opportunities come out of a particular need, or a set of needs and desires that can be addressed by changes in policies and physical changes in the right-of-way. Solutions are best when they can solve multiple goals.

In each situation, someone took action. Property owners, citizens, elected officials, or city staff can be instigators for better places. Projects in the public realm quickly become complex, and instigators must find support from a broad range of people. No matter where the instigation comes from, these actions required public outreach, efforts on the part of agency staff from multiple departments, enthusiasm from elected officials, and the enthusiasm of property owners. These projects require leadership and collaboration, tenacity, and patience. More and more of these kinds of projects are happening in a variety of places and contexts, and each innovative project eases the way for those that follow (Figure 7-1).

Figure 7-1

MINT PLAZA

Figure 7-2 Mint Plaza's flexible seating accommodates events and quieter times. © *CMG Landscape Architecture*

> **Our goal is to bring in a lot of people— to have a true public life there.**
> —*Michael Yarne, The Martin Building Company*

Mint Plaza transformed an alley near the heart of San Francisco's downtown into an asset for both local residents and the many people of all backgrounds who mix in the district. The design of Mint Plaza pushed the envelope for sustainable design practices with local agencies, and is now a model for handling stormwater in urban environments where hardscape surfaces predominate (Figure 7-2).

Neighborhood

San Francisco's Mid-Market District has seen highs and lows over the years. The commercial core, active Hallidie Plaza and the cable car turn-around at Powell Street lie on the northwest side of Market Street. The Civic Center is nearby and Yerba Buena lies just to the southeast of Market. But despite its proximity to these citywide assets, Mid-Market has languished, with vacant lots and buildings, seedy streets, and a variety of social problems (Figure 7-3).

The Old U.S. Mint block, at 5th Street and Mission, is at the healthiest edge of Mid-Market, at a confluence of people from all walks of life. The Westfield San Francisco Centre, on the other side of 5th Street facing Market, boasts the country's second-largest Nordstrom and some 200 other shops. To the south and southwest, according to Livable Cities Executive Director Tom Radulovitch, are the "social services that no one really wants in their neighborhood, but that are all essential things for the city."[1] For some, this confluence is what makes cities great, edgy, and interesting.

[1] "What Will It Take to Save Mid-Market?", San Francisco Appeal, by Susie Cagle, March 10, 2010; accessed at http://sfappeal.com/news/2010/03/what-will-it-take-to-save-mid-market.php.

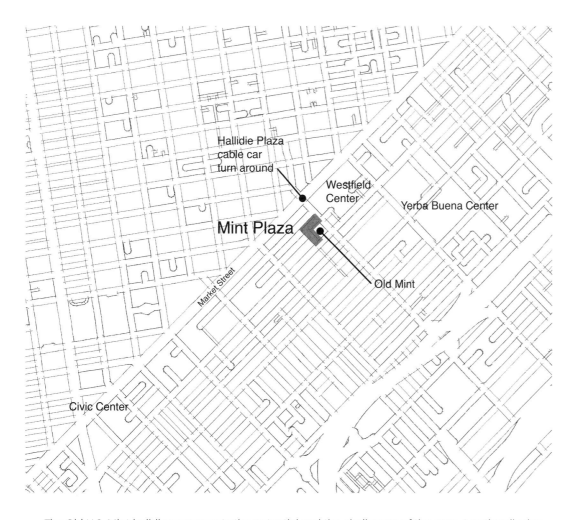

Figure 7-3 Mint Plaza Context.

The Old U.S. Mint building represents the potential and the challenges of the area. A nationally designated landmark with a proud history, it is a unique and underutilized asset. The U.S. Department of the Treasury vacated the building in 1994, and ownership was transferred to the City of San Francisco in 2002. It awaits transformation into a mixed-use cultural center spearheaded by the San Francisco Museum and Historical Society.

The geometry of the street system is an issue in revitalizing the neighborhood. Market Street separates the grids to the north and south, and the blocks on the south side are large—825 feet by 550 feet. These super-sized blocks have a negative impact on both vehicle and pedestrian connectivity. Traffic is concentrated on the streets, and pedestrians walk long distances between intersections. The neighborhood does have some alleys, with pieces of Jessie Street and Stevenson Street threading through the blocks.

Vision

Urban advocates had long seen the potential for a better public realm in the neighborhood. The area around the Old U.S. Mint building has been targeted for improvements in various plans and initiatives. The visions for Mid-Market included a more vibrant mix of land uses, with added housing, and a better pedestrian environment—all without displacing the people who live and work in the vicinity.

One step towards this vision happened in the late 1990s when the Martin Building Company began buying property in the neighborhood. The Martin Building Company specializes in development that incorporates historic preservation. The four buildings that they call the Mint Collection are clustered along the north side of the portion of Jessie Street that is now Mint Plaza. These buildings each have stories of their own. The Hales Warehouse building dates from 1926, and once held the offices and warehouse for one of San Francisco's early department stores. The Station House #1 was the firehouse for the San Francisco Fire Department, and the Haas Candy Factory was built the year after the Great Fire of 1906. The four buildings have been developed with 95 residential and live-work units.

The Mint Plaza project closed 290 feet of Jesse Street to traffic and created a new pedestrian plaza. Surrounded by historic buildings on three sides, the plaza is a needed "eddy" of pedestrian space in the midst of the City. The vision includes a mix of uses—the new housing in the renovated buildings, restaurants to activate the edges, pushcarts and weekly farmers' markets, and events with art and music. The vision brought together a mix of people, including residents from varied economic means. The Plaza would be a mix of the best of historic architecture and cutting-edge new design (Figures 7-4 and 7-5).

Process

Part of the process involved setting up the financing arrangements that allowed the funding of the design and construction of the project. The Martin Building Company led that effort, working with the City to create an arrangement that would allow the ownership of the underlying street to remain with the City, but allow the project to be constructed and maintained by a private entity.

The design process was a collaboration between the owner, the design team, and government. The design for the stormwater system required particular coordination, because standards for this type of development did not exist. The design team worked closely with the San Francisco Public Utilities Commission to create storm criteria design and performance standards.

Figure 7-4 Mint Plaza before the project. ©*CMG Landscape Architecture*

Figure 7-5 Mint Plaza as a pedestrian place. *Courtesy of the Friends of Mint Plaza*

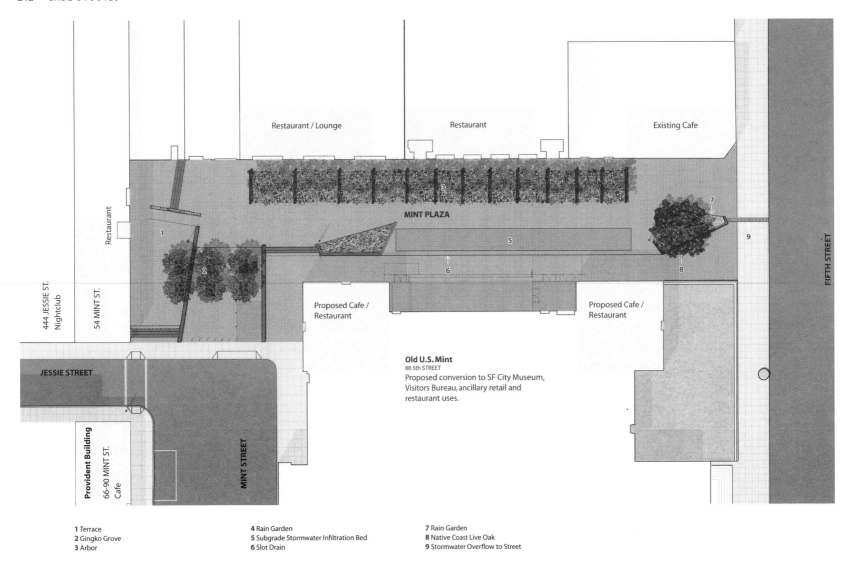

Figure 7-6 Mint Plaza site plan. ©*CMG Landscape Architecture*

Labels within the figure:

Restaurant / Lounge
Restaurant
Existing Cafe

444 JESSIE ST. Nightclub
54 MINT ST.
Restaurant

MINT PLAZA

Proposed Cafe / Restaurant

Proposed Cafe / Restaurant

Old U.S. Mint
88 5th STREET
Proposed conversion to SF City Museum,
Visitors Bureau, ancillary retail and
restaurant uses.

JESSIE STREET

Provident Building
66-90 MINT ST.
Cafe

MINT STREET

FIFTH STREET

1 Terrace
2 Gingko Grove
3 Arbor

4 Rain Garden
5 Subgrade Stormwater Infiltration Bed
6 Slot Drain

7 Rain Garden
8 Native Coast Live Oak
9 Stormwater Overflow to Street

Public input was an important part of the design process. The design team listened to community ideas, presented alternatives, and refined the design to take community needs into account. The enthusiasm for the project ran through the design team, the regulators, the owners, and the community.

The street closure was approved by the Board of Supervisors and the Mayor in April of 2007. While some valet parking routes were eliminated, removing the cars had little impact on mobility. There is a remnant of Jessie Street that still provides service access.

Design Features

Conger Moss Guillard (CMG) Landscape Architects and Sherwood Design, Civil Engineers, designed the Plaza. "Our primary design agenda was simplicity and flexibility," says Willet Moss of CMG. "And we were very committed to the stormwater component of the project." The width of the space, 54 feet, is much wider than a typical alley, and allows good access to sun. With activities along the edge and an open central space, the Plaza functions well for daily use and for a variety of special events.

The 18,000-square-foot Plaza has aggregate stone pavers and a 14-foot-tall steel trellis, planted with flowering trumpet vines, that runs along the north edge. A rain garden near 5th Street is planted with a signature tree that invites passersby into the Plaza. The western side of the Plaza terminates with a grove of trees visible from Mint Street. The open interior of Mint Plaza has bright-orange movable chairs available during daylight hours (Figure 7-6).

Environmentally responsible design was a high priority for the designers. The Plaza surface needed to manage a 3-foot grade change across the site, meet the levels of doorways at the edges, and direct surface water. Stormwater from the Plaza moves to one of two rain gardens or a slot drain that conveys water into an infiltration basin below the surface. The infiltration chamber is filled with drain rock and wrapped with geotextile filter fabric. The chamber was located to avoid digging up old utilities and remnants of old building footprints. A 100-year event backup chamber is integrated into the design of the seating bench along the rain garden (Figure 7-7).

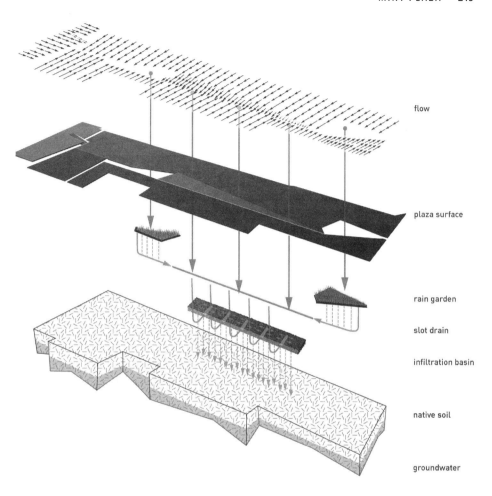

flow

plaza surface

rain garden

slot drain

infiltration basin

native soil

groundwater

Figure 7-7 Mint Plaza stormwater diagram. ©*CMG Landscape Architecture*

"We've calculated and observed that we can infiltrate as much as half a million gallons of storm-water back into the groundwater right underneath our feet, which is remarkable for a project that historically had zero infiltration—there wasn't a tree on the street," explains Bry Sarte of CMG Landscape Architects. This low-tech solution is applicable to other urban places that require large paved areas.

The project was awarded the 2010 National Award for Smart Growth Achievement by the U.S. Environmental Protection Agency, and a merit award from the Northern California Chapter of the American Society of Landscape Architects.

Funding and Management

The Martin Building Company formed a Community Facilities District (CFD), an entity allowed by California's Mello-Roos Act. The CFD levies a special tax on properties in the district to provide the initial funds needed to design and build projects with a specific benefit to the district. The City retained ownership of the street itself, which remains fully open to the public at all hours.

The developer established the Friends of Mint Plaza, a nonprofit organization that is responsible for the costs of maintaining the Plaza. The nonprofit works to provide programs in the Plaza, and is required to indemnify the City for any claims regarding the management of the space. Friends of Mint Plaza can generate revenue for maintenance and programming by renting portions of the space for events, or charging user fees.

The goals set by Friends of Mint Plaza for managing the space are worth relating in full, because the intent of the space is clearly reflected in those management goals:

- "Ensure that the Plaza becomes a treasured space, accessible to all and preserved for future generations of San Franciscans.

- Maintain the Plaza in a clean and orderly fashion that makes it a safe and inviting place for people of all ages and incomes to enjoy at all hours of the day.

- Activate the Plaza area through thoughtful and creative programming, including art exhibitions, live music and theater."[2]

The project's construction cost a totaled $3.5 million. The investment is hopefully a down payment on the bright future of the Mint Plaza neighborhood.

In the broader neighborhood, there is a Community Benefits District in place, funded by property assessments, that provides community guides, cleaning, and programming. The people involved in Mint Plaza play a role in the Central Market CBD and coordinate programming efforts with the Friends of Mint Plaza.

---

[2] Mint Plaza website, Friends of Mint Plaza Mission Statement, accessed at http://www.mintplazasf.org/mission_statement.php.

Lessons Learned

Making a project like Mint Plaza happen requires a catalyst, a funding mechanism, and the flexibility to permit innovative solutions.

- The enthusiasm of the Martin Building Company gave the project momentum. They have the long-term vision of contributing to urban, mixed-use living, refurbishing old buildings for new housing. Their efforts to create an amenity like Mint Plaza benefit not only their properties, but the larger neighborhood.

- Creating a set of mutually agreed-upon goals at the outset of the project helps guide projects through the myriad decisions that follow. These goals need to be at a high enough level to influence the detailed decision-making process, and broad enough to reflect the agendas of the variety of stakeholders in the project. They set the tone for a collaborative process.

- The funding mechanisms that allowed the project to be built were complex, but the mechanisms existed through state legislation that allowed private entities to take the lead on creating community benefits. Some states have more tools for creative financing than others. The right legislation can have a huge impact on the ability of both the private and public sector to make great cities.

Figure 7-8 Mint Plaza's farmers' market. ©*CMG Landscape Architecture, Photographer: Sharon Risedorph*

- Great projects need support from public agencies, because innovation almost always breaks some rules. From a design standpoint, the project broke ground on regulations for sustainable stormwater treatment. The collaborative mindset of the team members and regulators made this nonstandard design approach feasible. Determining storm design and other performance criteria by working directly with agency staff helped make Mint Plaza a model for other urban projects.

Mint Plaza has been a catalyst for changes to the immediate neighborhood and as a model for other spaces in the City. Drew Norton, at Sherwood Design, says that they are now working on another pedestrian plaza in a public street. The new project, Davis Court, benefits from the work done with regulators at Mint Plaza (Figure 7-8).

DESIGNER COMMENTS

"Mint Plaza is in the heart of downtown, in a confluence between Nordstrom and Skid Road. The moveable chairs are part of the social equity. You don't need to buy a cup of coffee to be able to sit there."

— *Willet Moss, CMG Landscape Architecture*

"We were fortunate to have great subsurface soils to work with. Much of the soil nearby is fill from after the [1906] earthquake, but the sandy soil here drains well."

—*Drew Norton, Sherwood Design, civil engineers*

"We point to it as an example and to show that creative stormwater design is highly compatible with urban design in areas that are hardscaped and dense. It really proves in concept what we're trying to make happen throughout the rest of the City."

—*Rosey Jencks, SF Public Utilities Commission*

NORD ALLEY

> **When a space is activated by people, it is transformed.**
> —*Todd Vogel*

The revitalization of Nord Alley in Seattle's Pioneer Square exemplifies the rewards of good ideas, bringing communities together, and tenacity. The idea is simple. Use the neglected spaces in the alleys as a resource. Work with the neighbors one step at a time to see what can be done, and keep leveraging the successes, the imagination, and the resources. As the alley transforms, relationships build, traditions are created, and others are inspired (Figure 7-9).

Neighborhood

Pioneer Square is Seattle's oldest neighborhood. Founding father Henry Yesler chose this tide flat between Elliott Bay and the wooded slopes to the east as the site for his lumber mill in 1852. The site was, and remains, one of the few flat spots in downtown Seattle.

The wooden buildings of early Seattle burned to the ground in the Great Seattle Fire of 1889, and a new neighborhood of brick and stone grew in its place. Planners chose to raise the level of the ground in the new fire-resistant neighborhood in order to solve drainage and plumbing issues, and the City regraded the adjacent bluffs to create a more even grade from east to west. The new buildings had entries at the existing low grade, and planned for grander entries at the new street level. This resulted in the unusual condition of an entire underground level still in place that was once at grade.

The heyday of Pioneer Square came in the 1890s when it became the center for outfitting adventurers heading to Alaska during the Klondike Gold Rush. As Seattle grew, downtown expanded to the north, and the area south of Pioneer Square was regraded and filled for the industrial uses connected to the port and the railroad. Pioneer Square slid into decline until the 1960s, when the demolition of some of the fine historic architecture mobilized preservationists. A 30-acre historic district protects the architectural legacy, but the economic condition of Pioneer Square has remained a challenge.

The stadium district lies just to the south of Pioneer Square, where a baseball stadium opened in 1999. A professional football and soccer stadium followed in 2002. These facilities bring tens of thousands of people to Pioneer Square in brief waves on game days. Sports fans patronize local bars and restaurants.

Figure 7-9 Nord Alley has become a community resource.

Figure 7-10 Nord Alley context.

Pioneer Square is home to a mix of art galleries, offices, and shops drawn by the neighborhood's character and relatively low rents. The missing piece for Pioneer Square has been housing (Figure 7-10).

Most blocks in Pioneer Square have alleys. The 16-foot-wide alleys are lined with turn-of-the-century brick buildings, and have been used for parking entries, exit doors, and dumpsters. With Occidental Park and the surrounding streets short of activities on most days, no one looked to the alleys for additional active space.

Vision

Todd Vogel, head of the International Sustainability Institute (ISI), bought two floors of the Nord Building in 2007. In addition to his own office space, he rented out space to other tenants, including nonprofits like pedestrian advocates Feet First. The adjacent alley was a derelict but intriguing space outside the Nord Building's back door. The new occupants began treating the alley with respect, cleaning and opening up windows, and putting up better doors. "When I moved into my building, I found a crack pipe the first day," says Todd. "But we started to open up the building, removing the boards from the windows. Simple things—cleaning things up. We bought plants for $10, a table and chair for $26. And right away, other people started respecting the space." (See Figure 7-11.)

The next step was to let a friend's band play in the alley, almost as a lark. But people came. The alley parties have become a highlight of Pioneer Square's First Thursday art walks. Performers of all kinds are draws for hundreds of people coming to the alley.

The alley got its name without much thought. They needed to call it something, and so the alley behind the Nord Building became Nord Alley. But in retrospect, Todd wishes that it could have been part of a larger process that would have helped build the community. But the name stuck, and a computer-savvy resident of the alley has made sure that Nord Alley is located on Google Maps. With several alleys in Pioneer Square interested in following the lead of Nord Alley, there are naming and community building possibilities for other alleys.

The International Sustainability Institute partnered with the City of Seattle, the Scan|Design Foundation, and the University of Washington's Green Futures Lab to bring Gehl Architects to Seattle to study how to make the City more walkable and bikeable. Gehl Architects, from Copenhagen, is one of the most

highly regarded urban design firms in the world. Working with architects from Gehl's office, dozens of University of Washington students inventoried Pioneer Square, documenting street furniture and trees, and counting pedestrians. The result is a valuable in-depth study of pedestrian patterns in the downtown area. A number of the ideas have been embedded in Seattle's Pedestrian Master Plan. The Gehl study spoke specifically to the potential of the alleys to be "the green lungs" of the City (Figure 7-12).

Figure 7-11 Simply adding a chair and table began to shift attitudes about thet alley.

Figure 7-12 The alley is adjacent to Occidental Park.

Clearing the Way for Activities

The dumpsters that for many years lined the alleys of Pioneer Square were major obstacles to healthy activities. People used them as screens, evident by the smell of urine and drug paraphernalia collected behind them. Removing the dumpsters was key to reusing the alley. This need led to the creation of the Clear Alley Program, largely developed by CleanScapes—a private waste removal company committed to sustainability.

Figure 7-13 Chris Ezzell's Waste Not sculpture hanging over the alley. *Photo courtesy of ISI, International Sustainability Institute*

Chris Martin, a former resident of Pioneer Square, founded CleanScapes in 1997 with the goal of cleaning up the alleys to make a better neighborhood. "Seattle has a perfect example of what an alley can be," he said, referring to Post Alley. Martin started with 5 pickup trucks and 25 employees, half of whom were once homeless.[3]

The City didn't originally want to remove the dumpsters. CleanScapes lobbied the City Council on the merits of removing the dumpsters, and a pilot program was developed to test the idea. Instead of using dumpsters, refuse is sorted into three bags—waste, recycle, and food waste. The bags are picked up daily, and in some locations, up to three times per day. Gary Johnson, of the Department of Planning and Development, believes that the pay-per-bag program makes you think differently about waste and encourages recycling. People are more thoughtful about filling up a bag they will have to pay for. With dumpsters, you pay the same amount no matter how much waste is inside.

Clean alleys have set the stage for new uses. Nord Alley has taken the most advantage of the opportunity, but other blocks and neighborhoods are starting to generate ideas and organize events.

Art as an Activator

One of the first changes to come to the newly clean alleys was to install art. Architect Chris Ezzell became the first to turn Nord Alley into a public art gallery. His two hanging sculptures were created out of recycled plastic bottles. Some 2,500 empty one-liter bottles hung over the alley spelling out the words "Waste Not" (Figure 7-13). A smaller sculpture hung near the entry at South Main Street to indicate that something different was happening in the alley.

The installation is an example of overcoming regulatory hurdles with creativity. Attachments to the historic facades, even on the alley side, required approval from the historic preservation board. The board denied permission to install the piece on the facade, so Ezzell created a frame out of metal

---

[3] "Cleanliness is right up our alley: Pilot program tries to reclaim Pioneer Square," *Seattle Times,* by Sarah Anne Wright, December 2, 2002.

rebar, tied into the old shutter hooks at the windows, and hoisted the piece overhead with climbing ropes.

The Alley Art Project builds on the momentum of the events held in the alley by installing permanent infrastructure for displaying art. Neighboring design firm Jones & Jones donated the design work for seven display boards on the alley walls. Glasshouse Studio, whose store adjoins the alley, donated more than $25,000 worth of glass globes installed well above reach. Students at the Pratt Fine Arts Center fabricated the steel panels and the brackets, carefully locating attachments to minimize new penetrations in the brick. Artwork is now rotating on the display boards, accompanied by opening celebrations (Figure 7-14).

Collecting Ideas and Making Them Happen

The International Sustainability Institute gathered a group of people interested in reclaiming the alleys to brainstorm ways of broadening support and generating ideas for how to make alleys that contributed to the walkability, activation, and sustainability of Pioneer Square. The result of the brainstorm was a competition, "How Green Is My Alley?" The long list of cosponsors is an indicator of the breadth of community buy-in on the idea: ISI, the City of Seattle, the Pioneer Square Community Association, the local chapter of the AIA, the People for Puget Sound, the Downtown Seattle Association, and Feet First.

The announcement of the winners was, in the new tradition of Nord Alley, held as a party. All the entries were on display, tables of food set out, and live jazz played. Ideas included creative ways of infiltrating stormwater, recycling containment, micro-commerce, micro-agriculture, and enterprise zones. Some ideas drew on new technologies such as smart phone applications, and energy monitoring systems. One envisioned trees that attract hummingbirds, and another proposed devices to capture light. A winning entry suggested that the alley host showings of the 2010 soccer World Cup. ISI decided to make that happen.

World Cup Alley was imagined as a way to attract people to Pioneer Square who don't typically come to the neighborhood, and bring them together to celebrate an international event that only happens once every four years. Enough funding was cobbled together to get a screen, a projector, seating, and help in publicizing the events. The time difference between Seattle and South Africa meant that many of the matches would be held at odd hours, or during the middle of the day when the sun would be over the alley. For $9 per day, ISI rented a truck, and put the 100-inch screen in the back. They put out portable seating and coffee, and hundreds of people came to watch. The event

Figure 7-14 Art of all kinds has found its way into the alley.

Figure 7-15 Hundreds of people came to the alley to watch soccer's World Cup. *Photographer: Jordan Lewis; Photo courtesy of ISI, International Sustainability Institute*

brought in families with young soccer fans who couldn't watch in the bars. Whole soccer teams came in uniform. Fans from the various countries in the matches found their way to the alley. People who live on the streets joined the crowd for the games. People from the nearby offices and people on jury duty brought lunch and watched over the five weeks of the World Cup (Figure 7-15).

> Seattle is not the USA's No. 1 soccer city without reason. Only in Seattle could soccer be used to help clean up alleys.
>
> —Soccer America Daily, *May 26, 2010*

The community of people interested in reusing the alleys has grown and prospered. Two interns at the Green Futures Lab collected data for 300 alleys in Seattle, and put out the Seattle Integrated Alley Handbook. Young architect Daniel Toole won a traveling fellowship to study alleys around the world, sharing his stories on his blog and through exhibitions.

Process

Activating the alley is really the same process as strengthening a community. The people who live and work in the block have new relationships that have formed in terms of the interest in the alley. A broader community has formed, including City staff, nonprofit organizations, university staff and students, local property owners, businesses, designers, and community activists. This wide range of people has been energized by the potential of creating and expanding uses in the alleys and other public spaces. It's about much more than the alley itself.

On the functional side, the activities in the alley require permitting from the City. Even though the City is supportive of activating the alley, the paperwork has to be done for temporary closures. Physical changes, like bolting into existing walls, require review and approval from the historic review board.

Todd describes the process for events: "The City's been great. And yes, there is a permitting hassle. We sit down, and they say you'll need this permit and this permit and this permit. They don't cut me any breaks, but now we just tick off the boxes." The City has made the alley closure process simpler and less expensive by creating a new designation of a "Festival Alley." This annual permit allows multiple events over the year without additional fees and process. The City still needs to be notified, but because creating events is easier and more affordable, there may be an increase in events throughout Pioneer Square and other neighborhoods with alleys in the future.

Design Features

The alley is 16 feet wide and 240 feet long, lined by historic brick facades. Nord Alley is just across the street from Occidental Park, the heart of the Pioneer Square neighborhood. But it is part of a series of open spaces including alleys, pedestrian streets, and park space. Just east of the alley is Occidental Mall, a street that was turned into a pedestrian connection in 1972. The heart of the neighborhood has an unusual amount of pedestrian spaces and low-volume, low-speed traffic. Combined with the historic architectural fabric, Pioneer Square has many design assets. The shortage of residents has been a challenge for many years in terms of long-term health of the neighborhood spaces.

Funding

The activities in the alleys have been funded by cobbling together a series of small amounts of money from grants, donors, and numerous volunteers. The funding and volunteer hours from diverse residents, professionals, and organizations has helped foster a community dedicated to success for the neighborhood and its alleys.

Lessons Learned

■ Spaces are full of clues that affect behavior. Boarded-up windows and trash were part of a cycle of neglect and criminal activities. For Pioneer Square, giving clues that the alleys are used and cared for was enough to turn the cycle from negative to positive.

■ "Do some small moves, and hope that they have traction," advises Todd. "What you need are little acupuncture points along the street that bring people in. The space looks totally different when it's full of people."

■ Simple moves can be leveraged, sparking changes in nearby spaces, other neighborhoods, and other cities. The small donations and volunteer efforts build relationships within the neighborhood and beyond. It takes recognition of the opportunities and a great deal of tenacity.

CENTRAL ANNAPOLIS ROAD

> **How can we serve the transportation function, but have the community as the centerpiece rather than the road?**

As cities sprawled outward from historic centers, roads brought large volumes of traffic through once-quiet communities. How can major through-routes, necessary for regional travel, have less impact on the communities they run through? Solutions to this common condition could help to heal divisions within urban neighborhoods, suburban districts, and historic Main Street communities. Central Annapolis Road, in Prince George's County, Maryland, is an example of the challenges of taming arterials that run through neighborhoods (Figure 7-16).

Figure 7-16 Sketch of potential future transit-oriented development. *The Maryland-National Capitol Park and Planning Commission, Prince George's County Planning Department*

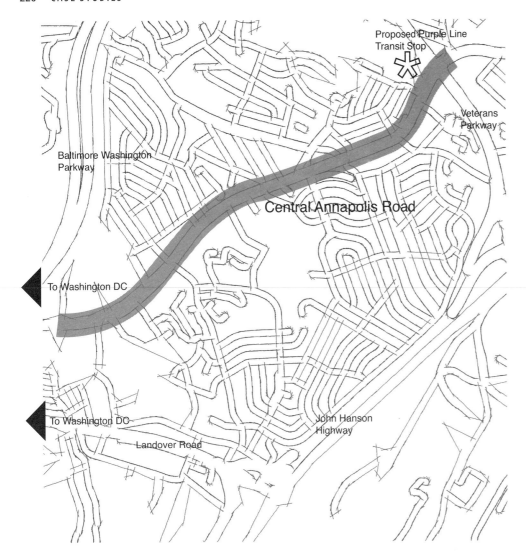

Figure 7-17 Central Annapolis Road context.

Context

Annapolis Road, on the outskirts of Washington, D.C., has received a great deal of thought from the State of Maryland and Prince George's County. Also known as Maryland State Route 450, Annapolis Road runs from the outskirts of the nation's capital east through Prince George's County for 30 miles to Annapolis. The impetus to reconsider the corridor came from the County, who was planning for future growth based on the principle that transportation and land use are tied together and must be well integrated to achieve County goals.

In some ways, Central Annapolis Road is a quintessential American road. A four-lane highway that people depend on for commutes and errands, it runs through shopping centers and residential zones. It is intended to connect places, not to divide neighborhoods.

The Annapolis Road Sector Plan aims to transform part of a major regional highway into a safe, attractive, environmentally sustainable neighborhood boulevard, while retaining its arterial functionality. Through a joint effort between the State Highways Department (SHA) and Maryland National Parks and Planning Commission (M-NCPPC), constructive input from traffic engineers informed the urban design recommendations at the outset (Figure 7-17).

Neighborhood

The portion of the route being studied as a Sector Plan comprises almost two miles between Veterans' Parkway (Maryland 410) and the Baltimore-Washington Parkway (Maryland 295). The segment begins on the west end at the interchange of Central Annapolis Road and Baltimore-Washington Parkway.

Capital Plaza Mall was built in the early 1960s near the intersection of Veterans' Parkway and the Baltimore-

Washington Parkway, taking advantage of the visibility from the two major roads. The mall was once a regional draw, but began a slow decline as newer malls pulled shoppers away. Capital Plaza Mall was finally demolished in 2007. Wal-Mart recognized the value of the crossroads location, and built its only store within the Washington Beltway on a portion of the site. Other auto-oriented businesses lie on this western end of the site near the Baltimore-Washington Parkway, giving a "strip" development character.

Along the middle of the Central Annapolis Road segment, the road divides a series of single-family communities—Glenridge, Woodlawn, Radiant Valley, Bellemeade, and Landover Hills. These are stable, family-friendly communities, developed primarily with single-family homes in the 1960s. There are several schools near the corridor—three public elementary schools, one middle school, two high schools, and several private schools. Three libraries, a recreation center, and neighborhood parks are additional destinations for people on foot, including children.

On the west end of the segment is more auto-oriented shopping. Maryland Transit Administration's proposed Purple Line, a light rail route connecting the communities just inside the Washington Beltway, is planned at the east end of the corridor. The Purple Line will connect the Metrorail Red, Green, and Orange Lines that radiate into suburban Washington. The station at Annapolis Road near Landover Hills would be the second-most easterly stop before the terminus at the New Carrollton Metro Center (Figure 7-18).

Figure 7-18 Existing conditions. *The Maryland-National Capitol Park and Planning Commission, Prince George's County Planning Department*

The Road

Central Annapolis Road functions as both a regional arterial and a local access road. It carries some 37,000 daily vehicle trips, including several bus routes. It may need to carry as many as 45,000 vehicles per day in the future. There are too many cars to employ the idea of a "road diet." It has a posted speed of 35 miles per hour.

Most of the corridor has more capacity than needed, even during peak times. Only the signalized intersection at Veterans' Parkway becomes a bottleneck for cars. The right-of-way is generous—mostly 120 feet wide, but up to 190 feet in segments. The road configuration varies between four lanes and six lanes, with intermittent medians. Portions of the median are as much as 60 feet wide. Sidewalks range from four to seven feet, and are on both sides for most of the corridor. Cyclists share the road with cars.

Even though Central Annapolis Road carries heavy traffic, it is also a primary route for pedestrians. The street patterns in the area are not laid out in a well-connected grid, so the arterial is often the only direct connection between destinations.

Pedestrians don't feel safe walking here. In fact, there were three pedestrian fatalities in the three years prior to the study. Street crossings are far apart, and can be far from where people want to cross. Bus stops, in particular, are not always located near street crossings. Because signals along the corridor are spaced an average of a quarter-mile apart, pedestrians resort to darting across the arterial at mid-block locations between traffic signals.

Cyclists are similarly challenged. With no bicycle lanes along Central Annapolis Road, cyclists opt for other routes or choose another mode of transport. The County's 2009 transportation plan recommends a side path for cyclists rather than bicycle lanes near the curb of the arterial, and identifies some residential streets in lieu of the arterial.

Central Annapolis Road contrasts with the nearby Baltimore-Washington Parkway. A limited-access roadway, the Baltimore-Washington Parkway has a full tree canopy and carries upward of 100,000 vehicles each day on a four- or six-lane section. As a limited-access road, there is no need for multiple curb cuts, vehicle-scale retail signage, and adjacent parking lots. Is there a way to shift Central Annapolis Road to something closer to a parkway, with its space-defining trees? How can a community interact with a boulevard-like road? And how can current conditions change over time to become more accommodating to pedestrians and the adjacent neighborhoods?

The corridor's community is modest; the racially diverse population has middle-class incomes below the County average. Residents have fewer cars than other parts of the County, and the T18 bus route that runs along Central Annapolis Road is one of the most heavily patronized in the country.

Process

The Maryland-National Capital Park and Planning Commission and the Prince George's County Planning Department engaged the architecture and planning firm Goody Clancy to study the Central Annapolis Road segment. The community came out in force, with some 120 interested citizens attending the kick-off meeting. Local residents were concerned about the speed of traffic and safety; they wanted more retail and entertainment options in the neighborhood, and cared about the quality of community life. The sentiment of one resident—"Make my neighborhood my home again"—captures the concerns of those living near a major arterial.

One of the concerns expressed in the public meetings was congestion. Interestingly, the road operates at a Level of Service A, which means that traffic is typically free-flowing. The perception of congestion must actually be associated with different, but related issues. With frequent curb cuts, highway-style signage and a wide open expanse of suburbanized landscape, the roadway feels exposed, inefficient, and unpleasant.

Reshaping a corridor and neighborhood with transit, new uses, and densities takes a great deal of planning and patience. The County's goal was a Sector plan that would rezone land along the corridor for transit-oriented development, for more walkable retail clusters, and stronger neighborhoods.

The State of Maryland's highway administration, SHA, has embraced context-oriented design, community input, and support. Residents, property owners, businesses, and county and state agencies need to define mutual goals and phased actions that include the transportation function of the road, the issues of zoning, land assembly, and infill development. SHA has been a leader in context-sensitive design for many years, and has outlined a thorough method of working with the community in its *When Main Street Is a State Highway* publication.[4]

When numerous agencies need to find joint solutions, it can be difficult to get everyone in the same room at the same time. The Central Annapolis Road team took advantage of an opportunity to bring agency leaders together with the design team and outside experts in a design workshop, the American Architectural Foundation's Sustainable Cities Design Academy.

During the two-day workshop, the team found that it would be possible to accomplish some early project goals by piggybacking on existing programs. SHA had upcoming maintenance projects to re-stripe the road, and could begin making some of the desired improvements, such as bike lanes, as part of the restriping. The State also could assist the project with sustainable landscaping. The State has found that reducing the amount of mowing along medians made new sustainable landscape cost-

---

[4] See also "Maryland Going 'Beyond the Pavement,'" *Washington Post,* by Lori Montgomery, Washington Post Staff Writer, September 15, 2000. The "Thinking Beyond the Pavement" program.

Figure 7-19 Street trees would be added to the median in an early phase. *The Maryland-National Capitol Park and Planning Commission, Prince George's County Planning Department*

effective. They were interested in finding metrics that supported funding. How much asphalt could be reduced? How much tree canopy could be added? Other financing options might be tapped, such as the Safe Routes to School program. The U.S. Forest Service might be a source of new trees.

One obstacle to implementing improvements was the inability for the County to take on maintenance along a State route. Although other counties had mechanisms in place to maintain SHA right-of-way, Prince George's County needs to establish a public-use easement for streetscape improvements outside their own right-of-way. Models for this type of easement exist, and are politically supported, but the idea needs completion (Figure 7-19).

Vision

The agencies and the design team addressed the areas of concern identified by the community. Safe crossings and additional street lighting were the highest priority. Some recommendations were relative-

Figure 7-20   A bike lane and a planted median as a buffer are added. *The Maryland-National Capitol Park and Planning Commission, Prince George's County Planning Department*

ly simple. For instance, signalized crossings in the central, residential portion of the segment are nearly half a mile apart. Bus stops were located in places that required a long walk to a signalized intersection, encouraging people to make unsafe crossings. The easiest solution was to relocate the bus stops. Simple amenities, such as benches, a place to stay dry, and posted schedules were recommendations that would have a real impact for a community with high transit usage.

In the longer term, Central Annapolis Road is moving toward a boulevard. More trees along the median and the edges will define the space of the road. Sustainable plantings and better use of the medians for handling stormwater will make the road more environmentally sound.

Shifting land use patterns can eliminate curb cuts and turning motions. In the mixed-use zones, the design team used the multiway boulevard concept. A multiway boulevard has fast-moving traffic in the center of the right-of-way, buffered by landscaping from slower-moving local service lanes. (See Taming Arterials Typology in Chapter 6 and Figure 7-20.)

Converting arterials to multiway boulevards can provide a quality pedestrian realm at the edges of a thoroughfare. With sufficient buffering, the land uses along the service lanes remain relatively unaffected by the faster traffic in the central zone of the right-of-way. The service roads become lower-volume, lower-speed streets that can support housing and mixed-use development along the property lines. The enhancements—landscaping, on-street parking, and refuge areas for pedestrians needing to cross—work for people on foot as well as for drivers.

Central Annapolis Road is an ideal candidate for a multiway boulevard. The width required for the through-lanes, service lanes, and medians is available. The boulevards can be built out concurrently with new mixed-use development over time. With future incremental development, where the service lanes begin and end will become an issue that needs to be resolved.

New land use approaches are being put into place in the Central Annapolis Road corridor by a comprehensive rezone that moves from single-family and auto-oriented commercial to a more walkable, mixed-use area. The mixed-use zones are critical to reshaping both the road and the corridor. At these denser locations, Central Annapolis Road shifts to a multiway boulevard with the local service lanes (Figure 7-21).

Lessons Learned

Central Annapolis Road still has a long way to go. But the lessons it teaches, even at the planning stage, can easily be applied elsewhere as communities take on the challenge of taming the regional arterials that run through them.

- Collaboration is essential. Transportation, land use, and environmentally sound practices need to work together for major reconsideration of a large road to work.

- Communities need to set the vision for their futures. "If communities don't want the changes that we are proposing, we don't do the project," says Greg Slater, Director of Maryland State Highway Administration's Office of Planning and Preliminary Engineering.

- Leadership is needed within agencies to provide the creative problem-solving to implement those visions.

- Plan for the long term, because it takes a long time to implement major changes. Central Annapolis Road will change as the light rail is completed and new development occurs, but the planning allows each incremental step to add up to a desired outcome. Plans need to be in place, especially where changes are foreseeable, such as the planning for new transit stations. Every stage along the way needs to function, both physically and for the community.

- The early, easier improvements can make a big difference in the life of the community. Finding some near-term funding to add trees in the median, or striping for a bike lane show that change can happen, and set the stage for the next increment of improvements (Figure 7-22).

Figure 7-21 This phase adds a local access lane, buffered by a planted median. *The Maryland-National Capitol Park and Planning Commission, Prince George's County Planning Department*

Figure 7-22 The long-term vision includes pedestrian-oriented land uses along the edge of the local access lane. *The Maryland-National Capitol Park and Planning Commission, Prince George's County Planning Department*

COMMENTS

"The collaborative process produced a workable strategy that was able to break down the ambitious and often politically contentious goal of downsizing a busy traffic arterial. We focused on achievable bite-sized phases of changes to the streetscape with clearly identified plausible sources of funding."

—*Ganesh Ramachandran, Senior Urban Designer, Goody Clancy*

"The reason this worked was because the transportation planning was there at the beginning, in a collaborative rather than a reactive role. If the community gives us the vision, then we can let the engineers dig in to solve the right problems."

—*Greg Slater, Director, Office of Planning and Preliminary Engineering, Maryland State Highway Administration*

"The community was interested in every inch of that road. We shaped our vision to capture that energy."

—*Bill Washburn, AICP, Planner /Coordinator for The Maryland-National Capitol Park & Planning Commission*

78TH AVENUE SE SHARED USE

> **We always knew this stretch of street had to be different.**
> —*Rich Conrad, Mercer Island City Manager (CSMI intro)*

The City of Mercer Island, Washington, set out to make a special place at the northern terminus of their "main street." The vision of a plaza that could serve both pedestrians and cars, that could function well on a day-to-day basis and for occasional festivals, was built with the cooperation of developers on either side of the block (Figure 7-23).

Figure 7-23 78th Avenue SE is now a shared-use street.

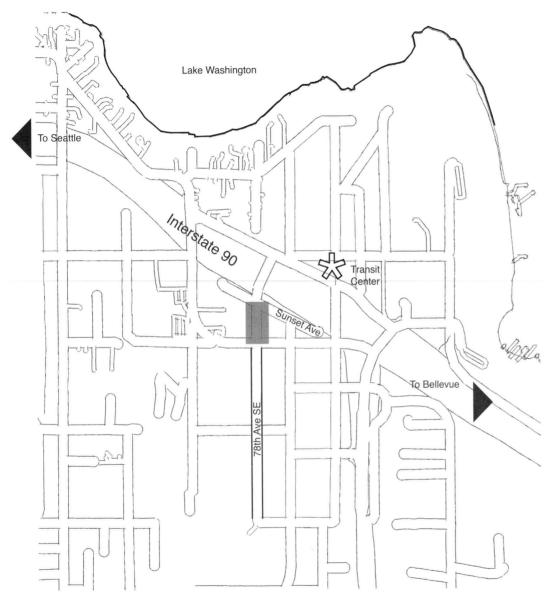

Figure 7-24 78th Avenue SE context.

Neighborhood

Mercer Island is the name of both the island in Lake Washington, and the suburban community of 24,000 located on the island. With Interstate-90 cutting across the north end of the island, Mercer Island is within easy reach of both Seattle and Bellevue, Washington. Most of the area is upscale, leafy, and suburban. The town center lies just to the south of the sunken, landscaped highway, and for many years, the town center was mostly surface parking and one-story convenience shopping. In many ways, it is ideally situated to be rebuilt into the kind of walkable, transit-oriented "urban village" that planners in the region are looking to foster (Figure 7-24).

In the broader context, State and regional planners have been working hard to manage the explosive growth of recent decades in the Northwest. In order to check sprawl and reduce auto dependency, work has been done in terms of land use planning and the retrofit of high-capacity transit systems. Light rail is coming to Mercer Island in the next decade, with a station on the I-90 corridor adjacent to the town center.

As part of the State's growth management planning, the population of Mercer Island is mandated to take part of the expected regional population increase. Incorporated cities, such as Mercer Island, are required to accept new residents into their communities in order to check growth in rural areas. The town center, with its adjacency to I-90, is a very attractive location for a compact, walkable, transit-oriented community.

Vision

Mercer Island's town center lay dormant as other suburban communities grew. Land use regulations based on a suburban model, with little development capacity and large parking requirements, were ripe for change by the mid-1990s. A series of workshops including planners, urban designers, and some 200 citizens resulted in a new Town Center Plan. It put forth a transformed downtown, with a pedestrian spine along 78th Avenue SE, new commercial development along the street fronts, and parking on the rear. The pedestrian spine led to a future transit station along I-90.

This vision served as the foundation for the City's Comprehensive Plan, required by the State as part of the Growth Management Act, and a subsequent revision of the zoning ordinance. The new zoning allowed more height and lot coverage, and reduced parking requirements.

Design standards were put in place. "Building designs that are urban in character and oriented to the pedestrian are encouraged," state the standards. "New development should increase the attractions and pedestrian amenities that bring residents to the Town Center."

The City began the transformation by concentrating on the land under their control—the street. Using Federal ISTEA (Intermodal Surface Transportation Efficiency Act) and local matching funds, the City redesigned 78th Avenue SE to favor pedestrians, actually removing lanes and doubling the width of the sidewalk to 12 feet, and adding pockets of on-street parking. Medians with street trees and plantings reduced the scale of the street, and slowed traffic (Figure 7-25).

Figure 7-25 The improvements done earlier established a pedestrian-friendly street with heavily landscaped sidewalks and median.

The pedestrian spine had a clear terminus on its north end where the highway, below grade, traverses the Island. A greenbelt with an outdoor sculpture gallery maintained by the City's Arts Council runs along the I-90 corridor. The last block of 78th Avenue SE comes to an end, and cars have little reason to drive on that block because the cross street, Sunset Highway, despite its name, is only a few blocks long. "We always knew this stretch of street had to be different," says Rich Conrad, Mercer Island City Manager. It was a waste of space for driving, and the perfect place for pedestrians.

The City's design standards called out the northernmost block of 78th Avenue SE as a specific Opportunity Site:

> One such opportunity site is the development of a public space on 78th Avenue SE between 27th Avenue SE and Sunset Highway. Envisioned in this area is a public-private partnership project with street improvements to create a viable civic gathering area that encourages public space amenities on adjacent private property with special pedestrian-oriented features that may accommodate vehicular traffic but could be closed off for community events. It is hoped that this space, combined with the art park, can become a key downtown plaza within the Town Center.[5]

Process

It took almost a decade for the expected development to materialize. A confluence of market forces brought developers into the City at about the same time, with plans in hand. The property owners for both the east and west sides of the northern-most end of 78th Avenue SE came in to the City with plans to develop within a few months of each other. This timing set up an opportunity for the City and the two developers to work together on the critical location at the end of 78th.

Direction for creating a pedestrian plaza came from the City Council. The City Manager and the Director of Development Services set the goals for the project:

- Replace existing asphalt street pavement with textured, colored, and/or scored concrete or pavers;

- Remove the vertical curbs and replace with smooth transition between future sidewalk and street;

- Provide enhanced or raised intersection and crosswalks across Sunset Highway to enhance pedestrian connection from 78th Avenue to the Sculpture Garden;

---

[5] City of Mercer Island, Town Center Development and Design Standards, Chapter 19.11, Section 19.11.010.B.1.d, Opportunity Sites.

- Provide removable bollards at each end of 78th Avenue SE so this 200-foot-long block of roadway can be closed to vehicles for pedestrian-oriented special events; and

- Provide on-street parking on one side of the street (Figure 7-26).[6]

---

[6] From Business of the City Council, City of Mercer Island, WA, AB4113, July 24, 2006, Proposed Design and Construction of Textured and Colored Concrete Street Improvements on 78th Avenue SE Between Sunset Highway and SE 27th Street.

Figure 7-26 78th is adjacent to the outdoor sculpture gallery.

It is significant that the elected officials supported the project, and empowered staff to find a way to accomplish the stated goals. City Council offered the ability to tap into the City's Beautification Funds to help build the streetscape. "It was hard to sell the idea that the City should spend money on this," according to Richard Hart, who was the Director of Development Services at the time. But a good private-public action should be a win-win situation for everyone. The City could point to the effect of the streetscape improvements along the 78th Avenue pedestrian spine as an example of public benefit.

The departmental structure also helped. Staff members involved in planning for the right-of-way are within the Development Services Group rather than in a separate transportation department. All the staff was engaged in making the project feasible and successful, finding ways to address concerns regarding utilities and fire access. The multidisciplinary firm KPG was brought in by the City as the consultant to design the plaza within the right-of-way.

The City used both "carrots and sticks" to work with the developers on either side of the block. An important incentive for the developers was the ability to use 78th Avenue SE on a temporary basis as lay-down space during construction, according to Patrick Yamashita, the City Engineer.

Mercer Island has a Design Commission made up of local citizens that reviews projects for compliance with the design standards. The projects on either side needed their approval, and because the pedestrian plaza was specifically cited in the design standards, the Design Commission had the regulatory tools to make sure that the developments would be part of the vision for the plaza.

Design Features

The design creates a central plaza that can be used by cars, with some parallel parking on one side. Retaining some level of access for cars was important to the property developers, but it is easy to close off the street for events. Staggered street trees will provide canopy as they grow, and landscaped areas help define a car-free zone next to the buildings. Plentiful seating is provided, and lighting continues the fixtures chosen for the Town Center.

The curbless street gave clues to the visually impaired by the use of bollards, a change in texture and landscape zones between sidewalk and the drivable plaza. Drainage occurs via an inverted crown, with a portion of the stormwater directed to the planters.

The developer of the mixed-use 77 Central building wanted to include a major sculpture along the pedestrian plaza. An art piece would be an appropriate tie-in to the Sculpture Gallery in the greenbelt. The Harold Balazs piece is set in a landscaped zone on the west side of the plaza..

"It was very different than a typical capital project," says Paul Feusel of KPG. "Instead of just meeting standards, the project was able to evolve." The technical issues were solved to the satisfaction of all the project stakeholders. Fire truck access is adequate, and no red paint was needed to denote a fire lane. "We don't do that here," says Yamashita. If people are parking where they aren't supposed to, the City can find ways to solve it through signage or enforcement, but it hasn't been a problem. The drainage worked within normal standards, partly because of the gentle slope of the street.

Funding and Management

Although the design of the street is different, the City of Mercer Island maintains the right-of-way (Figure 7-27).

Figure 7-27 Bollards and a shift in materials denote the drive zone.

Figure 7-28 Art, seating, lighting, and landscaping are integrated into the street.

Lessons Learned

- Even though there wasn't a specific process or set of design standards to build a shared-use street, everyone involved was willing to work together to make the project a success. It is possible to implement a vision through negotiations rather than a proscribed set of standards, if the will is there.

- The will to make a different kind of place in the right-of-way came from the top, with a vision shared by elected officials and key City staff. The leadership stayed in place over the course of the project, so that the vision stayed intact.

- The City set out to take advantage of a clear opportunity, rather than to do a shared street for its own sake. "We just slid it in and did it. We didn't advertise it as something different," says Feusel. And when it was completed, it didn't seem to be something that anyone should be afraid to do.

- The City understood from the streetscape work done earlier that putting resources into the right-of-way could have a real effect on the quality of the Town Center. This made the idea easier to "sell" to nay-sayers.

Mercer Island got the planning right—so much so that groups of planners and citizens interested from other places interested in improving their town centers tour Mercer Island as a model for their own town centers (Figure 7-28).

HIGH POINT

> ## What opportunities come with building new communities?

Seattle's High Point neighborhood offered the chance to create and test a new green neighborhood in an urban setting. Land use densities and arrangements, the street system, and a natural drainage approach to stormwater could all be planned at once to be mutually supportive. This required collaboration among agencies, designers, and the community. It meant flexibility on the part of City departments to use new approaches that will inform future development city-wide (Figure 7-29).

Figure 7-29 High Point's natural drainage integrates into a green neighborhood.

Figure 7-30 High Point context.

Context

The High Point neighborhood lies on a 120-acre site in West Seattle, about 6 miles from downtown Seattle. High Point was once comprised of temporary housing for the surge of workers who came to Seattle for jobs in its defense industry during World War II. After the war, the housing reverted to the Seattle Housing Authority (SHA). The housing that was meant to be temporary became home to many low-income families for the second half of the century. By the end of the 1990s, the housing and the neighborhood infrastructure were in poor condition and the neighborhood was struggling. The streets did not connect to the surrounding street grid. The relatively wide, winding residential streets were more typical of a low-density suburb than one of Seattle's close-in neighborhoods, setting the neighborhood apart from the surrounding community (Figure 7-30).

In the late 1990s, the SHA, in partnership with the High Point community stakeholders, the City of Seattle, and a team of designers, embarked on what would become more than a decade's worth of redevelopment projects funded through the Federal HOPE VI program. The goal for the HOPE VI program was to change the nation's approach to public housing by transforming largely subsidized housing communities into mixed-income neighborhoods with community assets. These neighborhoods included rental units available to low-income families through the Seattle Housing Authority, and market-rate, for-sale housing. The HOPE VI program provided an opportunity to completely remake three Seattle neighborhoods: Holly Park began reconstruction in 1995, followed by the Rainier Vista neighborhood redevelopment in 1999. High Point began in 2000.

Prior to redevelopment, there were just over 700 housing units at High Point. With the redeveloped site, up to 1,600 units of rental and for-sale housing units will be

completed, along with a library, parks, a community center, and a health center. Phase I, now completed, includes the major infrastructure, all of the rental housing and over half of the market-rate housing.
The Phase II market-rate construction has slowed because of economic conditions.

The Opportunity

High Point provided not only the rare opportunity to accomplish a large-site redevelopment project
within the city limits of Seattle—where such large sites are few and far between—but also to push the
boundaries on design, development, and green stormwater infrastructure.

The SHA and the design team had clear intentions to reinvent the structure of High Point from a
low-density, single-use neighborhood into a walkable community with onsite services and amenities.
Plans included a library branch, a medical and dental health center, and a neighborhood center that
hosted a Head Start program, family center, teen center, tutoring program, and job connection program. The project team also intended to improve the connections to transit, and make walking and
bicycling in the community easy and enjoyable so that car travel was not the only option.

One of the unique circumstances of the High Point neighborhood is its location in the Longfellow
Creek watershed. This four-mile-long urban creek flows year-round through West Seattle's Delridge Valley into the Duwamish River and Elliott Bay. Longfellow is one of only four natural waterways left within
the Seattle City limits that remain free-flowing. It was once full of salmon. City and community efforts
have aimed to restore the salmon runs to Longfellow Creek, with yearly fish releases by local schools,
and removal of fish barriers in the creek. In 1995, salmon returned to the creek for the first time since
1939. Fish populations include Coho salmon, cutthroat trout, and steelhead trout.[7]

As planning for the redevelopment of High Point began, the health of Longfellow Creek was identified as a priority for the City. High Point became an opportunity to improve the urban watershed as well
as an inspiration for rethinking development strategies.

Process

The SHA started with a strong vision of creating a mixed-income community with quality design and a
healthy environment. In order to realize the vision on the scale of this project, SHA recognized that the
existing land use and zoning restrictions constrained the desired use of the site. They began work with
the City of Seattle on rezoning the site from single family to higher-density residential with some capacity for mixed-use development.

---

[7] From the Longfellow Creek Community Website, accessed at http://www.longfellowcreek.org/cooper/cooper.htm.

The 1940s-era street grid needed to be integrated into the surrounding community. Within the neighborhood, the streets were curvilinear and confusing. Adjacent streets were typical of the 25-foot-wide north-south and east-west City street grid. Along with rezoning, a new street grid was created in order to reintegrate High Point into the surrounding neighborhood and encourage the surrounding community to visit the site.

Street width related to City code was evaluated as part of the project. The existing roadway design had road widths of up to 32 feet, which was wide enough to encourage drivers to speed through the neighborhood. High Point residents were concerned about excessive speed, especially with the large population of children in the community. Deviation from the City's current right-of-way width and road width standards was reviewed through the redevelopment process (Figure 7-31).

Figure 7-31 In the reconfigured neighborhood, the quietest streets are 25 feet wide curb to curb.

Design guidelines for the rental and for-sale developments were also developed by SHA and its design team. For rental units, the housing types were primarily ground-related because many of the occupants are large families, people with disabilities, or seniors. Garages and surface parking were set back, and front porches provided to offer places to sit so that neighbors could get to know one another and have "eyes on the street."

At the point in the planning process when the Master Plan had determined the street grid and housing concept, Seattle Public Utilities (SPU) approached SHA to integrate a natural systems approach (green stormwater infrastructure) into the neighborhood. SPU had success in implementing green stormwater infrastructure along a street length in north Seattle but had not yet implemented green stormwater infrastructure on such a large scale and within a higher-density neighborhood. In order to ensure successful design through construction and maintenance, SHA and SPU developed a partnership. New street design standards were developed through collaboration of the various City departments who ensured that all required infrastructure needs were met. This required a full look at the street cross-section from curb heights to cross-slope of the road to location of sewer, water, fire hydrants, electrical infrastructure, and alley locations. From the design charettes and discussions, the cross-slope of the road was "thrown" to one side with the electrical infrastructure on the uphill side and stormwater bioretention facilities and pervious concrete sidewalks on the downhill side.

Solutions

Lessons were learned from the first two SHA redevelopments. SHA understood the value of close cooperation between planners, residents, designers, and other community stakeholders. The neighborhoods are highly mixed in terms of ethnicities, native languages, and income levels, but SHA had practice at coordinating meetings with diverse communities in order to understand their concerns and priorities. One important lesson replicated from the earlier HOPE VI neighborhoods was making market-rate, for-sale housing and rental units all indistinguishable so that no group is stigmatized.

The infrastructure was reconsidered from scratch, with streets reconnected to the grid of the surrounding neighborhood. In replatting, the blocks were kept short to enhance walkability. Mature trees were identified for each block, and the layout of the streets and housing adapted to their location in order to preserve them. Most of the structures, roads, and utilities that were onsite were demolished, recycling old pavements and foundations. The project put in place a new street grid that reconnected to the surrounding streets, and over 21 acres of distributed open space, parks, and playgrounds.

Narrow Streets

The majority of the residential streets are 25 feet wide, with parking on both sides. This width and the ability to park along the street is consistent with the older adjacent neighborhood street grid. The SHA agreed to meet the SPU request to create a neighborhood plan that focused on improved water quality for Longfellow Creek, but asked the SPU staff to back them up in discussion with the other departments to allow permitting for the requested narrower streets.

This collaborative approach resulted in positive results for many partners. While Seattle's traditional street width would match the 25 feet, the Fire Department generally wants wider streets in order to ensure emergency access when on-street parking is fully utilized. The Fire Department also wanted space for the outriggers that are used to stabilize the trucks when fighting fires. Fire Department personnel were included in the early design discussions, and because they had years of experience providing emergency services to the same width of street, the 25-foot streets were approved. The design team listened to the fire department's issue of staging space and strategically placed fire hydrants and used cross-block alleys to further break down the street length, giving opportunities to pull over or stage emergency vehicles along the streets. The fire hydrant locations and cross-block alleys meant that there would be spaces that would be clear of parked cars.

Intersection Treatments

The vision for the redevelopment of High Point, under the guidance of Tom Phillips from the SHA, was a livable, healthy community. One of Tom's strengths as a leader was his ability to look at both the broad policies and the critical details of the project. When the design team explained the desire to have landscape nodes at the intersections, which required asking the Department of Transportation for a variance to their standard curb ramp design, Tom was supportive of this effort. While it took several meetings to discuss the details and refine the radii for slower turning movement, the successful application resulted in a subtle but improved intersection zone for the people living in the community (Figure 7-32).

Walks

Early discussions about the drainage approach considered walks on only one side of the street to allow more room for drainage. But the design team felt that walkability in urban communities was critical, and pushed to find a way to achieve both drainage and walkability goals. To do that, they needed to consider all elements of the right-of-way simultaneously, from utility location and separation requirements to road width and curb height, in order to make the most out of the space available. For example, pervious walks were placed on the low side of the street to maximize drainage. The other side kept a smooth condition for scooters, rollers skaters, strollers, and walkers (Figure 7-33).

Stormwater Design

High Point was designed and permitted through a mechanism called an integrative drainage plan (IDP) that allowed the design to include both the public and private areas. Seattle Public Utilities required this code approach to allow a stormwater solution that was not in the code language in 2001. The goal for

Figure 7-32   Landscape at intersections makes the streets feel greener.

Figure 7-33   Porous paving on the sidewalk adjacent to the swale.

the stormwater system was to simulate the hydrologic system found in pastures design, but with 14 to 35 units per acre of ground-related housing. The entire site, from the housing and parks to the gently sloping streets and biofiltration/retention swales, is designed to infiltrate stormwater runoff as close as possible to where it hits the ground.

The key element was to control the impervious area and utilize what were then cutting-edge low-impact development (LID) technologies. The key components of the natural drainage systems in the right-of-way at High Point include pervious concrete for public sidewalks along one side of the street and three types of bioretention swales within the right-of-way. The stormwater management treatment train includes conveyance, shallow bioretention, deeper bioretention swale, and a stormwater pond. The natural drainage elements along the streets are typically the third or fourth point of the system.

On the private side and within the housing development, components of the natural drainage system include downspout dispersion, infiltration trenches, soil amendments in all landscape areas, various types of porous pavements for vehicular and pedestrian areas, tree retention, rain gardens, and small-scale bioretention facilities.

The street is engineered to carry water to one side, so that it can move into the shallow vegetated bioretention swale cells. As water flows into these cells, it is cleansed through the plants and filtered through the two to four feet of compost gravelly soil below. Native and drought-tolerant plants—shrubs, trees, and grasses—are both attractive and effective as natural filters for rainwater. The stormwater design slows the flow of water, allows water to soak into the ground, filters and reduces pollution using the natural processes of soil and plants, reduces impervious surfaces, and creates a lush, green neighborhood (Figure 7-34).

Figure 7-34 Natural drainage swale during a storm event. Vegetation between the cells indicates that the swale is handling the water without overflowing. *Courtesy of SvR Design*

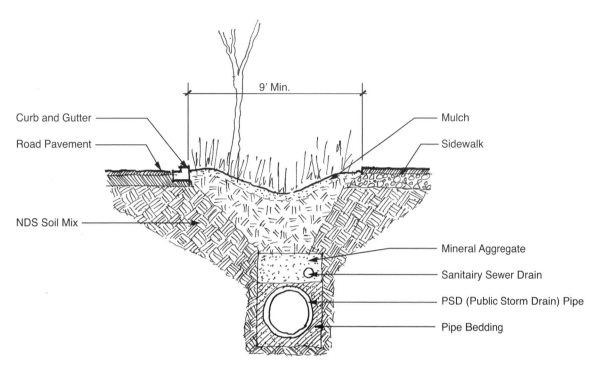

9' Min.

Curb and Gutter

Road Pavement

Mulch

Sidewalk

NDS Soil Mix

Mineral Aggregate

Sanitairy Sewer Drain

PSD (Public Storm Drain) Pipe

Pipe Bedding

Figure 7-35 Swale section.

Pervious concrete pavement was used for public sidewalks adjacent to the bioretention swale cells and along one public street. High Point was the first time that pervious concrete was used in a public street in the State of Washington. The pervious concrete allows rainwater to filter directly into the earth below, mimicking an unpaved condition (Figure 7-35).

Landscape

Prior to the redevelopment, over a thousand existing mature trees onsite were assessed and rated by arborists. By adapting the housing plan, new street grid, and grade changes for accessibility, 107 healthy, mature trees were saved and incorporated into the new development. In addition, more than 3,000 new trees were planted along the streets and open spaces.

Tom Phillips provided valuable insights into the design because of his attention to detail. He requested a street tree plan that had variety and provided consistent applications along each street. He wanted people to have many visual clues as to where they were as they walked through their neigh-

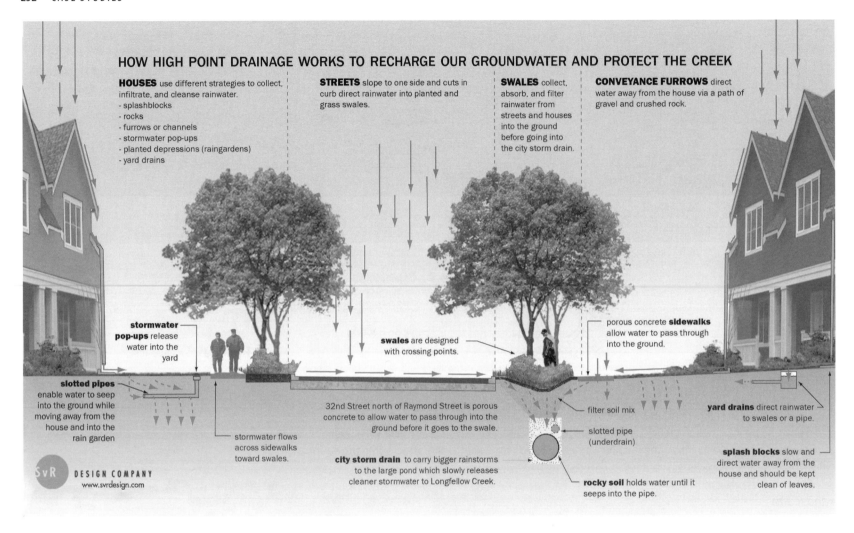

HOW HIGH POINT DRAINAGE WORKS TO RECHARGE OUR GROUNDWATER AND PROTECT THE CREEK

HOUSES use different strategies to collect, infiltrate, and cleanse rainwater.
- splashblocks
- rocks
- furrows or channels
- stormwater pop-ups
- planted depressions (raingardens)
- yard drains

STREETS slope to one side and cuts in curb direct rainwater into planted and grass swales.

SWALES collect, absorb, and filter rainwater from streets and houses into the ground before going into the city storm drain.

CONVEYANCE FURROWS direct water away from the house via a path of gravel and crushed rock.

stormwater pop-ups release water into the yard

swales are designed with crossing points.

porous concrete **sidewalks** allow water to pass through into the ground.

slotted pipes enable water to seep into the ground while moving away from the house and into the rain garden

filter soil mix

yard drains direct rainwater to swales or a pipe.

stormwater flows across sidewalks toward swales.

32nd Street north of Raymond Street is porous concrete to allow water to pass through into the ground before it goes to the swale.

slotted pipe (underdrain)

city storm drain to carry bigger rainstorms to the large pond which slowly releases cleaner stormwater to Longfellow Creek.

rocky soil holds water until it seeps into the pipe.

splash blocks slow and direct water away from the house and should be kept clean of leaves.

SvR DESIGN COMPANY
www.svrdesign.com

Figure 7-36 How High Point drainage works. *Courtesy of SvR Design*

borhood. This puzzle of variety and consistency led to thoughtful and deliberate discussion of each tree species through the season. The use of evergreens along the streets was intentional to add "spikes" and flowering trees were used to announce key locations. The low-level landscape was also carefully designed with the same concept of variety and sense of place. The landscape architecture aspires to create a vibrant walking environment that is as interesting in Seattle's bleak February as it is in early June (Figure 7-36).

Art

Bruce Myers, of Myers Sculpture, was selected as the artist for the site. Early in the planning process, Myers integrated his concept into the overall plan for health and watershed care. The art plan dispersed various elements across the 34-block neighborhood accentuating the "water trail" from the highest point on the site down to the pond park. Elements included bronze plaques at the curb cuts and on the lamp posts with images of the habitat that benefits from the stormwater system. Large boulders, some of which were recovered from the site, were polished and sandblasted with watershed images. A raindrop symbol was scored into the standard concrete sidewalk along the primary walking path and hand-made concrete splashblocks of various patterns from swimming salmon to cobbles were used for the downspouts dispersion. Through Myers' work, the neighborhood's relationship to the natural environment and stormwater is told.

The Pomegranate Center was also brought in to work with the community to integrate art into the neighborhood. Pomegranate and the residents created elements such as an amphitheatre, fencing for the market garden, and various covered shelters in the pocket parks (Figure 7-37).

Figure 7-37 Pomegranate Center worked with the community on the design of this amphitheater. *Photo courtesy of Pomegranate Center*

Maintenance

The enhanced street environment and the approach of integrating the stormwater management into the street system were unusual in this type of development at the time it was built. Even though this was a public (not gated) community, there were special considerations that would benefit from a defined maintenance program.

A High Point Natural Drainage, Landscape, Open Space, and Rights of Way Association is responsible for the public realm. Homeowners at High Point contribute to this association each month. An operations and maintenance manual was developed in the planning phase specifically for the LID tools or green stormwater infrastructure elements that were implemented throughout the site. Chemical fertilizers and pesticides are prohibited from use to prevent leaching into the stormwater and impacting the water quality. This manual has been updated a few times, incorporating the observations and experience of the onsite staff and design team.

Lessons Learned

In retrospect, using High Point as a testing ground for an early application of LID or green stormwater infrastructure on a large scale with dense ground-related housing was quite an undertaking, given that High Point is a community redeveloped to achieve a mix of housing types for a variety of incomes and ages. However, having an integrated and collaborative design team led by clear vision from the owner allowed a framework to take on each new element in a spirit of trust.

Based on the spirit of trust the lessons related to details are more fine-grained.

- It is worth the effort to collaborate with agency staff early and maintain an integrated disciplines approach.

- The attention to details such as the intersections does result in value.

- It took time to work out the regulatory issues for a noncodified approach.

- It was apparent that this shift to green stormwater infrastructure requires a new approach to site construction management and sequencing.

- The efforts in public outreach have value and extend well beyond the project limits and local community.

- Finally, maintenance planning is a design issue and it is never too early to frame the approach to maintenance.

BARRACKS ROW

Bringing a Main Street Back to Life

Washington, D.C.'s 8th Street SE, known as Barracks Row, is a success story in revitalizing an urban Main Street. Barracks Row began with a number of assets—a mix of residents, business, and institutions within walking distance, good transportation, and strong leadership. That leadership organized, and attracted the support of the City's transportation department, economic development office, and the National Trust for Historic Preservation's Main Street Program (Figure 7-38).

Figure 7-38 Barracks Row's wide sidewalk is well used public space.

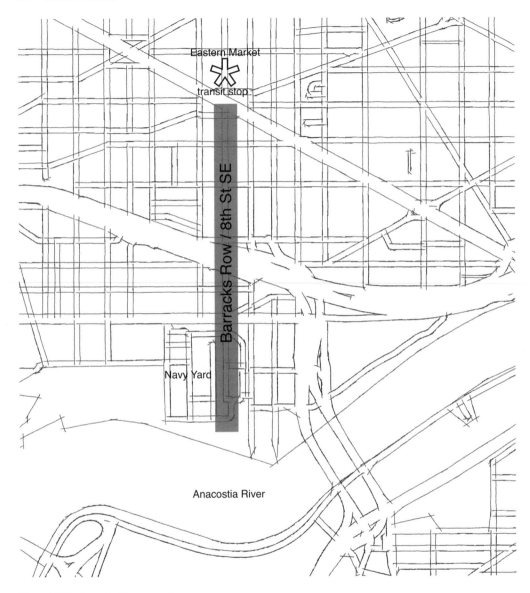

Figure 7-39 Barracks Row context.

Neighborhood

Located in Washington, D.C.'s Capitol Hill neighborhood, Barracks Row is the City's oldest commercial corridor. 8th Street SE runs from the historic Washington Navy Yard on the south along the Anacostia River, to Eastern Market on the north. The district's name comes from the United States Marine Corps Barracks, at 8th and I Streets, the location chosen by Thomas Jefferson for a post to guard the Navy Yards and the Capitol. 8th Street intersects Pennsylvania Avenue, the diagonal that connects to the Capitol (Figure 7-39).

The Barracks Row commercial district thrived for many years, with small businesses serving the workers at the Navy Yard, who mostly lived in the neighborhood. At its founding in 1799, the Navy Yard took advantage of the natural harbor on the Anacostia River. The Navy Yard expanded in 1845 as its work began to focus on testing and manufacturing weapons and ammunition. The area's population expanded and unlike other areas in the south, the neighborhood included a diverse mix of immigrants, American-born whites, and free blacks.

The Civil War brought an expansion of population, housing, and shops along 8th Street. A new Eastern Market was built in 1872 at the north end of the district. The population continued to grow, with a variety of primarily blue-collar workers, including those employed at the Naval Gun Factory. World War II was the peak of employment in the district; by 1962 the gun factory was closed and the Navy Yard converted to office and museum uses. The buildings of the neighborhood reflect the diversity of the people who have lived there over time, and display a variety of architectural styles from over the years.

The 1960s brought the construction of the Southeast-Southwest freeway and the separation of the north and the south parts of 8th Street. In 1968, after the assassination of Martin Luther King, Jr., the neighborhood was one of the areas of Washington, D.C., to suffer from rioting. 8th Street had still not recovered decades later.

Vision and Process

The rejuvenation of Barracks Row came about because of the local community and their ability to organize. For Barracks Row, the vision and the process were intertwined. When asked about the reason for the success of Barracks Row, James Dalpee, the former Executive Director, said: "The founders of Barracks Row Main Street, Linda Gallagher and George Didden, had a very strong vision of what the future could be like here. They were passionate about the revitalization, and determined to make it happen. The streetscape renovation, the first big change, was what led the way. It made businesses want to come here."[8] (See Figure 7-40.)

The early visionaries understood the potential of the district. Although it was dilapidated, the Barracks Row neighborhood had all the ingredients of a thriving place. There are over 15,000 households within a mile of Barracks Row. People work in the neighborhood, with 13,000 employees at the Navy Yard alone.[9] The area is well served by public transportation, with the Eastern Market Metro station at the north end of the district, and multiple bus routes.

In the 1990s, business and community members founded the Barracks Row Business Alliance with the intent of revitalizing 8th Street. The renovation of the abandoned Oddfellows Hall in 1998 by the esteemed Shakespeare Theater was an early victory. The Oddfellows Hall became the Shakespeare Theater's offices, rehearsal space, and classrooms for their acting academy.

The next year, the Barracks Row Business Alliance joined with the National Main Street Center of the National Trust for Historic Preservation to found the nonprofit organization, Barracks Row Main Street. Its mission is

8 The Hill is Home blog, July 30, 2009, interview with Nichole Remmert.
9 2010 Neighborhood Profiles, Washington, D.C. Economic Partnership..

Figure 7-40 Barracks Row Main Street offices are part of the mix along the street.

to benefit the broadest possible local community, to "revitalize 8th Street SE as a vibrant commercial corridor reconnecting Capitol Hill to the Anacostia River."[10]

The National Trust for Historic Preservation's Main Street program has been an extremely valuable resource to hundreds of communities, and has developed a comprehensive approach to revitalizing Main Streets. Barracks Row is a highly successful example of their trademarked Four-Point approach that combines organization, promotion, and economic restructuring with design.

Funding

Barracks Row Main Street approached local government to find resources to improve the neighborhood. The City transportation department, DDOT, had a street resurfacing project planned, and Ken Laden, Associate Director for the DDOT, was able to find funding to upgrade the project to include a renovation of streetscape for the six-block length of 8th Street SE.

Design Features

A study for the street began in 2000, with transportation consultants DMJM+Harris and landscape architects Lee and Associates. Parking was a primary concern of local businesses, and the design replaced parallel parking with angled parking to add spaces and make maneuvering easier. One block on the south end of the district was converted from one-way to two-way operations. Additional space was created for parking below the highway.

Meanwhile, the District of Columbia was recognizing the economic benefit of reinvigorating the City neighborhoods as economic engines. In 2002, the District of Columbia's Office of Economic Development created the DC Main Streets program in order to support lasting revitalization in the City's business districts. Barracks Row Main Street was well-placed to benefit from this assistance, and was selected as one of the five initial programs. The DC Main Streets program offers technical and financial assistance for neighborhood nonprofit organizations such as Barracks Row Main Street (Figure 7-41).

The new streetscape dramatically changed the feel of the neighborhood. The new sidewalks are 20 feet wide, with herringbone-patterned brick. The District's restaurants have made use of the sidewalk width by adding plentiful outdoor seating. A 5-foot border of blue stone runs along the curb between the tree pits. In an earlier design, landscape architect Jeff Lee alternated the blue stone with low grasses, but the community was skeptical of the mixing of hardscape and landscape, so the design kept to hardscape.

---

[10] Barracks Row Main Street website, http://www.barracksrow.org/what/mission

Figure 7-41 Wide sidewalks allow cafe seating, retail display, and plenty of space to walk.

New brick gutters and granite curbs were installed. Pedestrian-scale globe lights improved the feeling of safety after dark. Many of the street's Red Oaks were unhealthy and susceptible to blight. Only the healthiest were retained. The 92 new drought-resistant American Elms that now line 8th Street SE were donated to the project. The $8.5 million construction project was completed in December of 2003.[11]

Material changes indicate pedestrian zones at intersections, and the quality of the materials reflects the value placed on the pedestrian realm. These materials maintain their integrity over time, unlike the painted intersections that are commonly used (Figures 7-42 and 7-43).

Lessons Learned

The construction of the street was challenging for all concerned. During the 15-month construction period, businesses were disrupted, parking was difficult, and Hurricane Isabel blew through. Old streetcar tracks and coal chutes were discovered below the surface of the street. But DDOT and Barracks Row Main Street prioritized communication with the businesses along the street. The shared work of improving the District built a sense of community among the merchants. Ron Casidine, a manager at the Backstage Theater Store, said that the shared goals have brought the businesspeople of the District together. "The owners and managers on 8th Street are like family," he said.[12]

■ The neighborhood has highlighted its rich history. Cultural Tourism DC created a well-marked Heritage Trail, with 16 illustrated historic markers which tell the story of two centuries of local history. Barracks Row was composer and band leader John Philip Sousa's neighborhood, and his presence continues to be felt—the Marine Band is still stationed at the Barracks, and plays at the traditional Friday parades on summer evenings.

■ Streetscape improvements can be a catalyst for economic rejuvenation. By 2005, when Barracks Row won the Great American Main Street Award from the National Trust for Historic Preservation, 40 new businesses had come to 8th Street, and more than 50 facades had been restored, according to the June 2005 issue of *Restoring D.C.* (Volume 2, Issue 4). The sidewalks were filled with outdoor cafe seating, and nearly 200 new jobs had been created. Barracks Row continues to flourish.

Tom Litke, a consultant to nonprofits who has been involved in Barracks Row, summarizes the advice found in Sean Zielenbach's *Art of Revitalization*:[13] turning around a neighborhood requires good housing, political leadership, strong institutions and community organization. It also takes perseverance, and years.

---

[11] National Trust for Historic Preservation, Barracks Row in Washington, DC, accessed at preservation.org/resources/case-studies/gamsa/2005/barracks-row-washington-dc.html.

[12] "Barracks Row Revival," *The Common Denominator: Washington's Independent Hometown Newspaper,* March 8, 2004.

[13] Sean Zielenbach, *The Art of Revitalization: Improving Conditions in Distressed Inner-City Neighborhoods,* The Maxine Goodman Levin College of Urban Affairs at Cleveland State University, Garland Publishing, Inc.: New York and London, 2000.

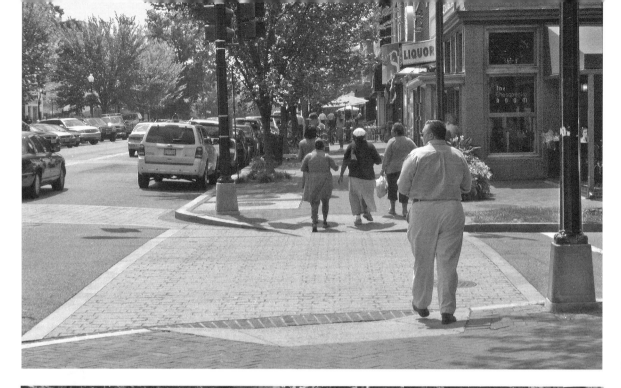

Figure 7-42 Materials indicate pedestrian crossing zones.

Figure 7-43 Cobblestones mark where an alley crosses the sidewalk.

Figure 7-44 The east side of the street, along the Barracks, is not a retail zone, but a pleasant, well-landscaped sidewalk.

Revitalization is extending outward from Barracks Row. To the north, the historic Eastern Market reopened in 2009 after being damaged by fire. Plans have been discussed for the portion of 8th Street south of the Southeast Freeway, and for the redesign of the area near the Eastern Market Metro station. These new plans may take some time to come to fruition, but with enough perseverance, success will breed success (Figure 7-44).

NEW YORK CITY

> **We have developed a plan that can become a model for cities in the 21st century.**
>
> —*PlaNYC*

PlaNYC was announced by Mayor Bloomberg on Earth Day, 2007. The City had come a long way since it was near bankruptcy in the 1980s. Population had increased from its low point, and the air and water are cleaner. But they still do not meet national environmental standards, the infrastructure is aging, and more residents are expected to move into the five boroughs (Figure 7-45).

Figure 7-45 New York City has converted part of Times Square's vehicular space to a pedestrian plaza. *Photographer: Payton Chung (Creative Commons License)*

Months of public outreach went into a plan that was both simple and bold. The City needed to create a functional, healthy, and environmentally sound place for an increasing number of residents, employees, and visitors. A series of goals were set out for land, water, transportation, energy, air, and climate change. These strong and clear policies set the framework for actions, funding, and implementation of projects that brought multiple benefits to the City and its residents.

The NYC Plaza Program

PlaNYC states that no one should live more than a 10-minute walk from a park. At the time the plan was created, over 2 million New Yorkers lived in places that did not meet the goal.[14]

14 City of New York, PlaNYC website, "About PlaNYC, Parks and Public Space," accessed at http://www.nyc.gov/html/planyc2030/html/theplan/public-spaces.shtml.

Figure 7-46 Willoughby Street Pedestrian Plaza offers public space in the right-of-way. *Photographer: Paul Iano*

With a finite amount of land and an expected increase in population, the right-of-way comes under scrutiny as a valuable resource in meeting a wide range of goals. Many residents were surprised to learn that the right-of-way comprised a third of New York City's land.

The Open Space Report in PlaNYC put forth a goal to create or enhance at least one public plaza in every community. "Our challenge," states the plan, "is to find more creative ways to make our neighborhoods greener and more active than ever."

Within the overall goals of the plan, the impetus to create new plazas comes from residents. "The program is bottom up," says Vaidila Kungys, of the Office of Planning and Sustainability: Public Spaces, with NYC DOT. "Community groups propose plaza sites that are consistent with their vision and goals for the neighborhood. At the same time, the program is funded as a city-wide initiative to improve the amount of open space and quality of life for New Yorkers so it meets local as well as city-wide goals."

The plan includes a case study of Willoughby Street in downtown Brooklyn. The opportunity for better use of the street came from a City DOT Deputy Commissioner noticing, while on jury duty, that right-of-way outside the window was full of illegally parked cars. Unused by either pedestrians or traffic, the area was next to the Jay Street subway station and the Fulton Street shopping area—a prime location for plaza space. In the summer of 2006, the Metrotech Business Improvement District (BID) and the City DOT partnered on the Willoughby Pedestrian Plaza pilot project. With a minimal budget, the City set out planters to block the cars, chairs, tables, bicycle racks, and umbrellas, and created a 7,000-square-foot park (Figures 7-46 and 7-47).

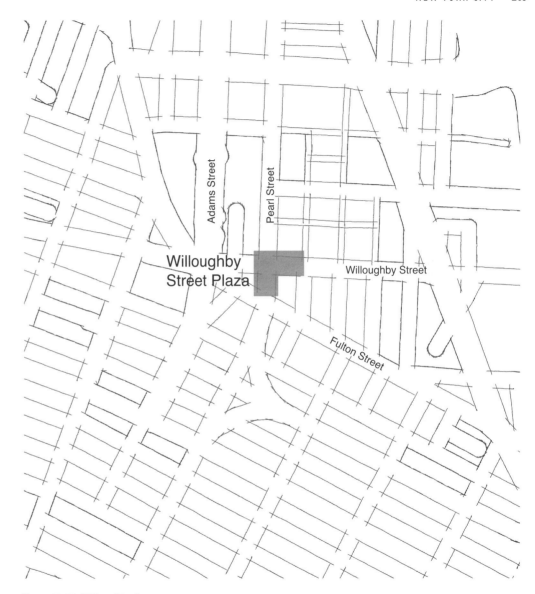

Figure 7-47 Willoughby Street context.

Figure 7-48 Planting a tree as part of the MillionTreesNYC program. *Photo credit to Michael Perlman, Chair of Rego-Forest Preservation Council*

As with almost every project, there were nay-sayers. Some community members feared that the plaza would bring vagrants and trash. Others marveled at the shift of attitude on the part of the DOT. As an experiment, there was very little to lose. No permanent changes were made for the pilot project. So often, this kind of experimentation is possible where more expensive and permanent projects are prohibitive. The pilot Willoughby Street Pedestrian Plaza was a resounding success, leading to a permanent park with higher quality furnishings. The innovative NYC Plaza program is creating new public spaces throughout the City.

Again, the goal is clear and bold. "The NYC Plaza Program will re-invent New York City's public realm," states the program description.[15] The combined amount of land in New York City's public rights-of-way, at 64 square miles, is about 50 times the land in Central Park. Non-profit organizations can apply to the Plaza Program, nominating candidate plaza sites. Selected non-profit organizations are responsible for maintenance, insurance, and programming. The non-profit must demonstrate how the plaza will be managed and funded over the long term through a funding plan. DOT contracts with a design team that works with the non-profit partners to create designs tailored to the needs and context of the site.

MillionTreesNYC

MillionTreesNYC is one of PlaNYC's 127 initiatives, many of which take advantage of the City's right-of-way. Of the million trees that the City aims to plant by 2017, 60 percent will be on public land, including the streets and plazas.[16] In order to fully stock New York's street, over 200,000 new street trees are anticipated for planting by the Parks Department. This ambitious plan benefits from numerous grants, the commitment of government and community organizations, nonprofits, and corporate sponsors. Private citizens are encouraged to plant trees and become tree stewards.

The many benefits of the trees include stories of people and communities working together to create a better city. The Get Involved section of the City website notes that, "With a million trees there comes a million stories of how each tree was planted and is being cared for." Wonderful stories and photos are posted from groups of coworkers, resident groups, individuals, and school kids, which will inspire personal efforts and make an enormous collective difference (Figure 7-48).

---

[15] www.nyc.gov/html/dot/html/sidewalks/publicplaza.shtml.
[16] Best Practice: Planting One Million Trees to Develop the Urban Forest, New York City Global Partners, March 25, 2011.

Leadership: Redefining a Twenty-First-Century Transportation Department

> "In an effort to better manage the public realm, DOT has established for the first time both the Art, Urban Design, and Public Plaza programs within Planning and Sustainability."
>
> —*NYCDOT Strategic Plan*

The imperatives of PlaNYC call for a different approach to the transportation department. The land under the purview of NYCDOT is some of the most valuable real estate in the world. With a low rate of car ownership and high rate of transit use, the idea of accommodating multiple modes of transportation is paramount. Making the most of space that is in such high demand means considering not only the functions, but the qualities of the spaces. NYCDOT recognizes that the streets are literally the front yards of urban residents. "We are committed," states NYCDOT in their 2008 Strategic Plan, "to creating more varied and lively streetscapes to make our streets great destinations."

Mobility: Bike Path Matrix

PlanNYC set out the goal of completing the City's 1,800-mile bicycle master plan. That bike plan dates from 2006, when New York City announced an ambitious, unprecedented agenda for creating a safe bicycle network. The joint announcement was made by the transportation commissioner, the health commissioner, the parks and recreation commissioner, and the police commissioner. Creation of a safe bicycle network for the City would simultaneously benefit diverse agendas. It was a safety report, Bicyclist Fatalities and Serious Injuries in New York City 1996 –2005, that spurred the notion of a better network of paths, lanes, and routes for cyclists.[17]

New York City's bicycle improvements are also rooted in planning documents and policy priorities. The New York City Bicycle Master Plan of 1997 laid out the rationale, goals, and an action plan for increasing bicycle ridership as an important component of the transportation system. The Plan outlined a City-wide network of over 900 miles of bicycle facilities, and design guidelines and multiagency initiatives to encourage and educate the public. Funding came in part from federal programs targeted to balancing transportation with nonmotorized sources, the Congestion Mitiga-

---

[17] www.nyc.gov/html/doh/downloads/pdf/episrv/episrv-bike-report.pdf.

Figure 7-49 A bike lane with a buffer from traffic that is part of the expanding network for cyclists in New York City. *Photographer: Payton Chung (Creative Commons License)*

tion Air Quality (CMAQ) program and the Transportation Equity Act of the 21st Century (TEA-21) (Figure 7-49).

New York has many advantages for cycling. The density and mix of uses means that many destinations lie within an easy bike trip. The land is relatively flat, and there are pleasant routes through the park system and along the waterfront. Particular issues to New York were improvements needed on the bridges, and better access for cyclists using transit for portions of their trip.

In 2008, the City implemented 90 miles of new bike lanes, contributing to an unprecedented 35 percent single-year increase in bicycle commuting. It was an impressive achievement: 200 miles of bike lanes implemented in three years, in all 5 boroughs, not to mention almost 5 miles of bike paths separated from car traffic lanes, 20 sheltered bike parking structures, and 3,100 bike racks. The City reports that between 2006 and 2009, commuter cycling increased 79 percent. Safety statistics showed results as well, with injuries to both pedestrians and cyclists down, and much less reported riding on sidewalks.[18]

Obstacles

The major difficulty in implementing the initiatives in PlaNYC is money, given that the economy in the early years of its implementation was in recessionary mode. The reduction in the capital budget meant that implementation of some items would take longer than planned. For instance, budget cuts reduced the number of Greenstreets that were planned.

One strategy to "do more with less" has been to focus on initiatives that are least capital intensive, for instance, increasing open space for communities by opening up the public schoolyards as playgrounds. As the implementation of the plan has occurred, the City has been willing to reconsider initiatives where benefits may not be worth the efforts and costs involved.

Lessons Learned

New York is an excellent model for creating a strong, clear policy framework. The goals are clear, and come along with actions for implementation. This kind of planning is impossible without supportive and strong leadership, not only to create the plan, but to follow through with it over the course of a number of years.

The City has also shown the value of experimentation, using pilot projects to test ideas and public acceptance. Change can be worrisome to people, but sometimes they are willing to accept experimental changes that can be reversed. Testing changes can be very helpful in formulating permanent solutions.

---

[18] www.nyc.gov/html/dot/html/bicyclists/bikenetwork.shtml.

Vaidila Kungys offers some lessons from New York's experience:

- Start small. Even small budgets can produce significant changes in reclaiming public space. Paint, planters, creative remarking of streets and movable chairs can make people places out of unneeded right-of-way.

- Leverage local resources. Nonprofits with roots in the community know the neighborhood better than agencies, and programs can be developed to make use of those assets.

- Integrate changes by reviewing current capital dollars and street reconstruction projects to find places to improve safety and enhance public spaces.

- Let local community groups compete for City resources. This competition should be within a clearly defined framework of a program and criteria for the City's priorities.

- Leaders can inspire organizational change. Without supportive leadership, it is difficult to move new programs forward.

- Get written community support early. Later, this is helpful if opposition arises.

New York is unlike many U.S. cities and towns in terms of its density and its comprehensive transit system. Where densities are lower, and destinations spread out, it can be more difficult to achieve the kind of activation that can happen in New York City. Nonetheless, the approaches taken in PlaNYC and the creation of public realm in the right-of-way can help lead the way as other cities develop more walkable, active urban spaces.

TERRY AVENUE NORTH

> **"How close can we get to a European-style pedestrian-oriented street?"**
> —*Grace Crunican, former Director, Seattle's Department of Transportation*

Figure 7-50 Terry Avenue North was redesigned to encourage pedestrian use.

In 2003, Seattle's South Lake Union neighborhood was on its way to wholesale changes in land use, development, and transportation networks. The industrial lakeside neighborhood was being transformed into one of Seattle's most prominent business and residential addresses.

Terry Avenue North was located at the heart of this change. Much of the property along the street was slated for redevelopment and there was a significant interest on the part of the community and the City to create a new type of streetscape for the six-block segment of Terry Avenue. Following a holistic neighborhood design exercise—the South Lake Union Public Realm Plan—Terry Avenue became the focus of a specific set of design guidelines that would shape future public and private investments (Figure 7-50).

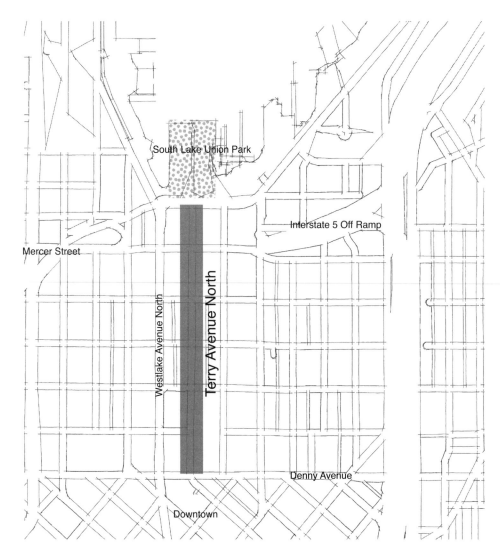

Figure 7-51 Terry Avenue North context.

Context

The South Lake Union neighborhood lies just a few blocks north of downtown Seattle, between the established residential neighborhoods of Queen Anne and Capitol Hill. Bounded by heavily traveled roadways, South Lake Union has felt disconnected from the surrounding neighborhoods and remained a low-density industrial area well into Seattle's boom times. In the mid-1990s, a citizen's initiative was placed on the ballot to turn this entire neighborhood into a park that would be flanked by residential and office development. This plan, called the Seattle Commons, went to the voters and failed.

Soon after, Microsoft cofounder Paul Allen's Vulcan Real Estate acquired some 60 acres of property in the South Lake Union neighborhood. Vulcan's plan, which has since moved forward, was to redevelop the area into a high-density residential and bio-tech hub with the companion goal of building new, sustainable infrastructure to support the future residents, employees, and visitors. The magnitude of redevelopment was huge, with Amazon.com's headquarters alone bringing 1.6 million square feet of office and 100,000 square feet of retail. Some 25,000 daytime employees were expected within a five-block radius with the near-term buildout.

During this same period of time, the City of Seattle acquired a significant property at the south end of Lake Union. In 2009, construction began on a new 12-acre waterfront park and community center. Additionally, the first line of the Seattle Streetcar network—the South Lake Union line—was planned to link the lake with this neighborhood and downtown, and major roadway improvements were proposed for the Mercer Corridor, an east-west street that provides a regional connection between Highway 99 to Interstate 5.

Terry Avenue North lies at the center of this evolving neighborhood. Because of its limited access, it has very little traffic. It is ideally suited to form a place for social connections in the midst of a denser, more active neighborhood (Figure 7-51).

The Opportunity

Terry Avenue North was identified by the City's Department of Transportation as an excellent candidate for a new streetscape model for a variety of reasons. First, Terry Avenue is a short segment of street designated as a nonarterial located within an industrially zoned area. With the lake on the north end, and Denny Way—a high-speed, high-volume roadway on the south end—Terry mostly served the access needs of the adjacent local businesses. Westlake Avenue, the parallel route to the west, takes most of the traffic volume.

Denny Way is not only heavily traveled, but cuts diagonally across the street grid of downtown and traverses a steep slope in this location. Cars have limited sight distance going up the hill, and are traveling extremely quickly going down the hill. For these reasons, Denny is a significant barrier for pedestrians crossing from South Lake Union to get to Seattle's adjacent downtown neighborhoods. One positive outcome is that left turns onto Terry from Denny are not allowed, ensuring that traffic remains local, low-volume, and low-speed. Since Terry is not a heavily trafficked street, trying something new here allowed the City and neighborhood to attempt something bold, without having an impact on the broader transportation network in the neighborhood (Figure 7-52).

Second, the right-of-way is unusually wide, ranging from 71 to 76 feet, and has an interesting character. The abandoned rail tracks and patches of brick paving reveal Terry's industrial past. The views toward Lake Union, downtown Seattle, and the Space Needle at Seattle Center provide interest and a sense of the street's location in the City.

And third, Terry Avenue North already functioned in some ways as a shared-use street, with little traffic. Cars parked next to the buildings and trucks parked perpendicular to the street. Without sidewalks, pedestrians walked in the street. This condition was comfortable because of the local-only traffic and low speeds. Cyclists avoided Terry because of the uneven pavement quality and the tire-grabbing in-pavement train tracks.

The idea of Terry Avenue North as a pedestrian street galvanized the public, private, and community sectors. The process of creating the Terry Avenue North Design Guidelines began in advance of upcoming construction on major new development projects and when final designs for a new streetcar were underway.

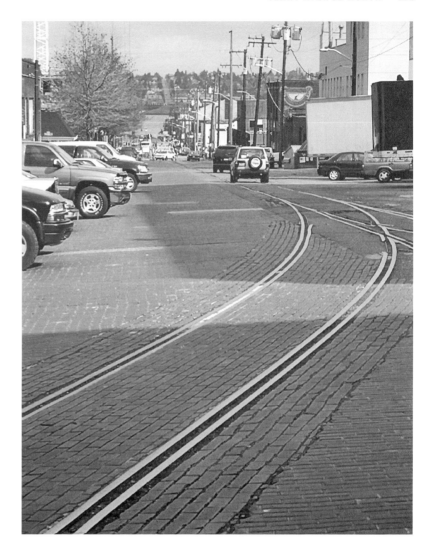

Figure 7-52 Terry Avenue North was part of an industrial zone near Lake Union.

MOVING FROM LINEAR TO CLUSTERS

The idea of clusters of space rather than narrow linear spaces was a fundamental and critical shift in approach to streetscape design. In most streets, the functions and the channels of movement are completely linear.

For Terry Avenue North, the idea of pedestrian use of the full right-of-way offered an opportunity to break out of standard design practices and more fully inhabit the street. The clustered design approach allowed for larger, nonlinear pedestrian spaces.

The plazas on the private side of the property line connect with the streetscape space, and pedestrians could comfortably cross from one side to the other along the full length of the street.

Larger groupings of landscaping allow for healthier environments for trees as well as larger species of trees. Grouped landscape and larger trees fill the volume of the street with landscaping, rather than a standard line of uniformly spaced trees.

Process

Even with the support of the area's highly engaged neighborhood organizations, the creation of the Guidelines required extensive community outreach and coordination between City departments. Community input was culled through a series of interviews with local property owners and tenants, public open houses, meetings with neighborhood groups, a website operated by the City, and input from the City's Design Commission.

The Guidelines had to be coordinated with multiple plans for a neighborhood under rapid development, plans for reconstructing major parts of the arterial system, and the fast-moving design process for the streetcar. As an identified "heart location," Terry was intended to be a social hub rich in amenities, including pedestrian-scale lighting, quality paving, landscaping, art, and open space fully available to the public.

The Guidelines were written to allow development over time, laying out a concept for the street so that developers would know the City's expectations of improvements in the street. They included street geometrics to assure consistency as the street built out over time. Instead of one palette of materials and a unified design, the Guidelines offered a number of options for materials to allow future private developers design flexibility. Because part of the character of the street originally comes from a mix of materials and uses, they encouraged variety within the overall palette.

The Guidelines were officially adopted by the City of Seattle in 2005. Subsequent developments were encouraged to follow them, and they were used as part of the design review processes required by the City (Figure 7-53).

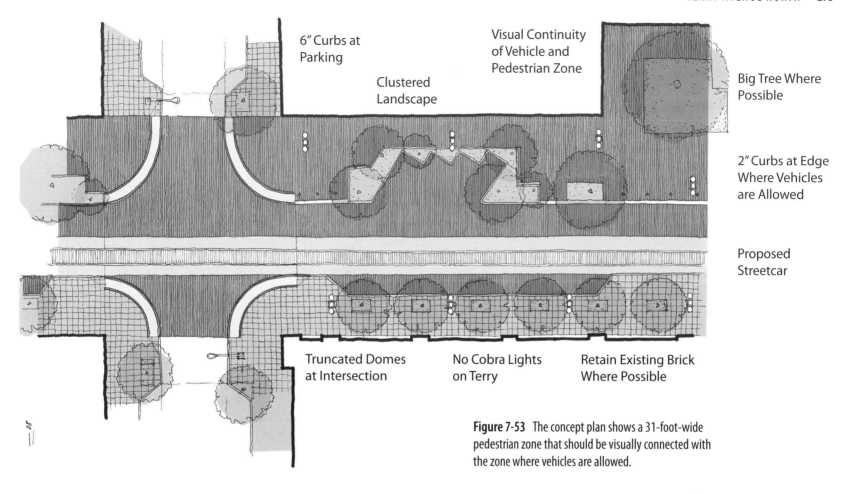

6" Curbs at Parking

Visual Continuity of Vehicle and Pedestrian Zone

Clustered Landscape

Big Tree Where Possible

2" Curbs at Edge Where Vehicles are Allowed

Proposed Streetcar

Truncated Domes at Intersection

No Cobra Lights on Terry

Retain Existing Brick Where Possible

Figure 7-53 The concept plan shows a 31-foot-wide pedestrian zone that should be visually connected with the zone where vehicles are allowed.

Solutions

Establishing Zones

Because Terry Avenue North would be built out over time along the six blocks, it was important at the outset to establish the configuration of the full buildout. The Guidelines established a clear priority for pedestrians with a 31-foot zone on the east side of the street. That zone accommodates a mix of pedestrian areas, landscaping, public art, street furniture, and clustered parking. Designers could choose

Figure 7-54 The streetcar connects the neighborhood to downtown.

how to allocate the uses so that the exterior and interior spaces were mutually supportive. A maximum of five parking spaces was set for a cluster of parking.

The vehicle zone of 23 feet allowed for two traffic lanes, including the streetcar. The 23-foot zone kept the option open for a two-way street in the future.

The pedestrian zone on the west side of the vehicle zone is a fairly standard design, with a sidewalk varying from 9 to 14 feet wide, based on the overall right-of-way width, a 6-inch curb, and parallel parking (Figure 7-54).

Water

Terry Avenue North has a grade change of 60 feet over its six-block length as it slopes toward South Lake Union. However, the lake no longer receives any of the natural runoff flow from the basin. Stormwater from the Terry Basin has been diverted into a 30-inch collection system that is a combined sanitary sewer and storm drain line.

The South Lake Union community has long been interested in becoming a more sustainable neighborhood. In 1996, the neighborhood council created "Waterflow Vision," sustainability guidelines that propose to "remake the community into a functional surface water landscape and ecosystem." There had been a longstanding community desire to use street and roof stormwater for irrigation of the South Lake Union Park, and ultimately, to return the water to the lake.

An interesting debate that occurred during the formulation of the Guidelines was the merit of reconnecting the lake and the water from the Terry Basin. Although the idea of reestablishing the connection to the lake was appealing, concerns arose about the potential harm caused by the turbulence from excess water during storm events, which could stir up the polluted sediment at the bottom of the lake and adversely affect salmon habitat. In addition, a major sewer overflow project intended to protect Lake Union and Elliott Bay from just this kind of stormwater influx had recently been completed.

Given this background, the Guidelines proposed to use the natural topography and the width of Terry Avenue North to emphasize visual representation of water flow through shallow runnels and landscape treatments that would store, convey, and treat the water through infiltration. Stormwater that exceeded the capacity of the landscaped areas would continue to be tight-lined into the underground system.

Materials

In discussions with the community, the character of Terry Avenue North was paramount. The industrial history was visible in the patches of brick and the rails in the street. The "gritty" nature of Terry Avenue was considered a positive attribute, and the intent of the Guidelines was to retain as much of the existing brick as possible, and to allow variation in the palette of new materials as the street was built out. This palette was selected for durability, ease of maintenance, and compatibility with the existing materials in the street.

Material choice is critical in creating a pedestrian street. The Guidelines drew on successful examples of streets that were already functioning as pedestrian streets, either by design or by circumstance. In each case the materials denoted space as favoring pedestrians. Local examples included the well-loved Pike Place Market, which essentially functions as a brick-surfaced pedestrian street. Westlake Plaza in downtown Seattle is surfaced with a pattern of pavers that extends across both pedestrian areas and the drive lanes. The visual continuity of quality materials made streets read as pedestrian, rather than vehicular in nature. Acceptable materials, per the Guidelines, included brick, new brick, granite pavers, and stamped concrete.

Accessibility

In trying to answer the original question posed by the project—How close can we get to a European-style pedestrian street?—meeting accessibility regulations turned out to be one of the biggest challenges. For example, in order to create a safe environment for people with visual impairments, federal regulations ask for 36-inch-wide warning strips with truncated domes. There must be a 70 percent color contrast between the warning strip and the adjacent pavement. In Seattle and other places, this has resulted in the installation of canary yellow tactile warning strips in curb ramps. The yellow retains its color contrast even over time which was not the case for the white tactile panels originally used as a City standard.

Removing the curb to create a consistent plane where cars and people mix runs counter to many standard practices. The separation of cars and people touches accessibility, safety, and liability issues that make regulators nervous. If visual continuity is the hallmark of a pedestrian feel in the street, there is an inherent contradiction in clear separation of uses.

The design team for the Guidelines tested a number of alternatives to keep the nonlinear feel of the street while providing visual and physical separation of pedestrians and cars. If the street were to be a curbless *woonerf,* a highly contrasted tactile warning strip would be required along its full length. This was deemed unacceptable as the brightly colored tactile warning strip was jarring against the palette of more muted, historically themed materials. Bollards are allowed in the Guidelines, but only intended for limited spaces, not as an element to line the street. Planters would serve as separators for parts of the interface between pedestrians and the zone where vehicles were allowed, and the six-inch curb at the diagonal parking spaces would solve the problem for additional length.

Where there were no landscape or parking zones, the design team felt that the best way to keep visual continuity was to retain, but de-emphasize the curb. Reducing the curb height from the six-inch standard to two inches along the pedestrian zone met the needs of the City, yet was unobtrusive. The curb would be a color that contrasts with the adjacent material. The Westlake Mall in downtown used a similar two-inch curb approach, setting a precedent for regulators.

At intersections, the City approved the use of pavers for tactile warning, rather than the yellow polymer strip, so long as the visual contrast was sufficient. The approved pavers were off-white and a dark charcoal gray to maintain a high contrast even over time.

Landscaping

Like most historically industrial streets, Terry had few trees along its length. The design team discussed various approaches to landscape that would take advantage of the larger spaces available, emphasize views toward the lake and the Space Needle, and possibly relate to the history of the street.

Figure 7-55 The width of the pedestrian zone allows offset landscape zones rather than only linear landscape.

The 31-foot-wide east zone of the street led to the "big tree" concept in the Guidelines. Landscape architect Shannon Nichol of Gustafson Guthrie Nichol Ltd saw the clusters of landscaping as a particular opportunity for trees that were larger than typical street trees. Both at the surface and below grade, this east zone could support and nurture very large tree species. The Bigleaf Maple (Acer macrophyllum) and Western Red Cedar (Thuja plicata) were called out as large native species that would provide iconic focal points in the urban setting. Their presence in Terry Avenue North would stand as symbolic homage to David Denny's sawmill, which once stood nearby.

The Guidelines called for linking the landscape palette of Terry Avenue North and the design of South Lake Union Park so that the street and the park were mutually strengthened (Figure 7-55).

Figure 7-56 Seating recycles wood from a remodeled older building on the street.

Lighting

Pedestrian lighting took its cue from fixtures already in place on the west side of the street. These fixtures, with lighting at a 15-foot height, would replace cobra lights between intersections. Two options were allowed for lighting along the wider east pedestrian zone in order to provide lighting levels where needed, to break up the linear feel, and to coordinate with tree locations.

Funding

The Guidelines were funded by the City of Seattle through a contract with a design team led by Weinstein A|U Architects and Urban Designers. The improvements to the street itself have been funded as part of adjacent development from private sector property owners. With the buildout of Amazon.com's headquarters in 2009–2010, a significant portion of the street was reconstructed.

The South Lake Union line of the Seattle Streetcar began service in 2007. A public-private partnership among property owners along the route, along with federal, state, and local government partners funded the streetcar construction.

Improvements in the right-of-way, according to the Guidelines, would be paid for by private property owners within the boundaries of their projects. Funded transportation projects would also be encouraged to follow the Guidelines. Although maintenance of the final improvements is technically a responsibility of the adjacent property owners, safety repairs can, by default, become a City of Seattle responsibility. The City engineering team, while a dedicated partner, was initially skeptical about the costs and responsibilities of ongoing maintenance due to the high-quality materials, unique design features, and unknown possible pitfalls of the Terry Avenue project (Figure 7-56).

Maintenance

Maintenance was a major topic of discussion throughout the development of the Guidelines and was often a driver of design decisions and material choices. In Seattle, as in most other cities in the United States, maintenance of the street elements falls to the City, while the adjacent property owner has the responsibility to keep the curb-to-building frontage portion of the right-of way in passable condition. When the materials used in the right-of-way differ from the City's standard palette of materials, a maintenance agreement between the private property owner and the City can be a condition imposed during the final permitting process.

In the case of Terry Avenue, with unique elements envisioned in the roadway as well as in the pedestrian zone and planting area, the City is responsible for the added maintenance of these elements—a situation that can easily result in higher maintenance costs when the repairs are needed. This can be a daunting situation for a maintenance manager who sees his or her budget shrinking over time due to budget shortfalls while the maintenance backlog throughout the City grows ever larger. These are a few of the factors that made the City engineers concerned about using a unique palette of materials in the right-of-way, and drove their interest in having maintenance agreements with adjacent property owners.

The City has become more comfortable over time with issues of maintenance in the right-of-way, although securing funding for maintenance will continue to be daunting. The push for sustainability in the right-of-way has relied on increased landscaping in order to meet new standards for storm drainage and plantings. In the case of Terry Avenue North, the maintenance of the right-of-way would be done as part of the same work as the maintenance of the adjacent public spaces on the private side of the property line.

Lessons Learned

Since the Guidelines were written, the streetcar and three blocks of Amazon's headquarters have been built out.

The 31-foot zone on the east side of Terry Avenue North, with its mix of uses, is successful in the way it functions and as a distinctive, well-used space. The public plazas, built as part of the new private development, have seating steps and prominent artwork and integrate well with the pedestrian zone. Two east-west pedestrian routes connect Terry Avenue North with Boren Avenue to the east. On sunny days, the steps and the plaza are full of people at lunchtime. Individuals and small groups regularly use the benches.

The clustered landscaping feels generously green, and the trees should grow well over time with much larger soil area than standard street trees. Seating near the landscape zone takes advantage of reused wood from the partially preserved Van Vorst Building. The small groups of back-in angled parking are screened by the landscape zones. As the adjacent blocks of Terry Avenue North are built out, the space should feel even more spacious.

On the west side, there is an area where the pedestrian space breaks out of a linear form. The streetcar shelters are adjacent to the curb, and landscape zones stagger between curb line and a zone west of the transit shelter.

Materials

The warm materials of the plaza on the east side reach out into the pedestrian zone, with a palette from the Guidelines. The blurring of plaza and pedestrian zone in the right-of-way is achieved with the use of materials. The success of the space is directly related to the quality of the materials, and the east side goes beyond the language of standard gray sidewalk. The west side stays with the two-foot-square standard concrete, and the extra width feels stark in comparison to the east side (Figure 7-57).

Vehicle Zones

In contrast to the successes of the pedestrian spaces, the vehicle zone is disappointing. The asphalt remains instead of the higher quality materials that encourage pedestrians to share the street.

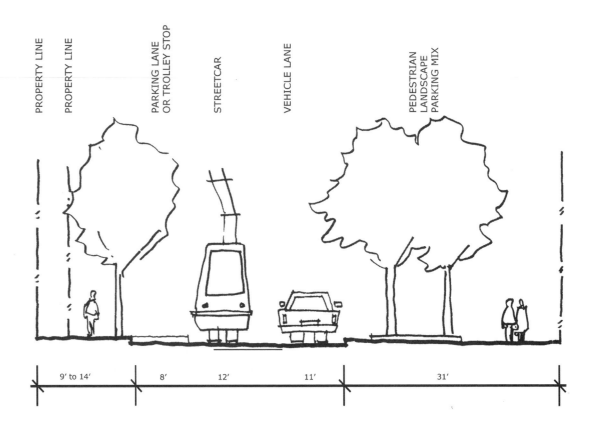

Figure 7-57 Zones, shown in section, looking north.

Lane markings also stayed in place even though Terry Avenue North is a one-way street. The streetcar tracks are placed in standard color concrete, with a raked finish as the only concession. The streetcar budget constraints drove the decision on materials.

Pedestrian/Vehicle Transitions

The two-inch curb works well on the east side of the street. But because the vehicle zone is asphalt, there is no visual continuity across the width of the right-of-way as intended in the Guidelines. However, everything is set up so that if the material in the vehicle zone were to be improved, the street would feel as intended.

Although the City approved using high-contrast pavers at ADA ramps, the installed material is the standard plastic truncated dome inlay. They are white rather than the yellow that appears throughout most of the City.

Conclusions

Looking back on the question of how close we could come to a European-style pedestrian street, the answer for this time and place was:

It is possible to accomplish an excellent pedestrian realm within the public right-of-way that blurs the line between the private side of the property line and the public side. Quality materials, seating, and landscaping can fill extra space. The quality of the materials is key, and if the standard language of vehicular traffic is used in the roadway, it is clearly not a pedestrian street. If either the private property owners or the City can find funding over time to improve the quality of materials in the vehicle zone, there is still a possibility to move from a grander pedestrian realm to a true pedestrian street (Figure 7-58).

Figure 7-58 Large landscape areas make the street almost park-like.

COMMENTS

"We love the way people are using the plaza and the wide pedestrian spaces. Terry Avenue feels like the center of an urban campus where people can enjoy being outdoors and mixing with each other."

—*Sharon Coleman, Real Estate Development, Vulcan*

"It sets up a fantastic rhythm, which is not a completely linear experience. When we show it to people they are very inspired. It has expanded the thinking of our client developers, who now see that good streetscape is an advantage worth paying for."

—*Guy Michaelson. Partner, The Berger Partnership, Landscape firm for the Amazon projects*

"We have definitely raised the bar in streetscape design. The east side of the street will hopefully be a new model, and we can continue to move closer over time to the idea of a *woonerf* across the full right-of-way."

—*Lyle Bicknell, Seattle Department of Planning and Development*

"In writing the Guidelines, the biggest challenge to creating a *woonerf* was the ADA (Americans with Disabilities Act). Now that it is built out, the two-inch curb and the pedestrian area are working very well. We came a long way toward the vision of the Guidelines, but the travel lanes still have too much of the language of traffic engineering for a fully pedestrian street."

—*Ron Scharf, Project Manager, Seattle Department of Transportation*

Chapter 8

WHAT'S NEXT

HOW FAR CAN THE IDEA OF REUS-ING STREETS GO? Visionaries imagine restored greenery, captured water, and new energy sources. When whole new districts and cities are envisioned, streets move beyond the idea of automobile use, coming full circle by turning back into places where people interact, and where natural systems are restored (Figure 8-1).

Figure 8-1 *From "Fight for Your Right of Way." Designers: The Miller Hull Partnership*

BIOPHILIC CITIES: MORE NATURE IN THE CITY

Nature holds the key to our aesthetic, intellectual, cognitive and even spiritual satisfaction.

E. O. Wilson, Biophilia

Our present physical, social, and economic structures are but a moment in human history. The automobile era constitutes roughly a century of human existence. In contrast, the natural landscape has provided for all aspects of our needs for some 200,000 years of human existence. Even the earliest cities began only a few thousand years ago. The world that we know—dependent on cars, trains, airplanes, large-scale agriculture, and nation states—is an anomaly, rather than a norm.

What does nature mean to human satisfaction, and what should it mean to cities as the population of the world expands and urbanizes? "We need nature in our lives; it is not optional but essential," argues Timothy Beatley in his book, *Biophilic Cities*. Biophilia "raises serious questions about what a city is or could be and what constitutes a livable, sustainable place."[1]

How can we bring back nature into our cities? Parks, green walls, and green roofs, all play a part. Certainly, the land in the right-of-way holds enormous potential to reintegrate nature into the places that we live and work. Examples discussed in earlier chapters include median plantings, "pollinator pathways," and increased tree canopy that support habitat in urban neighborhoods. Natural drainage systems are becoming standard common practice for a generation of civil engineers and planners.

Using the right-of-way to reconnect us to nature can be achieved by simple steps. Native-species plantings are friendly to habitat and appropriate to the climate. Trees serve a wealth of natural functions, supporting lichen, fungi, moss, insects, and birds. The importance of habitat for all of these important organisms, from the microorganisms up, has largely been forgotten in the creation of cities, and is in need of rediscovery.

As in so many cases, it is helpful to recognize what already exists, and use it as a model for what is possible. There are natural networks already in cities, and street grids successfully survive these natural interruptions where topography or water bodies prevent connections for vehicles.

San Diego, for instance, is shaped by its network of canyons. Because much of the canyon land has thus far defied development pressures, San Diego has retained natural forms, vegetation, and evidence of the watersheds in the City. Protecting the canyons has become a focal point for a range of civic groups. Their concerns for the future of the canyons in the City cover many topics—habitat, wildlife refuges, accessibility, openness to public use versus protection of fragile lands. But the City

---

[1] Beatly, Timothy. *Biophilic Cities: Integrating Nature into Urban Design and Planning,* Island Press, 2011, p. 3.

has formed itself around a connected natural system, and for San Diego, the biophilic city is there to nurture. For other cities, San Diego is one model of how interconnected systems, urban and natural, can coexist and flourish.

NEW TECHNOLOGIES

In addition to letting natural systems heal cities, new technologies can take advantage of urban rights-of-way. There is space, even with moving vehicles, to add solar panels and wind turbines. Solar-powered street lights, and even solar/wind hybrid lights are available on the market. With these technologies proven around the world and in the United States, the next step is to scale up the use of the right-of-way for energy production. In order to scale up, economic factors are as important as the development of new technologies.

Collecting Solar Energy

The U.S. Bureau of Land Management is finding a great deal of popular interest in utility-scale solar energy projects in the right-of-way, mostly in the sunny western states such as California, Nevada, and Arizona. How much impact could right-of-way solar energy collection have? The State of California alone has some 15,000 miles of highway.[2] The United States has roughly 4 million miles of roads, with 60 million miles of rights-of-way. Economist and energy specialist William Ellard calculates that the highway solar capacity, if fully developed, could generate several times the amount of electricity now used in the United States.[3]

The Oregon Department of Transportation put the first U.S. solar demonstration project on highway land in 2008. At the intersection of Interstate 5 and Interstate 205, almost 600 solar panels were installed, in collaboration with Portland General Electric (PGE) and US Bank. The solar panels supply power during the day to PGE's grid, and PGE returns power at night to light the interchange. Although this is a ground-breaking project in the United States, Germany and Switzerland have been using solar panels on highways for many years.[4]

---

[2] Caltrans Roadside Management Toolbox, California Department of Transportation, Caltrans website, 2011, accessed at http://www.dot.ca.gov/hq/LandArch/roadside/.

[3] William Ellard, "A New Use for Solar Energy - Highway Right of Way," in Seeking Alpha, December 13, 2008, accessed at http://seekingalpha.com/article/110509-a-new-use-for-solar-energy-highway-right-of-way.

[4] "First U.S. Solar Highway Installation Starts in Oregon," Environment News Service, August 9, 2008, accessed at www.ens-newswire.com/ens/aug2008/2008-08-09-091.html.

The roadway itself represents an enormous resource. Anyone who has walked barefoot on an asphalt road in the summer knows that there is plenty of solar energy in the pavement. The U.S. Department of Transportation gave the Idaho-based company, Solar Roadways, a grant to develop prototype panel that replace asphalt road surfaces with drivable solar panels. Solar Roadways founder Scott Brusaw is enthusiastic about using existing solar power technology in a new and practical way. If one mile of a four-lane highway were "paved" with a solar panel road, it would produce enough electricity to take 500 homes off the grid, even with only four hours of sunlight a day.[5]

The conditions for roadway surfaces are difficult, and the key to making the scheme work is finding a surface for the solar panels that has asphalt's traction qualities, with the ability to weather heat and cold. Penn State University's Materials Research Institute believes that they can design a glass surface to meet those specifications. The idea of including LEDs beneath the glass surface is another exciting possibility. The road could actually become the "information highway," with travel times, warnings, detour information, or directional arrows lit up in the LEDs below the surface.

The economics of such a solution are within the realm of feasibility. Asphalt is relatively inexpensive but has a short lifespan. If the glass solar panels can last long enough, the panels may hit a breakeven level if life-cycle costs are considered. With the ability to generate energy, the new technology may be realistic. Additionally, there is an obvious synergy with charging electric vehicles.

Harvesting the Wind

Roads and highways may be able to collect wind from both the weather and from passing vehicles. Turbines could be located overhead, on crossbars like those used for highway signs. They could be placed alongside the roadway or in medians.

Early tests for generating wind power in the right-of-way are already being performed. In Lincoln, Nebraska, the City and the University of Nebraska-Lincoln have partnered on a study to test wind generation as an energy source for the City's traffic signals. A wind generator has been installed at the intersection of Highway 2 and 84th Street.

One of the problems with wind power generation is that some places aren't very windy. But placing turbines near passing traffic might allow generation from highways. Mark Oberholzer's concept for smaller turbines in "jersey-barrier" style median structures won *Metropolis* magazine's 2006 Next Generation Design Competition.

Another idea for harvesting energy from roadways is to transfer the kinetic energy generated by passing vehicles into electricity. The technology utilizes piezoelectric crystals, which transform mechan-

---

[5] "Solar panel roads to power our homes," Gizmag, Jeff Salton, September 10, 2009, accessed at www.gizmag.com/solar-panel-roads/12780/.

ical stress into electrical charges. It is not a new technology. Discovered by Jacques and Pierre Curie in 1880, this effect is already used in everyday applications, including mobile phones and vehicle air-bags. The concept is being tested on roads in Israel and Italy.

Cleansing the Air

It is counterintuitive to think of streets as an opportunity to clean the air. But another potential function of the street comes from a cement product sometimes referred to as "smog-eating" concrete. The concrete contains titanium dioxide, which, in presence of light, breaks down air pollutants through a process called photocatalysis. The Italian company, Italcementi Group, has spent a decade working on the product, and has found reductions in pollution of up to 50 percent.[6] The best results have been in large surface areas and direct sunlight with high traffic flows. The smog-eating concrete was included in TIME Magazine's best inventions of 2008.

The photocatalytic concrete has been used in prominent architectural projects, in large part because the photocatalysis keeps the concrete bright white. American architect Richard Meier's Misericordia Church in Rome, for example, uses large precast concrete blocks with the self-cleaning surface to retain their white color.

Photocatalytic permeable pavers are now available in the United States, and were installed in Mary Bartelme Park in Chicago in 2010. These pavers allow stormwater to flow into the ground below, and reduce pollutants.

The photocatalytic concrete has been tested with success in Italy and Holland on roadways. Missouri Department of Transportation is testing the first U.S. application on 2,000 square feet of Highway 141, outside of St. Louis. The product is more expensive than regular concrete, and while effective, it will take a lot of smog-eating concrete to solve urban air pollution problems.

Visionaries: Living Cities

Visionaries of all kinds are conceiving future scenarios for the way we live. Using or combining cutting-edge ideas—low-technology natural solutions and the most optimistic cutting-edge technologies—these visions explore what cities might become.

Richard Register has been putting forward ideas for ecologically sound cities for decades. He follows in the footsteps of his mentor Paolo Soleri in developing visions of what an eco-city could mean. Eco-cities allow people to have a high quality of life, while minimizing the use of natural resources. He

---

[6] Italcementi Group, TX Active: Presentation of the first active solution to the problem of pollution, Milan, February 28, 2006, accessed at http://www.italcementigroup.com/ENG/Media+and+Communication/News/Corporate+events/20060228.htm.

envisions compact cities, with tall structures linked by bridges. Greenhouses and rooftop gardens top the buildings, and natural habitat corridors lie at ground level. His philosophy on transportation, which underlies the eco-city concept, is a piece of wisdom for all those involved in city building:

> Instead of thinking of going places, think in terms of being places. That is, think in terms of establishing desirable places close to one another. Transportation is what you have to do to get to places inconveniently located: the less the better.
>
> —*Ecocity Berkeley: Building Cities for a Healthy Future,*
> Richard Register, North Atlantic Books, 1987, p. 33

One interesting place to look for visions of the future is the Living Cities Design Competition. The International Living Building Institute, in partnership with the National Trust for Historic Preservation, invited people to radically reimagine neighborhoods, towns, villages, and cities. Part of the requirement of each living city is a rich, pedestrian-based street life. Teams developed visions for 69 different cities in 21 different countries. Richard Register's EcoCity Builders worked with partners in Nepal, Bangladesh, and the United States to develop a scheme for Kathmandu. First-place winners Daniel Zielinski and Maximilian Zielinski of the United Kingdom reconsidered Paris, France. According to the jury, their entry "welcomed and incorporated the present, instead of simply showing how the 'natural world' might colonize urban environments."[7]

Of particular note to reconsidered streets is the People's Choice winner, titled "Fight for Your Right of Way." Architecture firm Miller Hull Partnership, designers of the vision, used alternate streets in an urban neighborhood to bring back urban wilds, green streets, and creek streets. The green ways bring nature to with a five-minute walk of every resident. "Welcome to My Way Byway! See the light of day in the right of way. Take back the public way!" challenges the design team. The right-of-way is public land, and the living city belongs to the community. The City grid functions for circulation and access, but adds visible conveyance for all water systems (Figure 8-2).

BUILDING THE DREAM

Ecologically sound districts and cities are starting to actually be built around the world. Often triggered by concerns about climate change or the expectation of shift in the availability of energy, the pioneers of carbon-neutral are the first to test new technologies and products, and the marketability of green neighborhoods. They are exciting experiments that may not achieve all of their goals, but help pull us forward with commitment to bold ideas for the future.

---

[7] Living City Design Competition Winners Unveiled, April 29, 2011, Vancouver B.C., International Living Future Institute, accessed at ilbi.org/lcdc-winners.

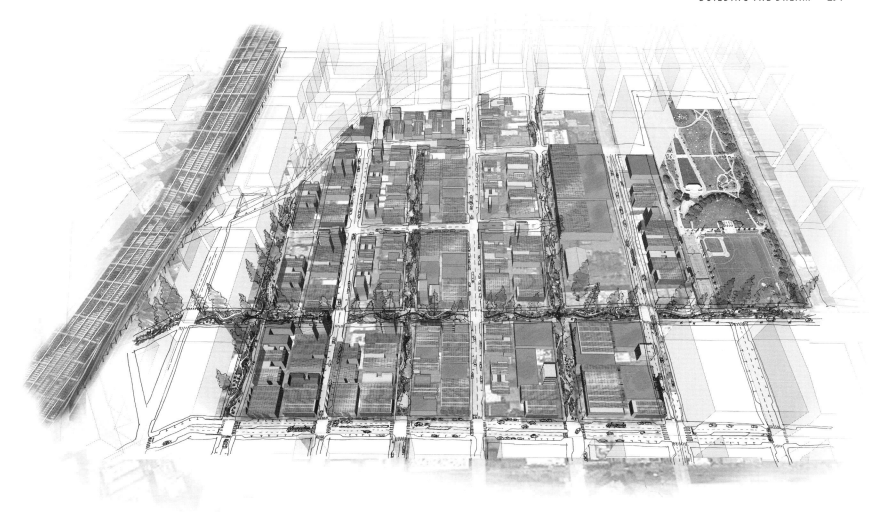

Figure 8-2 Aerial perspective from "Fight for Your Right of Way," Miller Hull Partnership's entry in the Living Cities design competition. *From "Fight for Your Right of Way."* *Designers: The Miller Hull Partnership*

Figure 8-3 Dockside Green in Victoria, B.C., focuses on pedestrians in the interior zone. *Photo courtesy of Dockside Green*

Figure 8-4 Dockside Green has a heavily landscaped street at its edge. *Photo courtesy of Dockside Green*

Dockside Green, Victoria

Victoria, British Columbia's Dockside Green set out to be North America's first carbon-neutral community. The master plan for Dockside Green received the first Platinum certification for LEED for Neighborhood Development. What do streets look like in such ambitiously green projects? The perimeter street includes a median planter and landscaped curb bulbs, but is recognizable as a city street. Inside the project, however, townhouses line the central green space, with a series of ponds that help retain stormwater and provide habitat. It is a shared pedestrian space, with paths and wooden bridges connecting to buildings and streets (Figures 8-3 and 8-4).

Treasure Island, San Francisco

Treasure Island, in San Francisco Bay, is slated for an ambitious development that pushes the envelope of sustainable design. Treasure Island was created in the 1930s by the federal government with fill dredged from the Bay, for use as an airport for Pan American's "flying boats" in the use at the time, such as the famed China Clipper. It is connected to Yerba Buena Island by a small isthmus, which allows access to the Oakland Bay Bridge. The island was used for the World's Fair of 1939–1940, and later as a navy base during wartime and up until 1997. Several hundred acres of the island opened up for development when ownership transferred to the City of San Francisco (Figure 8-5).

The development is a public-private partnership led by the City's Treasure Island Development Authority and Treasure Island Community Development, LLC. The design team includes master planners and architects Skidmore Owings & Merrill, CMG Landscape Architects, and ARUP. The strategies are similar to the Eco-City visions, with concentrated density, access to transit and open space, and pedestrian-dominated streets. The streets are angled in order to capture the most sunlight and to protect the streets from prevailing winds. The plan allows for more cars coming to the island, with over 10,000 spaces proposed, but hopes to discourage cars by charging a fee for vehicles during commute hours. Alternatives to driving include a new bus and ferry transportation terminal within walking distance of Treasure Island residents, and a pedestrian environment that attracts people to walk rather than drive.

In order to be a walkable community that can support needs such as a grocery store, the project builds density. According to the 2010 Draft Environmental Impact Report, the redevelopment plan

Figure 8-5 Rendering of sustainable development on Treasure Island, envisioned by SOM. *Courtesy of Skidmore, Owings & Merrill LLP/©AJSNY*

allows for up to 8,000 units, to be built over 15 to 20 years. The development is arranged in an "L" shape, with the commercial area and ferry terminal at the hinge.

A network of pedestrian, bicycle, and shared-use paths is a key component of the master plan. Routes connect the new ferry terminal and "Clipper Cove," and links to three of the remaining historic buildings. All of the residential units on Treasure Island would be within a 15-minute walk of the Transit Hub. Community facilities, markets, and the school would be a short walk or bike ride for the majority of the Island's residents. A "bike library" program would make bicycles available for residents and visitors, with bike lockers at major destinations. The Eastside District, facing Oakland, arranges the buildings around a 6-block long, 110-foot-wide central open space zone called the Eastside Commons.

The project proposes a new street designation for San Francisco—the Shared Public Way. This new typology is intended to encourage walking and cycling, and has no vertical separations such as

Figure 8-6 Plan of shared use street concept for Treasure Island. *Image courtesy of Treasure Island Community Development and CMG, Landscape Architects*

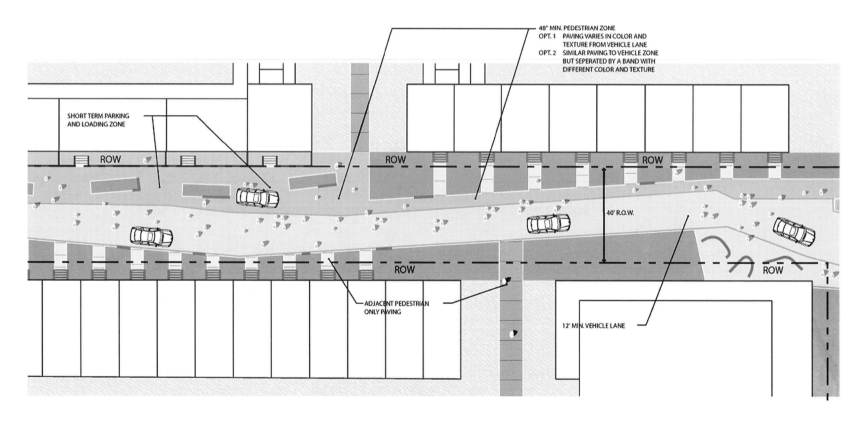

curbs. Strong enough visual and tactile clues are provided in order for the City to consider it a "nonhazardous" vehicle route. The streets on Treasure Island are new, and require approval from the fire department, utilities, public works, and the Mayor's Office on Disability. The design criteria for the shared-use streets were established through an inter-agency planning process. The parties involved have agreed to work together on design details, public outreach, approvals, and construction for the new type of right-of-way on Treasure Island. To do so, the group will need to work through issues of public safety, accessibility, liability, and maintenance through the final design and approval process (Figure 8-6).

Shared Public Ways on Treasure Island are also called "Mews." In section, the Mews are 40-feet wide, with a 20-foot zone where slow-moving cars share space with pedestrians. The Mews offer access within the larger blocks of the Cityside District, and on the south side of the historic hangars. Surface or architectural treatments differentiate the pedestrian-only areas from the pedestrian-vehicle zones. In order to bring in light, buildings adjacent to the shared-use ways need to step back above 40 feet in height. (See Figure 8-7.)

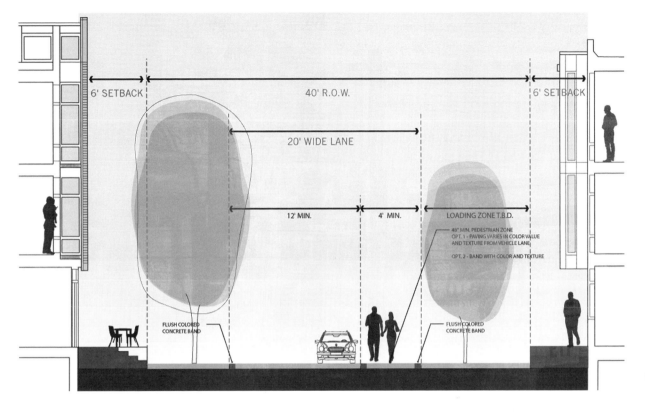

Figure 8-7 Section of shared use street concept for Treasure Island. *Image courtesy of Treasure Island Community Development and CMG, Landscape Architects*

Even before construction has begun, the process of envisioning Treasure Island has created change, as seen in the new shared-use street typology. But is this man-made island vulnerable to soil liquefaction in earthquake-prone San Francisco, the right place to concentrate efforts on sustainability? For some urban visionaries, there is an appeal to the new, the isolated, the island. Perhaps the idea of a clean slate is conducive to those who look for a utopian vision. The idea of a new bar for a sustainable district on Treasure Island has sparked imaginations and support, and maybe that's enough. Where opportunities arise, and support follows, there are lessons to be learned and new models that raise the bar everywhere.

Masdar City, Abu Dhabi, United Arab Emirates

Masdar City is not an island like Treasure Island. Instead, it is being built like an island in the desert. Masdar is about 10 miles from Abu Dhabi, in one of the world's most challenging climates. Foster + Partners, along with a team of consultants, led the master planning and the first stage of the project.

The ambitions are lofty. Masdar's goal is to become the world's first zero-carbon, zero-waste development, following the principles of One Planet Living. Masdar is not just about building housing for the growing population of the United Arab Emirates, but aims to be a showpiece of development for the future that would attract researchers, companies, and organizations working on renewable energy and clean technologies.

The designs employ ancient solutions to climate control, such as thick stone and mud walls. But these traditional wall types are to be covered with solar collectors. Pathways will be draped with fabric that converts sunlight into energy.

The master plan removed cars from the surface, leaving narrow, shaded pedestrian streets. People were to be shuttled in a system of driverless personal rapid transit–style system below the surface of the City. The "podcars" were to be powered by solar panels on the tops of buildings, with thermal storage allowing them to run day and night. But the system required building a full level beneath the City, which has turned out to be too much of a burden even with the enviable budget of the Masdar project.

CONCLUSIONS

The visions for the future share some common themes. Build enough density to support walkability, and make the pedestrian realm enticing. Look for new technologies, but rely on the wisdom of natural systems.

There are many stories of ways that people have found to use streets to make better communities. Regardless of the place or the scale, the same questions arise: Who makes the decisions in the public right-of-way? Who pays for improvements in the public realm? Who is responsible for maintenance? And who is liable if things go awry? How is it possible to change the status quo in order to make better use of streets?

The stories throughout this book have found ways to answer these questions, specific to each situation. Decisions regarding the public realm are complicated by their very nature. They may be made, in a way, by the individual decisions made every day. People decide to spend time walking or visiting the town center. Someone decides not to ride their bicycle to work because it feels dangerous. A gardening enthusiast digs up the median strip and invites the neighbors to join in.

Other decisions come from elected officials, agency staff, or institutions. Some of these are far-sighted and bold, and others are protective of the status quo. All of them are influenced, to some extent, by grassroots-led efforts when there are good ideas (Figure 8-8).

Some of the ideas for reusing streets are becoming more common, and it is much easier to convince decision makers that something is possible when others have done it to good effect. Ideas can be contagious.

Figure 8-8 Vancouver, B.C., planned for pedestrian-oriented neighborhoods in the housing built for the 2010 Olympics.

Figure 8-9 Looking ahead, when streets are transformed from cars-only to balanced green streets.

Often, when good examples exist, it is possible to see a good outcome and deal more directly with concerns. How did one city's fire department solve parking issues, or the need for space for riggers? How did the neighborhood group solve maintenance issues for their newly planted traffic circle? Can we actually save money with natural drainage systems? While each situation differs, there are valid concerns, reasonable solutions, and much to learn from those who have made it beyond the predictable obstacles.

For those who see possibilities in their streets, we leave you with these concluding thoughts and the hope that streets everywhere will contribute to stronger, healthier communities (Figure 8-9).

■ There is a lot of space to be put to work for the betterment of communities: With all that needs to be done to make cities walkable, desirable, and environmentally sound, the street cannot be left to just pavement and cars. As a significant portion of cities, the land that comprises streets can help solve the challenges of the future.

■ Change requires leadership and tenacity: For every successful reuse of a street, leadership and tenacity are fundamental ingredients. Leadership can, and sometimes must, come from multiple people with differing roles.

■ Change can come from many players: professional designers, agency staff, elected officials, and grassroots efforts. Many of the changes to communities come from within. Leaders and city staff often need to be challenged by people who care for places, and see the opportunities within their own neighborhoods.

■ Make sure the community is involved: Elected officials and decision makers need the input and buy-in of community members when trying to create change. There is often wisdom in local knowledge, and the community needs to be part of the caretakers of places.

■ Take advantage of the very specific opportunities of a place: Good placemaking brings out the character of a place, and never just applies a "one-size fits all" approach.

■ Learn from what others have been able to do, and create new examples of good ideas in action.

RESOURCES

CHAPTER 1: PLACEMAKING

City Repair, a nonprofit organization that aims to educate and inspire communities to creatively transform the places they live: www.cityrepair.org

Creative Placemaking by Ann Markusen and Anne Gadwa, White paper for The Mayors' Institute on City Design, a leadership initiative of the National Endowment for the Arts in partnership with the United States Conference of Mayors and American Architecture Foundation, copyright Markusen Economic Research Services and Metris Arts Consulting, 2010, available at: http://www.nea.gov/pub/CreativePlacemaking-Paper.pdf

The Death and Life of Great American Cities by Jane Jacobs, Modern Library Edition, Random House, 1993.

Project for Public Spaces, a nonprofit organization that helps people create and sustain public spaces: www.pps.org

Rudy Bruner Award, an award honoring urban excellence: www.brunerfoundation.org/rba/

Streetsblog, a nonprofit organization that provides a daily news source with information about sustainable transportation and livable communities: www.streetblog.net

Streetfilms, documenting livable streets worldwide: www.streetfilms.org

CHAPTER 2: MOBILITY

AASHTO Guide for the Development of Bicycle Facilities, current edition, American Association of State Highway and Transportation Officials: www.aashto.org

AASHTO Guide for the Planning, Design, and Operation of Pedestrian Facilities, American Association of State Highway and Transportation Officials, 2004: www.aashto.org

America Walks, a nonprofit organization leading a coalition of local advocacy groups for walkable communities from across the United States: www.americawalks.org

Bicycle Information Center: www.bicyclinginfo.org

The Business Case for Active Transportation, Economic Benefits of Walking and Cycling, Richard Campbell and Magaret Wittgens, Go for Green, The Active Living and Environment Program, Better Environmentally Sound Transportation, March 2004: www.best.bc.ca. Available at: http://thirdwave-cycling.com/pdfs/at_business_case.pdf

City of Portland's Twenty-Minute Neighborhoods, Portland Plan, Status Report, Twenty-Minute Neighborhoods, City of Portland Bureau of Planning and Sustainability, 2009: www.portlandonline.com/port-
landplan/index.cfm?a=246917&c=46822

Complete Streets: www.completestreets.org

Evaluating Non-Motorized Transportation Benefits and Costs, Todd Litman, Victoria Transport Policy Institute, October 2011: www.vtpi.org

Living Streets, DIY Community Street Audits: www.livingstreets.org.uk/

Nature in the City, Restoring San Francisco biodiversity, wildlife habitats & corridors: www.naturein
thecity.org

Pedestrian and Bicycle Planning: A Guide to Best Practices, Todd Litman, Robin Blair, Bill Demopoulos,
Nils Eddy, Anne Fritzel, Danelle Laidlaw, Heath Maddox, Katherine Forster, Victoria Transport Policy
Institute, Victoria, B.C., October 2011, available at: www.vtpi.org

Seniors and Transportation Options, Aging in Place, Stuck without Options, Fixing the Mobility Crisis
Threatening the Baby Boom Generation, Transportation for America, accessed via: http://t4america.
org/resources/seniorsmobilitycrisis2011/

Walkable Communities Institute: www.walklive.org/

Pedestrian and Bicycle Information Center: www.walkinginfo.org/

Walk Friendly Communities: www.walkfriendly.org

Walking the Walk: How Walkability Raises Home Values in U.S. Cities, by Joe Cortright, Impresa, Inc., for
CEOs for Cities, August 2009, accessed via: http://blog.walkscore.com/wp-content/uploads/
2009/08/WalkingTheWalk_CEOsforCities.pdf

CHAPTER 3: NATURAL SYSTEMS

"22 Benefits of Urban Street Trees," by Dan Burden, Glatting Jackson, and Walkable Communities, Inc.,
May, 2006: www.ufei.org/files/pubs/22BenefitsofUrbanStreetTrees.pdf

Bats in American Bridges, Bat Conservation International, Inc., by Brian W. Keeley and Merlin D. Tuttle,
Resource Publication No. 4, 1999: www.batcon.org/pdfs/bridges/BatsBridges2.pdf

Baltimore Ecosystem Study: www.beslter.org/

Biotope City Journal: www.biotope-city.net/

Ecological Consequences of Artificial Night Lighting, edited by Catherine Rich and Travis Longcore, Island
Press, 2006.

National Audubon Society: www.audubon.org/

U.S. Long Term Ecological Research Network, www.lternet.edu/

CHAPTER 4: ELEMENTS

AASHTO Guide for the Development of Bicycle Facilities, current edition, American Association of State Highway and Transportation Officials: www.aashto.org

AASHTO Guide for the Planning, Design, and Operation of Pedestrian Facilities, American Association of State Highway and Transportation Officials, 2004: www.aashto.org

AASHTO A Policy on Geometric Design of Highways and Streets, Current edition, also known as the "Green Book": www.aashto.org

Design and Safety of Pedestrian Facilities, A Recommended Practice, Current edition, Institute of Transportation Engineers (ITE): www.ite.org/

Pedestrian and Bicycle Safety and Mobility in Europe, International Technology Scanning Program, February 2010, sponsored by the Federal Highway Administration, in cooperation with the American Association of State Highway and Transportation Officials and the National Cooperative Highway Research Program: www.international.fhwa.dot.gov/pubs/pl10010/pl10010.pdf

Best Practices in Statewide Freight Planning, Requested by American Association of State Highway and Transportation Officials (AASHTO) Standing Committee on Planning, Prepared by Cambridge Systematics, Inc., Cambridge, Massachusetts, October 2003, available at: www.transportation.org/sites/planning/docs/nchrp33.pdf

Traffic Calming 101, Project for Public Spaces website: www.pps.org/articles/livememtraffic/

Traffic Calming Library, a searchable database of reports, articles and documents, Institute of Transportation Engineers (ITE): www.ite.org/ traffic/

CHAPTER 5: INFLUENCES

Professional and Research Organizations

American Architectural Foundation, (AAF): www.archfoundation.org/

American Public Health Association (APHA): www.apha.org

American Association of State Highway and Transportation Officials (AASHTO): www.transportation.org

American Institute of Architects, (AIA): www.aia.org/

American Planning Association, (APA): www.planning.org/

American Society of Civil Engineers, (ASCE): www.asce.org/

American Society of Landscape Architects, (ASLA): www.asla.org/

Association of Pedestrian and Bicycle Professionals: (APBP) www.apbp.org/

City of Seattle Right-of-Way Improvements Manual: www.seattle.gov/transportation/rowmanual

Environmental Protection Agency, Smart Growth and Sustainable Communities: www.epa.gov/sustainability/

Institute of Transportation Engineers (ITE): www.ite.org/

National Recreation and Park Association (NRPA): www.nrpa.org/

Transportation Research Board (TRB): www.trb.org/

Topics

Active Communities

ACES, the Centers for Disease Control and Prevention initiative to promote walking, cycling and accessible recreation facilities: www.cdc.gov/physicalactivity/professionals/environment/aces.html

Active Living Research, a national program of the Robert Wood Johnson Foundation: www.activeliving-research.org/

Let's Move, an initiative from the White House to raise a healthier generation of kids: www.letsmove.gov/active-communities

Complete Streets

National Complete Streets Coalition: www.completestreets.org

Context Sensitive Design

Context Sensitive Solutions (CSS), website to assist practitioners, developed in cooperation with ITE, the Federal Highway Administration, the Environmental Protection Agency, and in partnership with the Congress for the New Urbanism, 2011: www.ite.org/css/

Green Factor

Seattle Green Factor:www.seattle.gov/dpd/Permits/GreenFactor/Overview/

Biotope Area Factor (BAF): www.stadtentwicklung.berlin.de/umwelt/landschaftsplanung/bff/index_en.shtml

Green Infrastructure and Low Impact Development

California Stormwater Quality Association (CASQA), Low Impact Development Portal: www.casqa.org/LID/tabid/240/Default.aspx

Green Infrastructure, website developed by The Conservation Fund, with funding provided by USDA Cooperative Forestry and the Surdna Foundation: www.greeninfrastructure.net

Low Impact Development Center, a nonprofit organization dedicated to furthering the advancement of Low Impact Development technology: www.lowimpactdevelopment.org/

U.S. Environmental Protection Agency, Managing Wet Weather with Green Infrastructure: http://cfpub.epa.gov/npdes/home.cfm?program_id=298

Safe Routes to School

National Center for Safe Routes to School, funded by the U.S. Department of Transportation Federal Highway Administration and maintained by the National Center for Safe Routes to School within the University of North Carolina Highway Safety Research Center in partnership with the American Association of State Highway and Transportation Officials, America Walks, the Governors Highway Safety Association, the Institute of Transportation Engineers, and Toole Design Group: www.safe-routesinfo.org/

CHAPTER 6

Residential Streets

Guidelines for Planting City Boulevards, Vancouver, British Columbia: http://vancouver.ca/engsvcs/streets/greenways/guidelines.htm

Urban Gardeners Guide, Metro Blooms, Minneapolis, Minnesota, www.metroblooms.org/guide_blooming boulevards.php

City Repair http://cityrepair.org/ Includes Portland's City Ordinance #175937, Conditions of Revocable Permit to Modify City Intersections, and Painting Logistics: http://cityrepair.org/how-to/placemaking/intersectionrepair/

Paint the Pavement, St. Paul, Minnesota "How to" section and "Resources," www.paintthepavement.org/

Green Streets

City of Portland Bureau of Environmental Services. Their web-based library includes Sustainable Stormwater Management Solutions, Fact Sheets and Brochures, the Portland Watershed Management Plan, and City Standard Details: www.portlandonline.com/bes/

City of Seattle, Seattle Public Utilities, Green Stormwater Infrastructure: www.seattle.gov/util/About_SPU/Drainage_&_Sewer_System/GreenStormwaterInfrastructure/index.htm

Town of Edmonston, The Green Street Project. The work done in Edmonston is available on the website as Open Source files, and includes this note: "Planners, engineers, elected officials, and advocates of other communities are encouraged to download, replicate and improve upon these ideas. Credit to Edmonston or the engineers is appreciated but not necessary.": www.edmonstonmd.gov/Going-Green.html

Pollinator Pathways: www.pollinatorpathway.com/

Urban Bee Gardens: http://nature.berkeley.edu/urbanbeegardens/

Blue-Green Fingerprints in the City of Malmo, Sweden: Malmo's Way Toward a Sustainable Urban Drainage, by Peter Stahre, author, for Malmo stad and VA SYD, 2008, available at: www.vasyd.se/SiteCollectionDocuments/Broschyrer/Publikationer/BlueGreenFingerprints_Peter.Stahre_webb.pdf

Green Infrastructure Program, Cincinnati, Ohio: http://msdgc.org/wetweather/greenreport.htm

Green Infrastructure Plan, New York City: www.nyc.gov/html/dep/html/stormwater/nyc_green_infrastructure_plan.shtml

Alleys

Alleys of Seattle, Daniel Toole's blog on alleys: http://alleysofseattle.com/

City of Baltimore, Alley Gating & Greening Program, City of Baltimore website: www.baltimorecity.gov/Government/AgenciesDepartments/GeneralServices/AlleyGatingGreeningProgram.aspx

City of Chicago, "Green Alley Handbook", available via City of Chicago's website: www.cityofchicago.org/city/en/depts/cdot/provdrs/alley/svcs/green_alleys.html

City of Melbourne, Greening Melbourne's laneways: www.melbourne.vic.gov.au/Environment/WhatCanI-Do/Pages/GreeningLaneways.aspx

Community Greens, an initiative of Ashoka: www.communitygreens.org/

Green Futures Lab, Activating Alleys for a Lively City, Mary Fialko and Jennifer Hampton, in collaboration with the University of Washington Green Futures Lab, the Scan Design Foundation and Gehl Architects: http://greenfutures.washington.edu/publications.php

Main Streets

The Boulevard Book:, History, Evolution, Design of Multiway Boulevards, by Allan B. Jacobs, Elizabeth MacDonald, and Yodan Rofe, The MIT Press, Cambridge Massachusetts, 2002.

"Road Diets: Fixing the Big Roads", by Dan Burden and Peter Lagerway, Walkable Communities, 1999: www.walkable.org/assets/downloads/roaddiets.pdf

"Road Diet Handbook: Setting Trends for Livable Streets", by Jennifer Rosales, Parsons Brinkerhoff, 2009. Available at ITE Bookstore, or as a summary at: www.oregonite.org/2007D6/paper_review/D4_201_Rosales_paper.pdf

Washington State Department of Transportation website, SR99—Shoreline Aurora Ave–N Corridor Transit/HOV Lanes, retrieved February 23, 2011: www.wsdot.wa.gov/projects/sr99/shoreline_ncthov/

Thoroughfares

"Designing Walkable Urban Thoroughfares: A Context Sensitive Approach", Institute of Transportation Engineers and the Congress for New Urbanism, pdf available through: www.ite.org

The Boulevard Book:, History, Evolution, Design of Multiway Boulevards, by Allan B. Jacobs, Elizabeth MacDonald, and Yodan Rofe, The MIT Press, Cambridge Massachusetts, 2002.

Shared-Use Streets

Pedestrian Facilities Users Guide—Providing Safety and Mobility, Publication No. FHWA-RD-01-102, U.S. Department of Transportation, Federal Highway Administration, Research and Development. Turner-Fairbank Highway Research Center, McClean VA. March 2002. (Note: discussion of *woonerfs* begins on page 80.) Available to download via Google Books.

Home Zone Concepts in New Jersey, prepared by Alan M. Voorhees Transportation Center, New Jersey Bicycle and Pedestrian Resource Center, Edward J. Boustien School of Planning and Public Policy. Prepared for New Jersey Department of Transportation, November 2004.

Festival Streets

Farmers Market Coalition Resource Library: www.farmersmarketcoalition.org/resources/

National Trails, Streets as Trails for Life: www.americantrails.org/resources/health/streetspenalosa.html

The Ciclovía Movement, History and Resources: www.atlantastreetsalive.com/about/the-ciclovia-movement

CHAPTER 7

Mint Plaza

Livable City, advocacy for more livable, accessible San Francisco: http://livablecity.org

Mint Plaza: www.mintplazasf.org/

SPUR, San Francisco Planning + Urban Research Association, member supported non-profit: www.spur.org/

Nord Alley

Alley Network Project, coalition to transform Seattle's Pioneer Square alleys into assets: http://alleynetworkproject.com

International Sustainability Institute, nonprofit organization designed to bring worldwide sustainability to the Puget Sound region: www.isiseattle.org/

Central Annapolis Road

Central Annapolis Road Sector Plan and Sectional Map Amendment, Prince George's County Planning Department: www.pgplanning.org/Projects/Ongoing_Plans_and_Projects/Community_Plans_and_Studies/Central_Annapolis_Road.htm

Sustainable Cities Design Academy, program of the American Architectural Foundation to support and advance sustainable design practices: www.archfoundation.org/aaf/aaf/Programs.SC.htm

78th Avenue SE

State of Washington Growth Management Plan, information available at Municipal Research and Services Center of Washington: www.mrsc.org/subjects/planning/compplan.aspx

Transit-Oriented Development Case Studies, City of Seattle Department of Transportation: www.seattle.gov/transportation/ppmp_sap_todstudies.htm

High Point

Environmental Protection Agency, National Awards for Smart Growth Achievement. High Point was a 2009 winner; Mint Plaza and NYC received this award in 2010: www.epa.gov/smartgrowth/awards.htm

The Sustainable Sites Initiative (SITES), an interdisciplinary effort by ASLA, the Lady Bird Johnson Wildflower Center at The University of Texas at Austin, and the United States Botanic Garden to create benchmarks for sustainable design, construction and management. High Point is one of the case studies included.

Barracks Row

Barracks Row Main Street, www.barracksrow.org

National Trust for Historic Preservation, www.MainStreet.org

New York City

Million Trees New York: www.milliontreesnyc.org

New York City Pedestrian Plaza Program, Pedestrians & Sidewalks: www.nyc.gov/html/dot/html/sidewalks/publicplaza.shtml

PlaNYC 2030: www.nyc.gov/html/planyc2030/html/home/home.shtml

Streetsblog, New York City: www.streetsblog.org/

Sustainable Streets, City of New York Department of Transportation website: www.nyc.gov/html/dot/html/about/stratplan.shtml

Terry Avenue North

South Lake Union Neighborhood Plan, City of Seattle: www.seattle.gov/dpd/Planning/South_Lake_Union/NeighborhoodPlanUpdate

Terry Avenue North Design Guidelines, available at the City of Seattle website: www.seattle.gov/DPD/Planning/South_Lake_Union/OtherPlanningDocuments

CHAPTER 8

Biophilic Cities, *Integrating Nature Into Urban Design and Planning,* Timothy Beatley, Island Press, Washington D.C., 2011; website at: biophiliccities.org

Biophilic Design: The Theory, Science and Practice of Bringing Buildings to Life, by Stephen Kellert, Judith Heerwegen, and Marty Mador, eds., Hoboken, NJ: John Wiley and Sons, 2008.

Living Cities Design Competition, on the website of the International Living Building Institute: https://ilbi.org/resources/competitions/livingcity/brief

"Solar Highways: Oregon Department of Transportation travels a long road to power highway lights with renewable energy," *Rebuilding American's Infrastructure* magazine, by John Ochway, May 2010: www.rebuildingamericasinfrastructure.com/magazine-article-rai-may-2010-solar_highways-7856.html

INDEX

A

AASHTO, 80, 93, 94
Accessibility, 60, 79, 192, 278
Activation, 15, 221, 270
Adopt-a-Median, 119
Air quality, 44, 49, 93, 289
Alleys, 114, 139–153, 217–224
Americans with Disabilities Act (ADA), 59, 132, 191, 200, 283, 284
Amsterdam, 100
Albuquerque, New Mexico, 121–122
Ashville, North Carolina, 187
Asphalt, 58–59, 77
Austin, Texas, 47–48, 194
Axis Alley, 145–146

B

Baltimore, Maryland, 41, 145–146, 147–149
Barracks Row Business Alliance, 257
Barracks Row Main Street, 257, 258
Beatley, Timothy, 286
Bellevue, Washington, 180
Berlin, Germany, 44
Bertolet, Dan, 2
Bergmann, Sarah, 134
Best Management Practices, 125–126
Bicknell, Lyle, 284
Bicycles, 32–33, 90
    boxes, 63
    culture, 100–101
    facilities, 90
    lanes, 61–68
    parking, 66–67
Biophilic cities, 286

Biotope Area Factor, 44
Bioswale, 74–75 (*see also* Swale)
Boulder, Colorado, 21, 186
Boulevards, 176–178
Boulevard gardens, 115
Buffer zone, 54
Burden, Dan, 74
Burgdorf, Switzerland, 186
Business districts, 103–104
Business Improvement Districts, 98

C

Cape Town, South Africa, 203–204
Chicago, Illinois, 146–147, 160
Chief Sealth Trail, 56
Ciarlo, Catherine, 124
Ciclovías, 203
Cisterns, 45–47, 49
City Beautiful, 177–178
City Repair Project, 117
Clay, Grady, 139, 150
Clear Alleys Program, 144
Climate, 6, 9–10, 84–85, 159
CMG Landscape Architects, 213–214, 216, 293
Coastal Rail Trail, 56
Codes, 93
Coleman, Sharon, 284
Columbia City, Missouri, 145
Comfort, 9
Community Greens, 147–148
Complete Streets, 87, 94, 179
Concrete, 58
Conrad, Rich, 238
Context, 84

Context Sensitive Design, 87
Context Sensitive Solutions, 87, 93, 94
Community interaction, 4
Community gardens, 117
Copenhagen, Denmark, 10, 20–21, 81
Crime prevention through environmental design
    (CPTED), 13
Cross disciplinary design, 85–86
Crosswalks, 61, 101
Cul-de-sac, 185
Culture, 99–101
Curb and gutter, 54, 77–78, 283
    curb bulbs, 164
    curb radii, 164–165
    curbless street, 200
Cycletracks, 62

D

Dalpee, James, 257
Dark sky, 48
DC Main Streets, 258
Density, 192
Denver, Colorado, 113
Detroit, Michigan, 153
Distribution centers, 105–106
DMJM + Harris, 258
Dockside Green, 292
Doherty, Sarah, 145–146
Drayton, Bill, 147

E

Economy, 4, 103–105
Edges, 6–7
Edmonston, Maryland, 132–134
Emergency access, 152, 192
Equity, 101–102
Ezzell, Chris, 220

F

Farmer's markets, 195
Fenton, Mark, 101–102
Festival Market Place, 201–202
Festival streets, 114, 188, 193–204
Feusel, Paul, 240
Fire trucks, 31, 248
Flagstaff, Arizona, 48
Food, 93, 151, 158
Food vendors, 97–98
Freight vehicles, 92, 105
Fruitdale Street, 155

G

Garbage removal, 22
Gehl Architects, 11, 142, 218
Gilman Gardens, 117–118
Goody Clancy, 229
Greenways, 64
Green Book, 95
Green infrastructure, 45, 49, 95, 245, 247, 254
Green Garage, Detroit, 153
Green Grids, 129
Green Light for Manhattan, 17–18
Green streets, 114, 123–138
Growing Vine Street, 45
Growth management, 88, 236–237
Gustafson Guthrie Nichol, 70

H

Habitat, 47, 49
Hamilton-Baillie, Ben, 184
Health, 4, 92, 93, 101–102, 152
Hinman, Curtis, 131
Ho, Suenn, 198
Home zone, 184
Hoselton, Charlie, 117–118
HOV lanes, 91

I

Indianapolis, Indiana, 119
Industrial areas, 105
Institute of Transportation Engineers, 94
International Sustainability Institute, 218, 221
Intersections, 59–60, 248, 249

J

Jacobs, Allan, 177
Johnson, Gary, 220
Jones & Jones, 221

K

Kungys, Vaidila, 265, 270
Kunstler, James, 5

L

La Pierre, Curtis, 200
Land use, 100
Landscape, 251, 278–279
Lane width, 167–168, 246
Leadership, 110, 267
Lee and Associates, 258
Level of Service, 27–28
Liability, 107, 152
Lighting, 152, 192, 280
Litke, Tom, 260
Living Cities Competition, 290
Los Angeles, California, 150–151
Louisville, Kentucky, 17
Low impact development, 250, 254
Lowney, Ben, 121–122

M

Maintenance, 107, 152, 192, 254, 280
Main Streets, 114, 154–170
Malmo, Sweden, 136

Mangum, Oklahoma, 145
Maplewood, New Jersey, 163
Martin Building Company, 210, 214, 215
Martin, Chris, 220
Masdar City, Abu Dhabi, 296
Materials, 107, 277, 282
Maynard Avenue Green Street, 49
Medians, 164
Medieval streets, 7–8
Melbourne, Australia, 142–143, 152
Mercer Island, Washington, 235–239
Michaelson, Guy, 284
Miller Hull Partnership, 285, 290–291
Million Trees New York, 266–267
Minneapolis, Minnesota, 115–116
Mixed-use development, 88
Monderman, Hans, 184
Moss, Willet, 213, 216
Myers, Bruce, 253

N

National Trust for Historic Preservation, 103, 255,
        257–258
National Trust Main Street Center, 103
Neighborhood green ways, 64–65
Netherlands, 185
New York City, New York, 2, 194, 263–270
        Bicycles, 33, 101, 267
        Green Light for Manhattan, 17–18
        Million Trees NYC, 266
        Plaza program, 264–266
Niagara Falls, New York, 135
Nichol, Shannon, 279
Norton, Drew, 215, 216

O

Oakland, California, 155
Olin, 161
Olmsted, Frederick Law, 177

Ortiz, Adam, 132–134
Ortygia, Italy, 7

P

Parking, 79, 128, 169–170, 275–276
    Angled, 55
    Bicycle, 66
    Requirements, 92
PARK(ing) Day, 16
Parklets, 19
Parkways, 176
Pasadena, California, 156
Paseo, 99
Pavement to Parks, 19
Pavers, 59
Pedestrians, 8, 34, 89–90
    measures, 37
    plazas, 15
    streets, 20–21
    zones, 275
Perry, Kevin Robert, 121, 125
Personal vehicles, 91
Philadelphia, Pennsylvania, 177–178
Phillips, Tom, 248, 251
Phoenix, Arizona, 6
Pike Place Market, 21, 187–188, 201–202
Placemaking, 2–3, 5
PlaNYC, 263–266, 269, 270
Policy, 87, 93, 269
Pomegranate Center, 253
Pollinator Pathway, 134–135
Portland, Oregon, 25, 120, 141,161
    bicycles, 33
    Davis Street, 197–199
    green streets, 123–127
    Share-it-Square, 116–117
Porous pavement, 76
Philadelphia, Pennsylvania, 45
Phoenix, 6

Prince George's County, Maryland, 225–226,
    229–234
Priority Pedestrian Zones, 186
Private uses in public space, 97
Public process, 108–109
Public realm, 4, 11

R

Radulovitch, Tom, 208
Rain Gardens, 76
Rainwater, 92
Ramachandran, Ganesh, 234
Rebar, 16–17; 19
Register, Richard, 289–290
Regulations, 108
Road diets, 178–179

S

Sadik-Khan, Janette, 18
Safety, 13, 61, 64, 69, 127, 148, 269
St. Gallen, Switzerland, 187
San Diego, California, 56, 286–287
San Francisco, California 118–119,
    Pavement to Parks, 19
    Mint Plaza, 208–216
    Treasure Island, 293–295
Sarte, Bry, 214
Scenic Byways, 172
Scharf, Ron, 284
Seattle Housing Authority (SHA), 245–248
Seattle, Washington, 56, 94,117–118, 127–131, 135,
    144, 179, 187
    High Point, 243–254
    Lander Street, 199–200
    Nord Alley, 217–224
    Terry Avenue North, 271–284
Service vehicles, 92
Shared use streets, 55, 182–184
    commercial, 186

residential, 185
Treasure Island (San Francisco), 294–295
Shared space, 114
Sharrows, 62
Sherwood Design, 215, 216
Shoreline, Washington, 173
Sidewalks, 52–53, 248
Signage, 68–69, 192
Signed routes, 62
Simpson, Buster, 47, 126
Siskiyou Street, 120–121
Skateparks, 160
Skidmore Owings & Merrill, 293
Slater, Greg, 234
Snohomish County, Washington, 186
Snow removal, 152
Soils, 85
Solana Beach, California, 56
Solar energy, 287–288
Stahre, Peter, 137
Stormwater, 95, 119–121, 152, 248, 252, 254
Street classification, 27
Street Design Concept Plans, 96
Street furniture, 70–71
Street lighting, 48, 71, 132, 146, 152, 192
Streets
    proportions, 5–6
    residential, 114, 115–122
    volumetric character, 5
    width, 7, 246, 247
Sustainable Cities Design Academy, 229
Swales, 74–75, 76, 78, 96, 250–251
Switzerland, 186, 187

T

Term Ecological Research Network, 41
Thoroughfares, 114, 171–181
Through-routes, 57
Tolling, 91

Toole, Daniel, 222
Traffic calming, 164
Trails, 56
Transit, 10, 31–32, 91, 158
Transportation demand management, 91
Transportation management plans, 91
Transportation planning, 91
Travel lanes, 57
Trip chaining, 104
Trees, 6, 10, 22, 47, 71, 74, 159, 164, 177, 178, 274
    benefits of, 49–50
    as part of natural systems, 42–44,
    and streetscape, 54, 55,
Tree roots, 58, 59, 74
Trucks, 30, 57, 165–166
Trust for Public Land, 151

U

United Kingdom, 185
United States Federal Highway Administration, 185
Urban heat island, 49
Urbanization, 40
Utilities, 21–22, 152

V

Vancouver, British Columbia, 115, 150, 188, 189
Vancouver, Washington, 134
Vehicle zones, 275–276, 282
Victoria, British Columbia, 292
Vogel, Todd, 217, 218, 223, 224

W

Walk zone, 52–54
Walking school bus, 4
Walking as transportation, 89–90, 92
Walkscore ™, 26, 37
Washburn, Bill, 234

Washington, D.C., 140, 255–262
Water quality, 45, 49, 248
Weinstein A|U, 280
Wind energy, 288–289
Woonerf, 99, 114, 184, 185–186, 187, 192
World Cup Alley, 221–222

Y

Yamashita, Patrick, 240, 241

Z

Zoning, 88, 89–90, 229, 237